Hate Crimes

The Rising Tide of
Bigotry and Bloodshed

Hate Crimes
The Rising Tide of
Bigotry and Bloodshed

Jack Levin
and
Jack McDevitt

Plenum Press • New York and London

Library of Congress Cataloging-in-Publication Data

Levin, Jack, 1941-
    Hate crimes : the rising tide of bigotry and bloodshed / Jack
  Levin and Jack McDevitt ; foreword by Morris Dees.
        p.   cm.
    Includes bibliographical references and index.
    ISBN 0-306-44471-2
    1. Hate crimes.   I. McDevitt, Jack, 1953-   . II. Title.
  HV6250.25.L48   1993
  364.1--dc20   92-43230
                                                          CIP

10 9 8 7 6 5 4

ISBN 0-306-44471-2

©1993 Jack Levin and Jack McDevitt
Plenum Press is a division of Plenum Publishing Corporation
233 Spring Street, New York, N.Y. 10013

Printed in the United States of America

To victims of hate crimes everywhere,
whose pain is too often
minimized or ignored

Foreword

Over the past few years, the number of attacks against people because of their race, religion, sexual orientation, or ethnic origin has increased at an alarming rate. Historically, immigration and economic hardship have inspired racial tension and violence. A few years ago, hate crime was literally a black-and-white issue, usually involving white perpetrators and black victims. Today, we see a significant increase in black-on-white attacks. Other contemporary conflicts reflect the growing friction generated by the increasing diversity in our society.

America's racial and ethnic diversity increased more dramatically over the past decade than at any other time in history, according to the U.S. Census Bureau. Today, nearly one in every four Americans claims African, Hispanic, or Native American ancestry, and ethnic enclaves exist even in remote rural communities. This new diversity enriches our culture and challenges stereotypes about what it means to be an "American." But it also complicates race relations.

Compared with the overwhelming problems associated with the illegal drug epidemic and gang-related violence, hate crime may seem relatively insignificant. But even incidents that do not involve violence, such as vandalism and harassment, have the potential to disrupt entire communities and spark violence. The fight against hate crime is challenging and demands the attention of every citizen. For legislators, it means refining laws to address the serious threat of hate crime. For educators, it means finding ways to open the channels of cultural understanding among children. For police, it means increased attention to acts of hate violence. For neighborhoods, it means strengthening the bonds of community to embrace diversity and reject acts of bigotry.

Jack Levin and Jack McDevitt have done a masterful job outlining the hate crime problem, as well as the different approaches to effectively combat these extraordinary crimes. This illuminating and well-researched book provides the tools necessary to understand the dimensions of violence based on hatred. I challenge anyone interested in the future of our country to read this book.

Morris Dees
Klanwatch and Southern Poverty Law Center
Montgomery, Alabama

Preface

It has become nearly impossible to keep track of the shocking rise in brutal attacks directed against individuals *because* they are black, Latino, Asian, white, disabled, women, or gay. Almost daily, the newspapers report new and even more grotesque abominations. These "hate crimes" have become a growing threat to the well-being of our society—on the college campus, in the workplace, and around our neighborhoods. As ugly as this situation is now, it is likely to worsen throughout the remainder of the decade and into the next century as the forces of bigotry continue to gain momentum.

Thus, the focus of this book ranges far beyond the issue of free speech—whether an angry youngster has the right to shout a racial slur at someone who is different or to scrawl a homophobic epithet on the sidewalk. We emphasize that many hate crimes consist of not only nasty talk or mischievous pranks, but also violent assaults and even murder. Moreover, unlike attacks motivated by greed, jealousy, or lust, hate offenses can be regarded as acts of domestic terrorism. A cross burned in the front yard of a particular black family sends a frightening message to *all* blacks; an assault against one woman signals women *everywhere* that they could be next. In effect, an attack inspired by bigotry says in unequivocal terms to each and every member of the victim's group that "the same thing could happen to you."

In the past, hate crimes have too often been discussed as if they were all of one type. While it is true that they are all motivated by bias or bigotry, such attacks actually include a wide variety of criminal behaviors, vastly different in their severity and in their impact on the broader community. In this book, we introduce a typology that differentiates various kinds of hate offenses. Hate crimes are actually many different types of offenses with a common foundation in bigotry, and we hope that by appreciating this, communities, public officials, and criminal justice agencies will be able to respond to them more effectively.

We also believe that the only way to prevent the increasing violence motivated by bias or bigotry is for individual groups to join together in coalitions. While efforts at reclaiming cultural identity are important and should be maintained, the most meaningful strategies for reform are those initiated by a temporary alliance of victimized groups. So long as groups targeted for hate crimes see themselves as competing with one another for sympathy and attention, the bigots will continue to win. Hate crime offenders are usually not specialists. They may focus their hatred on a particular group in an effort to drive its members from the community or the workplace. Should the "need" arise, however, they typically shift their attention to other "outsiders." It is therefore imperative that *all* vulnerable groups band together and demand an end to violence.

We stress throughout the book that crimes motivated

by bigotry usually arise not out of the pathological rant-ings and ravings of a few deviant types in organized hate groups, but out of the very mainstream of society. This may be an uncomfortable position to accept, because it places the responsibility for our predicament on ourselves rather than on *them*. Yet, the implication is clear: As a society, as a community, and as individuals, we must all be willing to take some responsibility for making changes if we are to stem this rising tide of bigotry and bloodshed.

Acknowledgments

We acknowledge a number of individuals who have assisted us through the development and preparation of this book. First we want to thank Lieutenant William Johnston, Commander of the Boston Police Department's Community Disorders Unit, who has dedicated his career to fighting hate crimes and has taught thousands of police and public officials (as well as the authors of this book) that hate crimes are among the most serious of all offenses. We also acknowledge the activities of advocacy groups across the country, particularly the Anti-Defamation League of B'nai B'rith, the Southern Poverty Law Center, the National Gay and Lesbian Task Force, and the National Institute Against Prejudice and Violence, whose members have worked for years, with little public encouragement, to document and address the suffering of hate crime victims.

In conducting the research for this book, we depended on the assistance of a number of individuals. We are particularly grateful to Michael Levin of the New York Institute of Technology, whose research assistance for this book was indispensable. We also thank Glenn Pierce and

Robyn Miliano of Northeastern University's Center for Applied Social Research for their support in developing and refining many of our ideas about hate crimes.

Other colleagues and associates who contributed important suggestions include Arnold Arluke, Michael Brown, Morris Jenkins, Leonard Brown, Mervin Lynch, Debra Kaufman, Robert Fuller, Robert Croatti, Skip McCullough, Robin Chandler, and Patricia Golden (who died unexpectedly as we completed this book, but whose memory continues to inspire optimism about the future of race relations) of Northeastern University; Paul Bookbinder and Richard Robbins of the University of Massachusetts, Boston; William Levin of Bridgewater State College; Dan Bibel of the Massachusetts Crime Reporting Unit; Paul White of the Bureau of Justice Statistics; Yoshio Akiyama, Bob McFall, John Jarvis, and Tony Pinnozotto of the FBI Uniform Crime Reporting Program; Michael Lieberman of the Anti-Defamation League of B'nai B'rith; Sally Greenberg, Lenny Zakim, Pearl Matinson, and Ellen Betteman of the Boston Office of the Anti-Defamation League of B'nai B'rith; Danny Welch of the Southern Poverty Law Center; Brian Flynn and Dan O'Leary of the Boston Police Community Disorders Unit; Massachusetts Attorney General Scott Harshbarger; Richard Coles of the Civil Rights Division of the Massachusetts Attorney General's Office; Massachusetts Governor William Weld; Pricilla Douglass and Don Gorton, Co-chairs of the Massachusetts Governor's Hate Crime Advisory Committee; Sheri Liebowitz of Suffolk University; Kevin Berrill of the National Gay and Lesbian Task Force; Gail Padgett of the Community Relations Service; Brian Levin of Stanford University; Joan Weiss of the Judicial Research and Statistics Association; Sally Hare and Brenda Goldberg of Carolina Coastal College; Hank Tischler of Framingham State College; William

Holmes of the Massachusetts Committee of Criminal Justice; Phil Lamy of Castleton State College; Bill Lancaster of the Investigative News Group; Paul Kissman of the Sharon Public Library; Deena Weinstein of De Paul University; Philip Jenkins of Penn State University; Bruce McCabe, Tom Palmer, and Marjorie Pritchard of the *Boston Globe;* Shelly Cohen of the *Boston Herald;* John Snell of *The Oregonian;* Daniel Goleman of *The New York Times;* Melodie Howard of the *Jewish Advocate;* Sharon Shaw Johnson of *USA Today;* Bobbie Levin of the Jewish Community Center in Springfield, Massachusetts; students at Northeastern University, Worcester Polytechnic Institute, the University of Rochester, Salem State College, and Roger Williams College; the staff of Boston University Hospital; Carol Goodman-Kaufman of Hadassah; Dan Frio of Wayland High School; Scott Wolfman of Wolfman Productions. In addition, we owe a debt of gratitude to the Bureau of Justice Statistics and the Boston Foundation for providing funding for some of the research cited in this book.

We also acknowledge the valuable input of Bill Stone, Alan Rosen, Heather Walcutt, Daniel Weiss, Eric Silverman, Paul Maas, Paula McCabe, Jason Landau, Deborah Baiano, Louis Kontos, Karen Lischinsky, Kevin Borgeson, Kim McInnis, Michele Eayrs, Michael Kozack, Gail Pessas, Bizhan Monavarian, George Parangamilil, Lewis Chow, Monica Cantwell, Marilyn Churchill, Kitty Walsh, George Bradt, Louise Lafontaine, Deb Ross, Kim McCarthy, Samantha Bouchard, Rich Sparaco, Steve Ostervitz, Shana Baxter, Lisa Sanbonmatsu, Paul Phillips, Josh Shafran, Myron Lench, Lin Dawson, and all of the students who have participated in the prejudice panel for Sociology of Prejudice.

In addition to our students and colleagues at Northeastern University, we are indebted to President Jack Curry, Provost Michael Baer, Vice Provost Daryl Helman, Dean Robert Lowndes, College of Arts and Sciences, and Dean James A. Fox, College of Criminal Justice; the Office of University Communications with special thanks to Terry Yanulavich and Mary Breslauer, members of President Curry's Diversity Commission, William Frohlich of Northeastern University Press, members of the Society Organized Against Racism, members of the "Isms" committee, and especially Vice President John O'Bryant, whose untimely death ended a brilliant career.

Finally, we thank our children—Michael, Bonnie, and Andrea Levin, and Sean and Brian McDevitt—and most of all, our wives, Flea and Jan, who have endured our absences and, more importantly, whose insights are reflected throughout this book.

JACK LEVIN
JACK MCDEVITT

Contents

CHAPTER 1

Reign of Terror

It was June 18, 1984. Outspoken radio personality Alan Berg had spent another routine morning behind the microphone at superstation KOA in Denver, exchanging verbal barbs on the air with assorted lunatics, activists, survivalists, racists, and shut-ins. Later in the day, the bearded and graying talk show host picked up his ex-wife Judith Lee who had flown in from Chicago to spend the weekend visiting her parents and Alan. The couple passed the afternoon together, catching up on the details of one another's lives. They drove to Alan's fashionable apartment, dined together at a popular restaurant in a western suburb nearby, and then stopped at a 7-Eleven store to buy dog food for Alan's shaggy Airedale.

Just before 9:00 P.M., Berg dropped Judith at the Cherry Creek shopping center, where she had parked her car for the afternoon. He then drove alone toward his modern, three-story townhouse on Adams Street. Denver was unusually warm on this late-spring evening. The moon was hidden behind a thick layer of clouds, and more clouds were predicted for the following day.

Berg maneuvered his black Volkswagen beetle into the lighted driveway in front of his apartment, turned off the engine, and pulled up the emergency brake. Taking a last drag from his cigarette, he opened the door. The street was dark and quiet as he picked up the 7-Eleven bag from the seat next to him and began to step to the pavement. He was suddenly distracted by the headlights of an approaching car, then an explosion of gunshots. Before he could have known what hit him, Berg's six-foot-two, 150-pound body lay face up in a pool of blood, killed by thirteen bullets from an automatic MAC-10 pistol.

When the police arrived on the scene, Berg's right leg was inside his VW, and his hand still gripped the paper bag he had carried. Several cans of dog food had rolled into the street. (1)

It didn't take a multimillion-dollar task force to discover that Berg had been murdered or why. His assailants turned out to be members of a neo-Nazi hate group that awarded points to its "Aryan Warriors" for killing Jews, blacks, government officials, and reporters. One of the Nazis at the scene of the crime later bragged that "Berg went down so fast it was like someone pulled the rug out from under him." (2)

Berg's controversial show on Denver's KOA radio had been the talk of the town, but not all of the talk was complimentary. The fifty-year-old ex-criminal lawyer routinely berated racists, urging them to phone and express their venomous points of view. "Any Nazis out there?" the chain-smoking, coffee-addicted talk show host would ask on the air. "I'm a Jew and I'd like to talk to you."

Nazis frequently obliged him. So did Klansmen and members of the Aryan Nations. Over the airwaves, they blamed the hard economic times on "Jew Rothschild bankers," claiming that the "Zionist Occupation Government"

(ZOG) exercised total control over the economic resources of the United States. They challenged the authenticity of the Holocaust, suggesting instead that the atrocities committed by the Nazis had been fabricated by Jewish organizations in a bid to arouse the sympathy of the world. Some decried the "mongrelization" of the white race and expressed disdain for civil rights legislation. Others predicted that God would soon eliminate both Jews and blacks from the face of the earth . . . the sooner the better, they said.

And Berg challenged every one of his bigoted callers. He belittled them, debated with them, poked fun at them, and then usually hung up on them. Berg was both popular and despised, but he was always provocative. As a rival talk show host recalled after his death, Berg "made a living making enemies on the air." (3) Earlier in his career, his "enemies" had gotten him suspended and fired, had mailed indignant letters to the Federal Communications Commission, and had sent bomb threats to Berg's office at the station. The subject of the program Berg was scheduled to discuss the morning *after* his murder was gun control.

Investigators were convinced that Berg had been ambushed by five members of a neo-Nazi hit squad, but they were also sure that the evidence was lacking to obtain murder convictions at the state level. The alleged ringleader of the group, thirty-one-year-old Robert Jay Mathews, was the founder and leader of an organized hate group calling itself *Bruder Schweigen*, the Silent Brotherhood. His primary objective was, by means of murder, armed robbery, and counterfeiting, to fund the racist activities of the white supremacist movement. Mathews was later killed in a gun battle with federal agents. The other four alleged perpetrators—David Lane, Bruce Pierce,

Richard Scutari, and Jean Craig—were already serving time on charges of federal racketeering by the time the investigation had gotten underway. Whatever proof prosecutors had against the four racists was strictly circumstantial, based mainly on the testimony of members of hate groups who were willing to turn state's evidence in return for reduced sentences on other charges. Witnesses claimed that Berg had in fact infuriated racists in his audience by ridiculing them, and that he had been singled out for execution by the Silent Brotherhood.

Several months after Berg was assassinated, FBI agents located the murder weapon at the home of an Aryan Nations director near Hayden Lake, Idaho. Bullets from the gun matched slugs taken from Berg's body and other bullets found at a house near Troy, Montana—the home of one of the defendants, Bruce Pierce. (4)

Lacking evidence to convince a jury "beyond a reasonable doubt," the district attorney in Denver dropped the idea of obtaining murder indictments. But federal prosecutors, relying instead on an often-used tactic, charged the three men and one woman in federal court with having conspired to violate Berg's civil rights by killing him. (It is generally easier to prove a conspiracy to murder than the murder itself.) After thirteen days of proceedings involving more than thirty-one witnesses, Lane and Pierce were found guilty by a federal jury. Scutari and Craig were acquitted.

One thing was clear about Berg's execution: It was a "hate crime"—a legally prohibited activity motivated by Berg's being "different." Thus, hate offenses are directed against members of a particular group simply because of their membership in that group. (5) The basis for an attack may be a victim's race, ethnicity, religion, sexual orientation, or gender—indeed, any physical or cultural characteristic which, in the mind of offenders, separates the victim from themselves. The victim's individual characteristics are, from the attacker's point of view, all but irrelevant. The killers of Alan Berg could have cared less that their victim was tall and thin, liked baseball, lived originally in Chicago, or had a family. All that seemed to count was the fact that Berg was "a loud-mouthed Jew."

Unlike Berg's murder, most hate crimes do not involve organized hate groups, whose members are dedicated to the goal of achieving racial purity. Perpetrators usually are not card-carrying members of any racist organizations; they do not wear uniforms, armbands, or sheets; most have never even heard of the Aryan Nations or the Silent Brotherhood.

Hate crimes are more often committed under ordinary circumstances by otherwise unremarkable types—neighbors, a coworker at the next desk, or groups of youngsters looking for a thrill. The typical hate crime is more like the Howard Beach case, an incident that raised the consciousness of New Yorkers, white and black alike, on how hate crimes develop. It showed that brutal attacks can take place spontaneously without the help of organized groups.

It was December 19, 1986. "There's niggers on the boulevard. Let's kill them," shouted an enraged John Lester as he raced through a birthday party of white teenagers in Howard Beach, New York. It was six days before Christmas, shortly after midnight, and a cold winter's night, but Lester was ready to attack. Earlier that evening, he had exchanged racial insults with three young black men whose 1976 Buick had broken down on Cross Bay Boulevard and who were searching without luck for a train to carry them back to Brooklyn. Making the best of a bad situation, the hungry trio agreed to stop at the New Park

Pizzeria at 157th Avenue, one of many Howard Beach pizza shops. That turned out to be a fatal decision.

A largely Italian-American working-class community, Howard Beach is set apart from the rest of New York City by Kennedy Airport and Spring Creek Park. Its unpretentious row houses are distinguished from one another by tidy gardens and little more. But the residents of Howard Beach are fiercely loyal to the area they call home.

The slender and gentle-looking Jon Lester, a junior at John Adams High School, had a pernicious side to him that was not apparent at first glance. The only one among his friends in Howard Beach to have a criminal record, Lester had been previously arrested for possessing a loaded .32-caliber handgun.

When he found out that night that the black men hadn't left *his* neighborhood, Lester was livid. His immediate response was to organize his friends at the party into a posse for the purpose of running these strangers out of town. Armed with baseball bats, a tire iron, and a tree stump, the twelve teenagers jumped into three automobiles and sped in the direction of the pizza shop.

It was now 12:40 A.M. Spotting their assailants moving toward them, the three black men attempted to escape. One managed to elude the hunting party by brandishing a small knife and then, in the confusion of the moment, running into the darkness northward on Cross Bay Boulevard.

But twenty-three-year-old Michael Griffith wasn't so lucky. After being chased through the deserted streets of Howard Beach by his white pursuers, he was beaten severely. Then, in a desperate effort to escape, Griffith scrambled over a concrete barricade bordering the Belt Parkway, darted across its three eastbound lanes, and was then immediately struck by a car driving westbound. Griffith's mangled body shot fifteen feet in the air before hitting the cold asphalt of the Belt Parkway. He died instantly.

The Howard Beach teenagers then spotted the third black man, Michael Griffith's stepfather, Cedric Sandiford, as he ran up 156th Avenue. Surrounding their prey, the angry mob assaulted him again and again, beating him unmercifully with the bats, the tire iron, the tree stump, and their fists, until his battered body slumped to the ground. The tall black man survived by pretending to be unconscious or dead, but he sustained a number of serious injuries. (6)

On December 21, 1987, one day after a memorial service for Michael Griffith on the first anniversary of his death, and after twelve days of deliberation, a jury consisting of one black, two Asian-Americans, six whites, and three Latinos arrived at a verdict in the Howard Beach incident. In a decision that left many New Yorkers astonished by its leniency, Jon Lester and Scott Kern, both 18, and Jason Ladone, 17, avoided a murder conviction and instead were found guilty of having "recklessly caused the death of another," a lesser offense. A fourth defendant was cleared of all charges. In a plea bargain with one of the teenagers who admitted his participation in the Howard Beach attack, Robert D. Riley was permitted to plead guilty to assault rather than murder in exchange for his testimony against his fellow defendants. Seven other white teenagers accused of having participated in the Howard Beach attack have been indicted and await trial.

It is often easy enough to determine whether or not a particular criminal act is a hate crime. In the brutal murder of Alan Berg, the motivation was obvious and clear-cut, the bigotry so blatant that it virtually hits you in the face. In the Howard Beach attack, the hate-inspired violence was so intense that it is impossible to overlook.

In offenses against property, the hatred may be literally spelled out for everyone in a community to view. During the Gulf war, for example, a Los Angeles delicatessen owned by an Arab-American was set ablaze. Before igniting the fire, the arsonists scribbled a message on a wall: "You Fuckin' Arab, go home." (7) Or, in 1985, a black man who had recently moved to Bismarck, North Dakota, received a threatening letter and woke one morning to find a cross burning on his lawn. The message was clear: "Get out now or you're a dead man." (8)

In assaultive hate crimes, the attack is often excessively violent. In Bangor, Maine, for example, three teenage boys beat senseless a twenty-three-year-old man whom they believed to be gay. Then, they threw him off a bridge to his death on the rocks below. The three youths later boasted to their friends that they had "jumped a fag and kicked the shit out of him and threw him in the stream." (9) Some hatemongers make a career of attacking people who are different. On the night of August 20, 1980, Joseph Paul Franklin, a thirty-nine-year-old former member of the KKK and American Nazi Party, gunned down two young black men as they jogged alongside two white women in a Salt Lake City park. Ten years later, when asked from his prison cell to explain why he had committed the murders, Franklin replied, "I'll say that it was just because they were race mixing." Franklin was later connected to thirteen killings across the United States. In 1984, he was convicted of bombing a synagogue in Chattanooga, Tennessee, and in 1986 was sentenced to two more life terms for killing an interracial couple in Madison, Wisconsin. (10)

Alan Berg was slain by members of an organized group whose raison d'être was to rid the world of "subhuman" blacks, "mongrels," and Jews. In Michael Griffith's death, teenagers translated their racism into brutal vio-

lence. The incident would in all likelihood never have happened had the three "intruders" been white. But hate
crimes aren't always so easily labeled as such. When violence is perpetrated by youngsters in the neighborhood, it
can become difficult to determine motivation. Was it a bias
crime—an act of hate-inspired violence? Or, was it an indiscriminate attack that could have been directed against
anyone, regardless of race, religion, or gender? The Central Park jogger is a case in point.

It was an unseasonably warm, moonlit April evening;
New Yorkers took advantage of the weather by remaining
outside after dark. Some made small talk with neighbors
while passing time on their front stoops. Others strolled
the streets of the city, window-shopping for luxurious
items beyond their means or simply enjoying mingling
with the wide range of humanity. Still others jogged.

A young, blond-haired woman of slight build was
taking her nightly exercise. At 10:00 P.M., she ran at a brisk
pace along a secluded extension of 102nd Street, in the
direction of the brightly lit and busy pathways surrounding the Central Park reservoir in the heart of Manhattan.
The lush greenery and winding paths attracted joggers
throughout the city, and she would soon have plenty of
company.

But not the kind of company the young woman expected. Without warning, she found herself completely
surrounded by a pack of snarling, angry young men, apparently in their teens, who dragged her 200 feet down the
side of a muddy ravine and flung her to the ground on the
edge of an isolated pond. She screamed and struggled in
vain, her attackers unmercifully ripping off her clothes,
binding her hands, and gagging her with her own sweat-
shirt. For almost thirty minutes, some of the teenagers
held her down while others savagely raped her. They si-

lenced her muffled screams by smashing her senseless in the face and head, first with their fists and then with rocks, a brick, and a metal pipe. They slashed both of her legs with knives and wrapped her shirt around her neck in ropelike fashion. Then, when there was nothing else to do, they left her for dead.

Brutally disfigured and bleeding profusely, the young woman lay unconscious for three hours on a pathway by the side of the pond. When passersby finally discovered her, it was 1:30 A.M. She was close to death, having lost three-quarters of her blood. Her body temperature had plummeted to 80 degrees.

The police initially suspected that the Central Park jogger assault was a crime motivated by racial hatred. All of the attackers were of minority status—black or Hispanic youths from surrounding neighborhoods—and the victim was a white, relatively well-to-do Wall Street executive. Yet, the Central Park jogger was not the only person to be victimized in the park on the evening of April 19. One hour before they encountered her, the pack of teenagers had joined forces with dozens of other youthful delinquents to engage in a reign of terror. They had pelted cars and cyclists with rocks and bottles and had assaulted joggers and homeless people.

The only explicitly racial incident occurred when the gang taunted a couple on a tandem bicycle with racial slurs—"Whitey" and "Fucking white people." But several dark-skinned Hispanics were also harassed. Indeed, one Hispanic victim, after being robbed, was punched and kicked into unconsciousness. And then, the pack of teens decided to "get a woman jogger." As more and more was learned about the case, it became increasingly clear that the basis of the hate crime against the Central Park jogger was the fact that she was a woman. Her gender, even more than her race, had been a reason for choosing her as a victim. The perpetrators were looking for someone they could sexually assault.

Recent research strongly suggests that hate crimes reported to the police have certain characteristics that distinguish them from other types of offenses. First, hate crimes tend to be *excessively brutal*. A study of 452 hate crimes reported to the Boston police (11) found that fully half of them were assaults (see Appendix A). The remaining 50 percent consisted of acts of vandalism or destruction of property (for example, painting a swastika on a synagogue or throwing a rock through a window). Thus, one of every two hate crimes reported to the Boston police was a personal attack. This statistic is surprising when compared with the national figure on the nature of crimes: nationally, only 7 percent of all crimes reported to the police are assaults. (12) Hate offenses are much more likely to entail personal violence.

The *hatred* in such crimes gets expressed when force is exercised beyond what may be necessary to subdue victims, make them comply, disarm them, or take their worldly goods. Almost three-quarters of all assaultive hate crimes—unlawful personal attacks, even if only with threatening words—result in at least some physical injury to the victim. The relative viciousness of these attacks can be seen by comparing them to the national figures for all crimes, in which only 29 percent of assault victims generally receive some physical injury. By contrast, many victims of hate crime assaults—fully 30 percent—wind up requiring treatment at a hospital because of the severity of their injuries. For assaults of all kinds, this figure is only 7 percent. Once again, it appears that hate crimes are particularly violent.

Clearly, the brutality of the Central Park attackers

alerts us to the possibility that extreme hatred was being channeled into vicious behavior. For thirteen days, the twenty-eight-year-old woman lay in Metropolitan Hospital in a comatose state, precariously clinging to life, her disfigurement so complete that even close friends were unable to identify her. She suffered brain damage, multiple skull fractures, and countless cuts and bruises over most of her body including her face. According to one physician who observed her at the time, "She received a blow so severe that . . . her eyeball had exploded back through the rear of its socket." (13)

Miraculously, however, the recovery of the Central Park jogger was much faster and more complete than anyone would have hoped. Less than two months after the attack, she was released from Metropolitan Hospital to undergo a program of rehabilitation at a private hospital in Wallingford, Connecticut. After six months of intensive therapy, she was able to resume her job as a Wall Street investment banker and once again to jog. But the Central Park jogger never regained her memory of the attack, permanently lost her sense of smell, sometimes suffers from double vision, and occasionally has trouble walking. Plastic surgery hides only her most obvious scars.

A second characteristic of hate crimes reported to the police is that they are often apparently senseless or irrational crimes *perpetrated at random on total strangers*. As a society, we fear random violence against strangers even more than violence that has a logical basis. For example, if it is reported on the evening news that a drug deal "went bad" and one of the participants killed the other, we react with very little fear or even concern. After all, criminals are killing criminals over territorial disputes. And because *we* are not criminals, and therefore not competing with them in business, *we* feel perfectly safe and secure.

In sharp contrast, a story about random violence, such as unexplained attacks against innocent bystanders in a public place (for example, a public park or a post office), engenders widespread fear and anxiety. The reason for this is complex, but one element is that the violence is committed by a stranger against someone he has never met before. This makes all of us feel vulnerable as potential victims. Any one of us could be next.

In the Boston study, approximately 85 percent of all hate crimes involved offenders whose identity was unknown to their victims. In a few cases, the offenders remained unidentified and so might have been an acquaintance, but the vast majority definitely attacked total strangers. By contrast, the National Crime Survey, a national study of crime victims, reports that 61 percent of all crimes of violence are committed by strangers. (14)

When it comes to hate crimes, a potential victim cannot rationalize his or her future safety by saying, for example, "I don't use drugs, so I won't ever be hurt in a situation like that." Rather, for all members of a group under attack, the mere decision to leave home automatically puts them at risk of being victimized. This threat infuses all daily activities, both inside and outside of an individual's home, and is extremely difficult to eliminate. Even the arrest and conviction of an offender may not necessarily relieve this fear. Because the victims did nothing personally to precipitate the previous incident and never knew why they were chosen as victims, how can they feel sure that the same thing won't happen again? Wherever they go, they carry the reason for their victimization with them. They might be attacked again, whether in the office, at a restaurant, or at a bus stop. Even home is not a safe haven. At any moment, a rock might come smashing through the window, flung by an irate neighbor who despises gays, blacks, Asians, or Jews and simply cannot tolerate their presence on his block.

If a crime occurs because a victim's behavior—for example, moving into a neighborhood or attending a particular school—offends the perpetrator, then the victim does have recourse. He or she might be able to retreat, conceding defeat in the face of harassment and persecution. However, the cost in both psychological and economic terms may be prohibitive. In a larger sense, we all lose when victims are frightened away by the acts of hatemongers. To assure our own rights, we must also be able and willing to protect the constitutional rights of all citizens, including those groups we, as individuals, may dislike.

Psychologists suggest that rape is a crime of violence; it frequently becomes the means for men who feel belittled and powerless to express their need for control and dominance. Given the brutality of the assault, this interpretation seems clearly to fit the rape of the Central Park jogger. In one sense, it might be argued that all rapes are hate offenses, because they are invariably linked with the gender of the victim. Yet, not all rapes are directed against women in general. In date or acquaintance rape, where two people know one another, at least on a casual basis, a victim may be chosen because of her particular characteristics that the perpetrator finds either repulsive, appealing, or both. He might not have chosen just any woman for his sexual offense.

In stranger rape, however, the victims are often *interchangeable*, their individual characteristics being irrelevant or at best secondary in determining why they were chosen for victimization. Being female is frequently primary, even if the rapist targets only prostitutes, teenage girls, socialites, brunettes, or the like. Under such conditions, then, rape may indeed qualify as a hate crime.

The Central Park jogger was probably selected *not* because she liked to exercise, *not* because she was five-foot-five in height, *not* because she was an investment banker on Wall Street, and *not* because she had graduated from Wellesley College. The anger of her assailants could not have resulted from anything that she had said to them, because no personal conversation took place before the attack. Their anger could not have been a result of their prior relationship, because they had none.

It is possible, of course, that the Central Park jogger's race and presumed economic status were also factors in her selection as a victim. Joggers are often upper middle class and white; the perpetrators were neither. Consequently, a poor black woman may not have been attacked. Still, the Central Park jogger was an interchangeable victim, one who just happened to be at the wrong place at the wrong time. Almost any other female jogger—and especially any other white female jogger—would probably have been similarly at risk.

Many states are presently in the process of deciding whether or not to include gender as a basis for determining hate motivation. Indeed, eleven states now consider as hate crimes any attack against a woman that is motivated primarily by her gender. The controversy revolves around exactly which crimes against women qualify. Should, for example, all sexual assaults be counted as hate offenses?

The fact that hate crime victims are interchangeable may help to focus the debate. With respect to race, *any* black family that moves into certain neighborhoods will likely be attacked. With respect to sexual orientation, *any* man thought to be gay who happens to walk down a particular street will in all likelihood be assaulted. Similarly, gender-motivated hate crimes should include those attacks in which the offender is looking for *any* woman. By this criterion, acquaintance rape and acts of domestic violence, no matter how despicable, would be excluded from consideration as hate offenses. Only random attacks against women would be included.

The state of California has attempted to apply the interchangeability criterion by specifying that to be considered a hate offense, any crime against women must include an articulated threat by the offender against women in general. Therefore, the offender must say something to the effect that "I am beating you because you are just like all other women and I hate all other women."

Though well-intentioned, the California criterion for establishing interchangeability in crimes against women places too restrictive a burden on the police, who during the course of their investigation must uncover a threat against women in general. Just like other criminals, hatemongers don't always state the motivation for their crimes in the presence of their victims. In place of this rigid standard, victim interchangeability should probably be determined by offender statements made not only to the victim, but also in the presence of friends, relatives, or even the police while being interrogated.

Another characteristic of hate crimes is that they are usually *perpetrated by multiple offenders*. This is a group crime frequently carried out by youthful perpetrators operating together for the purpose of attacking the members of another group.

In most situations, violent crimes are perpetrated by individuals acting alone. In fact, according to the National Crime Survey, only about 25 percent of all crimes of violence are committed by more than one offender. By contrast, 64 percent of hate crimes reported to the police involve two or more perpetrators. Indeed, most are carried out by a group of four or more offenders who attack their victims in a gang. In contrast to gang warfare in which teenagers fight teenagers, however, the targets of hate crimes are not necessarily in their teens or early twenties. Many victims are over thirty, and some are young children.

In the Central Park jogger episode, dozens of teenage boys had congregated on the evening of April 19 to go "wilding"; that is, they got together strictly for the "hell of it," to harass and attack strangers for sport, because they had nothing better to do. Early in the evening, the entire pack of youths roamed the park taunting and harassing victims at random. Then, while most of the boys left the park, at least six of them, ranging in age from fourteen to seventeen, splintered off from the others and continued to look for victims. These are the boys who assaulted the twenty-eight-year-old Central Park jogger.

Lt. William Johnston, who investigates hate crimes for the Boston police, suggests that most hatemongers act in groups because "they are basically cowards." He believes that the experience of being in a group offers the encouragement that may be necessary for offenders to attack a wholly innocent victim. (15)

Johnston is correct when he emphasizes the importance of groups in perpetrating hate offenses. Clearly, there is safety in numbers. The hatemongers who instigate an altercation believe that they are less likely to be hurt in a group because they have their friends to protect them. The group also grants a certain degree of anonymity. If everyone participated, then no one person can easily be singled out as bearing primary responsibility for the attack. Because they share it, the blame is diluted. Finally, the group gives its members a dose of psychological support for their blatant bigotry. Feeding initially on the hatred of one or a few peers, escalation becomes a game in which members of the group incite one another toward ever-increasing levels of violence. To do his part and "prove himself," therefore, each offender feels that he must surpass the previous atrocity.

The case of the Central Park jogger epitomizes how difficult it is at times to determine whether or not an attack is a hate crime. At one end of the continuum, there are numerous offenses that are unequivocally crimes of hate directed against individuals strictly because they belong to a group or category. At the other end of the continuum, however, there are some offenses for which it is difficult, if not impossible, to determine the extent to which hate is a motivating factor.

The attack on the Central Park jogger has all of the elements that define hate crimes. It was a crime committed by multiple offenders who employed excessive brutality against a total stranger. The ambiguity concerns the basis for the attack, whether it was really motivated by gender, race, both, or neither.

In many hate offenses, there is a "spillover" effect that can easily give the appearance of indiscriminate violence, at least at a superficial level. The offenders' anger may be so intense that it generalizes onto in-group members as well. It is conceivable, for example, that the wilding youths who assaulted the Central Park jogger set out exclusively to molest and harass whites or women, but were so caught up in the frenzy of the group experience that almost anyone present would have been victimized.

It is also possible that the youngsters involved in that attack actually set out to get even, in some abstract sense, with "society at large" or "humanity"—and especially with that segment of society that has "made it." Thus, they lashed out against "yuppies"—those privileged whites who apparently have the leisure to jog at whim. In their minds, race becomes an indicator of class; white means wealthy.

After all, many who commit hate crimes are at the margins of their community. They have dropped out of school either spiritually or physically and see little likelihood of ever making it in terms of the American success ethic. But if they can't succeed in a middle-class sense, then they can at least garner the respect and approval of their friends. Peer influence therefore becomes crucial to their sense of belonging and self-esteem.

A recent offense against property clearly qualifies as a hate crime. Here a spill-over effect seems to have occurred. At twenty-seven different locations in Wellesley and Dover, Massachusetts, two young men left ethnic and racial slurs—swastikas, "Adolph lives," "White only," "Final solution," and the like—on homes, cars, roadways, and retail stores. At the home of a Greek-American family in Dover, they painted a row of swastikas and the words "fuck Greeks" on the driveway. Yet the pair also vandalized the car of a racist skinhead they had known who probably would have agreed with their views on Jews, blacks, and Greeks.

Was this a mistake? Were the perpetrators simply attempting to be offensive? Or, was their hatred so extreme and out of control that any target was better than none?

In the pages that follow, we shall raise and answer these and many other questions about the causes, conditions, and consequences of hate crimes. What are the origins of hate crimes in society and within the individual? Are all perpetrators "sick" deviant types, or do they actually reflect aspects of the dominant, mainstream culture in which they live? What can the criminal justice system do to combat these offenses? Can the police be convinced that the victimization of groups whose members have historically been antipolice deserves their serious attention? Can prosecutors and judges be persuaded to treat hate crimes as serious violations of law rather than "childish pranks"? Will administrators in prisons and jails be willing to deal with the racism and homophobia that presently run rampant in their institutions? And, finally, what can we as individuals do to assure that hate crimes do not destroy us or our way of life?

CHAPTER 2

Nasty Pictures in Our Heads

Learning to hate is almost as inescapable as breathing. Like almost everyone else, the hate crime offender grows up in a culture that defines certain people as righteous, upstanding citizens; while designating others as sleazy, immoral characters who deserve to be mistreated. As a child, the perpetrator may never have had a firsthand experience with members of the groups he will later come to despise and then victimize. But, early on, merely by conversing with his family, friends, and teachers or by watching his favorite television programs, he learns the characteristics of disparaging stereotypes.

Columnist Walter Lippmann long ago coined the term *stereotype* in referring to certain "pictures in our heads"— the generalizations that we carry around with us concerning different groups of people. All members of group X are "dirty" and "lazy." All members of group Y are "money-hungry," "powerful," and "shrewd." All members of group Z are "illogical," "emotional," and "submissive."

These stereotypes are so powerful, so widely accepted, and so enduring that, based solely on the above

unattributed characteristics, many people can easily identify groups X, Y, and Z. Even if they personally do not
agree that these images are correct, many people probably
still recognize that the "pictures" are often associated with
African-Americans, Jews, and women, respectively.

To some extent, the tendency to generalize about other people is probably universal. Almost everybody, based
on personal experience that may or may not be limited,
makes at least some generalizations about what other
groups of people are like. The beliefs that we call stereotypes are, however, of a different order. First, every member of a stereotyped group is seen as a rubber stamp of
everyone else in that group. Individual differences are totally obscured. Second, stereotypes usually cannot be
modified by contradictory evidence. No argument or evidence is compelling enough to change the hatemonger's
mind. He is emotionally invested in believing the worst
about the members of a stigmatized group. And, third, the
person who accepts the validity of a nasty stereotype isn't
simply trying to make sense of his world. More likely, he is
looking for a convenient excuse to express hostility, to
attack and brutalize the people he despises.

Clearly, stereotypes tend to be all encompassing. That
is, they are applied without regard for individual characteristics to each and every member of a group. From this
viewpoint, there is no good reason to get to know "them"
on a personal basis. After all, "to know one Latino is to
know them all . . . to be familiar with one Asian is to be
familiar with each and every one of them."

By contrast, those who stereotype often also recognize a necessity to handle exceptions to the rule: those
cases they inevitably encounter in everyday life that simply don't fit their stereotyped preconceptions. For example, two freshmen—one black, the other white—recently

roomed together in the dormitory of a large northeastern university. Both had grown up under a system of rigid racial segregation in their neighborhoods, churches, and schools; and both initially expressed negative beliefs about members of other races. Neither had previously had a close relationship with a person of another race. Both were apprehensive about whether they would get along. Yet, after two months, they had developed a close friendship. When later questioned about their compatibility, both students expressed very positive regard for their roommate and yet continued to hold stereotyped beliefs about one another's racial groups. Each of them reasoned as follows: "My roommate is a great guy, but he's *different:* other members of his group simply can't be trusted." In a sense, then, by assuming that one case is unusual, the presumed exception allows a bigot to accept the "special case" while he continues to believe the stereotyped image.

The rule of exceptions also minimizes the impact of a bigot's exposure to the successful members of a despised group. How does a white racist—someone firmly convinced of the intellectual superiority of Caucasians—explain Bill Cosby, Barbara Jordan, or Martin Luther King? He really doesn't have to explain anything. After all, a *few* exceptions can always be found (and, if forced to explain, he can always talk about some blacks having "white blood" or getting special treatment). At the same time, the presence of a few exceptional cases in the mind of a hate-monger also helps him to disregard the possibility of economic inequities between racial groups. He reasons, "Why can't they all be like Bill Cosby and pull themselves up by their bootstraps? If Cosby made it, so can the rest of them. But I guess they'd rather burn buildings and loot stores."

To understand the meaning of a stereotype, one must

also be familiar with its social and historical context. During warfare, the enemy is called "bloodthirsty," but our fighting force is "courageous," even if both sides violate the same rules of battle. In the business sector, male bosses are sometimes seen as "motivated" and "assertive," whereas female bosses under the same conditions may be considered "pushy bitches." Having rhythm may be flattering when attributed to someone white, but it may not always be taken as a compliment by a black American who recognizes that the image of "the musical and ignorant black" was employed to justify slavery. Having power and wealth may sound like a laudable goal (indeed, the fulfillment of the American Dream), but not necessarily when ascribed to Jewish Americans, whose ancestors were kicked out of several countries or even exterminated because they were charged with being too rich or having too much power.

Indeed, the stereotype of Jews as unscrupulous, aggressive, and overly powerful continues to be accepted by millions of Americans. In fact, while many anti-Semitic beliefs have declined over the decades, a few have actually seen more widespread acceptance—in particular, that "Jews are always stirring up troubles with their ideas," that "Jews have too much power in the business world," that "Jews are more loyal to Israel than to America," and that "Jews have too much power in the United States." These are the very stereotypes that best express growing anxiety among Americans in general about *being able to compete for scarce resources* and moral outrage that a particular group might be getting *more than its share—"at my expense."* (1)

Even though verbalized in an apparently harmless joke or an innocuous television sitcom, therefore, stereotypes are often more pernicious than they might at first appear to be. Time and time again, they have been used to *justify* atrocities committed against members of stigmatized groups. Thus, the image serves an important purpose: adult men couldn't be beaten, enslaved, or murdered with impunity, but those considered subhuman or childlike could be enslaved and treated as though they were animals.

Throughout history, many groups have been *infantilized*. So long as they "stayed in their place" and played the inferior role to which they were assigned, they were stereotyped as children or infants. (2) For example, women have traditionally been regarded as "girls" who should remain at home—in the kitchen and bedroom—where they "belong," or so it was said. The particular image varied from generation to generation, but the intent was always the same—to keep women in a subservient position in their relations with men. To be in style, women of the 1920s were asked to look like children. Some wore their dresses cut to look like the shirts worn by little boys some ten years earlier. Others bobbed their hair like a baby's, hoping to give their face the appearance of "a small child: round and soft, with a turned-up nose, saucer eyes and a pouting 'bee-stung' mouth." During the 1960s, young women similarly dressed as if they were little girls. They wore very short ruffled frocks and made up their eyes to create a baby-faced look. Miniskirts, baby-doll nightgowns, and lacy baby-doll dresses all made "grown women look like toddlers with a glandular affliction, or like severely retarded nubile teenagers." (3)

Also much like children, women were viewed as diminutive or as the weaker sex and therefore in need of masculine protection, often whether they wanted it or not. Just to make sure that they remained weak enough, stylish women of the nineteenth century were expected to wear tight corsets to achieve the stylish hourglass figure. Those women who complied may have been in high fashion, but they suffered weakness, shortness of breath, and back pain, sometimes severe enough to cause disability (and therefore greater dependency on men).

Race has also served as a basis for infantilization. During slavery, the "Little Black Sambo" image depicted black American men as boys who lacked either the sophistication or the intelligence to fend for themselves—hence, the justification for what was popularly believed to be a "white man's burden": because some whites regarded blacks as inherently inferior, slavery was widely considered as absolutely essential for the survival of the black race. (4)

The members of a group are typically infantilized only as long as they conform to a docile and obliging role vis-à-vis those in positions of power. If the members of a stigmatized group get "too uppity"—perhaps even rebellious—they are no longer stereotyped as having the characteristics of children, but are instead regarded as animals or demons. In a word, they are *dehumanized*. After all, you cannot kill children, regardless of how much they misbehave; but it is perfectly acceptable—perhaps even obligatory—to slaughter an animal or to kill "the devil."

During the European witch craze (from the late fifteenth to the mideighteenth centuries), women who dared challenge the prerogatives traditionally assigned to men or who competed against men in the work force were summarily labeled as witches and then burned at the stake or crushed to death under heavy rocks. According to some estimates, millions of women may have been destroyed as witches. At the turn of the century, Irish immigrants who competed with native-born Americans for jobs were depicted in editorial cartoons as nothing more than fully clothed apes, while Jewish newcomers were portrayed in caricature as giant octopi whose tentacles enveloped the world. Members of organized hate groups have long contended that Jews are the descendants of Satan and that blacks are a different and inferior species they call "mud people." (5) During the 1960s and early 1970s, leaders of the women's movement were sometimes stereotyped—in cartoon fashion sporting horns, a tail, and the look of evil in their eyes—as ugly and vicious "she-devils." (6)

Stereotypes turn particularly nasty whenever a vulnerable segment of society is regarded as threatening the power, prestige, or privileges of the dominant group. After having experienced a lengthy period of rising acceptance of or at least tolerance for racial and ethnic equality throughout society, Americans are now increasingly concerned instead with cutting their economic losses in relation to other groups. Most Americans, in principle, continue to support equal treatment of blacks and whites in jobs, housing, schools, and public accommodations. But when it comes to supporting these efforts through action, enthusiasm begins to wane. In other words, at an abstract level, most Americans believe in equality, yet in practice we really don't want it—not if it means personal sacrifice!

What is more, because economic conditions have recently worsened, the opposition to measures that promise racial equality in some areas has either remained very strong or actually increased. Even today, few whites object to integrating schools or neighborhoods when a small number of blacks is involved. But when substantial numbers of blacks move into a classroom or a neighborhood, whites feel *threatened* and so reject integration. (7)

While black Americans tend to view themselves as victims of white society, white Americans typically no longer acknowledge the persistence of prejudice and discrimination in the lives of blacks. In this way, whites are able to downplay their own responsibility for why blacks tend to have worse jobs, lower incomes, and poorer housing than whites and, at the same time, to justify their own opposition to programs—for example, affirmative action—designed to achieve racial parity. (8)

Where a perceived threat is economic, so are the stereotypes applied to a particular group in order to explain its inferior status. Thus, according to a recent national survey sponsored by the National Science Foundation, a majority of white Americans say that blacks and Latinos are more likely than whites to "prefer to live off welfare" and less likely to "prefer to be self-supporting." More than half of the respondents also characterize both blacks and Latinos as lazier, less intelligent, and more prone to violence than whites.

Though Asians fare somewhat better in the survey, they too are characterized in a negative light by a sizable minority of Americans. In fact, 46 percent of the respondents claim that Asians are more likely than whites to prefer living off welfare, 34 percent that Asians are lazier, 36 percent that Asians are less intelligent, and 30 percent that they are more violence-prone. (9)

Even more threatening to whites, as well as to subjugated groups, is the complimentary image of Asians as the "model minority"—that set of newcomers who have been spectacularly successful in American society. This stereotype obscures important pockets of poverty within the Asian-American community and also exacerbates the resentment felt by Americans who simply aren't "making it" themselves. After all, even if Asians are "lazy" and "unintelligent," they are also believed to be inordinately successful. Why? How is it possible for a group of Americans to excel economically despite their presumed defects of motivation and intellect? *Perhaps Asians are the undeserving recipients of extraordinary treatment.* This is precisely the unsubstantiated charge that many Americans make in an effort to explain what they believe to be an unfair advantage for Asian-Americans. For example, a rumor that recently circulated among blue-collar workers throughout the United States was the claim, totally without basis in reality, that all Asian newcomers received the gift of a new automobile from the American government.

In some cases, the inordinate success of a few Asians has been used to justify withholding aid from all Asians. For example, most colleges and universities no longer grant Asian-Americans special consideration in their admissions process and in their awarding of financial assistance. Indeed, certain institutions of higher learning have actually "rigged their admissions standards to handicap Asian students." (10)

The importance of the personal threat in the stereotyping process can be seen in the acceptance of vicious beliefs concerning a range of groups whose members, having challenged the status quo by their new visibility, are currently the targets of hatred. As more and more Americans have grown fearful of contracting AIDS, for example, they have also stereotyped lesbians and gays as "a pervasive, sinister, conspiratorial, and corruptive threat." The traditional view of gays as essentially laughable—"as queens, fairies, limp-wrists, and nellies"—could hardly have put them at so much risk. But to stereotype gays as the destroyers of civilization is to make life easier for potential gay-bashers everywhere, who seek some kind of justification and support for their criminal behavior. (11)

Many people have a distorted view of social reality, because they usually don't bother to validate or test their beliefs about others in any systematic way. Thus they can go through a lifetime clinging to old stereotypes that are patently false, without the slightest hint that they are essentially being inaccurate and unfair.

Because Ivan Boesky was implicated in an insider trading scandal, anti-Semites conclude that Boesky engaged in shady business practices because he is Jewish. Protestants and Catholics accused of the same offense are somehow dismissed, because they don't fit the stereotype. If an Italian-American makes headlines because he is a member of organized crime, everybody remembers that he is of Italian descent. If a Frenchman gains the same notoriety, we don't remember his ethnic identity at all, because it seems irrelevant. If a rapist turns out to be black, some whites attribute his sexual deviance to his race. If a black police officer risks his life to arrest the rapist, the same whites forget about the color of the officer's skin. Or they treat him as an exception to the rule.

The distorted perception of the reality of life in America can be easily demonstrated by questioning even the most sophisticated individuals about elementary social facts. For example, what percentage of the population of the United States is black? Hispanic? Jewish? According to a recent Gallup national survey, the average American estimates that 30 percent of the population of the United States is black (actually, the figure for those who regard themselves as black or African-American is less than 13 percent); that 25 percent of all Americans are Hispanic (actually, the figure is close to 8 percent); and that 15 percent of our population is Jewish (actually, the figure is only 2 percent maximum).

What difference does it make that so many Americans have a distorted view of social reality? That they operate on the basis of false stereotypes? That they are misinformed about other people and maybe about themselves?

The answer lies in the relationship between the way we define the world and the decisions we make about it.

Commonly stereotyped as "unscrupulous, aggressive, and too powerful," if Jews are mistakenly believed to make up 15 percent of our population, then the myth of a dominant Jewish presence in banking or the press sounds more plausible. *Maybe we had then better restrict Jews so they can no longer work for banks and newspapers.* If blacks who are often regarded as violence-prone are also thought to constitute 30 percent of all Americans, then we might support making our inner cities into armed camps: *Let's spend less for social programs and more for police intervention.* Not only do stereotypes sometimes confirm our worst suspicions—in this case, that minorities are taking over—they also suggest that hatemongers take action to limit the influence of those minorities.

Whatever the causal factors responsible for hate offenses, those who attack other human beings because they are different would like *validation* in doing so. To an increasing extent, hatemongers find solace, if not inspiration, in the humor, entertainment, music, and politics that we share as a people, in a growing culture of hate that is being directed wholly toward the members of our society. (12)

CHAPTER 3

Hatred Is Hip

We laugh and the world laughs with us; at least some people in the world laugh with us. *Others weep*—those who are the butt of the joke. We clap along with the beat of a popular tune on FM radio. It makes us feel happy, excited, uplifted . . . *but at whose expense?* Perhaps at the expense of those groups maligned in the lyrics. We feel a surge of solidarity and self-esteem in response to the ravings of a bigoted, charismatic politician . . . *but somebody suffers*—usually the innocent people on whom all our personal problems are blamed. Hatred has become an integral part of American mass culture, finding expression in its art, music, politics, and humor.

Our popular culture both reflects and affects the attitudes and concerns of Americans. We may therefore look to recent changes in music, humor, art, and politics to identify larger trends in public attitudes that might not otherwise be so obvious, at least to a casual observer.

Bigotry is back. There has been a disturbing increase recently in the use of negative stereotyping to characterize various minority groups in the United States. Hatred has become hip; intolerance is in. What used to be whispered behind closed doors about blacks, gays, Jews, women, and the elderly is now openly flaunted between total strangers. Whether or not intended as such, we are in the midst of a growing *culture of hate:* from humor and music to religion and politics, a person's group affiliation—the fact that he or she *differs from people in the in-group*—is being used more and more to provide a basis for dehumanizing and insulting that person.

Sociologists and psychologists have long recognized the role of humor in subtly communicating malice under conditions of competition and conflict. Put-down jokes are designed to make one's adversary appear ludicrous or absurd. At the group level, racial humor is primarily created to attain some sense of self-esteem and solidarity at the expense of another racial group. (1) Under the guise of *merely joking,* individuals can give voice to racist ideas and emotions, yet maintain that they are only having a little fun. (2)

These racist jokes remain with the listener and may be retold time and time again to much wider audiences. Moreover, even if they are not retold, the racist ideas on which such humor is based tend to remain with the audience as a subtle reinforcement of society's stereotypes.

Among stand-up comics who capitalize on our sense of collective intolerance, Andrew Dice Clay has recently made the art of slurring women, gays, and minorities a highlight of his raunchy routines. He makes his audience laugh at the expense of newcomers, for example, by referring to Asians as "urine-colored people with towels on their heads." (3) Clay's slurs directed against women have sparked some outrage: when the comic hosted "Saturday Night Live," Nora Dunn, a former cast member, and singer Sinead O'Connor both refused to perform on the same stage, claiming that Clay's appearance would provide a legitimate arena for the sexist ravings of "a hate-monger."

But Andrew Dice Clay is hardly the Lone Ranger among contemporary comics who have made minorities, women, and vulnerable people the butt of their humor. In fact, a new form of "attack comedy" has recently emerged, in which the most downtrodden, least fortunate members of our society are verbally assaulted. During the 1960s, comics Lenny Bruce, Dick Gregory, Richard Pryor, and George Carlin were notorious for denigrating others in a humorous format. But they typically directed their anger against the establishment elements in society whose members could easily protect themselves—the wealthy, the powerful, and the prestigious—or against the prejudices, hypocrisies, and mindless slogans these comics ascribed to mainstream society. Bruce regarded his comedy as a vehicle for achieving social change. (4) Like Dick Gregory, he used humor to attack popular establishment targets—the military or the president—and to provoke his audiences to question their commonly held beliefs. His humor provided an alternative perspective.

In sharp contrast, modern "attack" comics like Andrew Dice Clay, Sam Kinison, Eddie Murphy, Bobcat Goldthwait, and Jay Charboneau make no pretense of having some higher purpose. Without restraint, they aim their savage barbs simply to achieve an effect—to make their audiences cringe, squirm, and, of course, laugh at the expense of those who cannot defend themselves from exploitation and cruelty.

Sometimes the victim is a defenseless individual; other times, it is an entire group of vulnerable people. In his stand-up routine, Kinison used to joke about a famine in Africa: "Of course those silly motherfuckers in Ethiopia are dying," he moaned. "Whoever told them to live in a desert? Human beings are not supposed to live in the fucking desert!" During a television performance, Don Rickles points to an elderly woman in the audience: "Hi there, Ma'am. I spoke to the home . . . you go in Friday." (5)

The culture of hate has permeated popular music as well, especially in the lyrics of recordings directed specifically to younger audiences. In the language of the streets, rappers like Ice-T, 2 Live Crew, and N.W.A. ("Niggas with Attitude") express a violent sexual theme supported by the view that women are "whores" and "bitches" who are "only asking for it anyway." In the extreme case, the rap lyrics fuse sex and violence, so that one becomes a metaphor for the other. In a recent hit number, for example, N.W.A.'s "Eazy-E" describes in sexual terms how he went to his girlfriend's house, knocked down the door, and blasted her with an assault rifle. Some rap violence is also directed against gays. In the song, "Watcha' Looking At?" by Audio Two, for example, a man who appears to be gay is warned that his sexual orientation is enough to get him punched in the face.

Popular musicians have also cast aspersions on groups that are different in terms of race or ethnicity. Calling himself "Supreme Allied Chief of Community Relations," Professor Griff (a member of the rap group Public Enemy) once told the press that "Jews are wicked. They create wickedness around the globe." Although no longer permitting Griff to give interviews to the press, Public Enemy nonetheless released a single, "Welcome to the Terrordome," in which the Christ-killer, anti-Semitic theme was espoused. (6)

On the whiter side of the pop music ledger, the lyrics of some "heavy metal" records emphasize violence, sexism, power, and hatred. In Motley Crue's song "Live Wire," for example, all of these themes come together in a scene of brutal assault and murder. (7) Moreover, the heavy metal rock band Guns N' Roses sold more than four million copies of "G N' R Lies," whose lyrics are blatantly anti-black, anti-immigrant, and antigay. In "Used to Love Her," the same group attempted to justify violence against women by depicting a young man being incessantly nagged by his girlfriend until he could take it no more and so killed her. A *Newsweek* reporter summarized the way Guns N' Roses leader Axl Rose defended his beliefs as follows: ". . . he's mad at immigrants because he had a run-in with a Middle Eastern clerk at a 7-Eleven. He hates homosexuals because one once made advances to him while he was sleeping. And, he uses words like 'niggers' because you're not allowed to use words like 'nigger.' " (8) Reflecting the same order of defiance in her teenybopper fans, rock idol Madonna, who brought us such controversial classics as "Like a Virgin" and "Like a Prayer," has, in a little number titled "Hanky Panky," extolled the pleasures of being spanked by men. (9)

Religious leaders have given expression to anti-Semitism. In the 1980s, the president of the Southern Baptist Convention, later insisting that he was only teasing, remarked in a radio sermon that "Jews got funny-looking noses." Louis Farrakhan, leader of the Black Muslim sect known as the Nation of Islam, once referred to Judaism as a "dirty religion." Speaking at Madison Square Garden in 1985, Farrakhan remarked, "The Jews talk about 'Never again' . . . listen, Jews, this little black boy is your last chance because the Scriptures charge you with killing the prophets of God. . . . You cannot say 'Never again' to God, because when he puts you in the oven, 'Never again' don't mean a thing." (10) Minister Farrakhan's denigration of Jews is reminiscent of the inflammatory speeches of Iran's Ayatollah Khomeini in which he attributed all of his nation's problems to America and called all Americans "the world's Satans."

The culture of hate has invaded the political arena as well, and commentators who might otherwise deserve a reputation for decency are willing to express their bigoted remarks to anyone who will listen. For the most part, these political leaders are *not* at the lunatic fringe. On the contrary, they attract large and diverse constituencies and are located more or less in the mainstream of American public opinion. Some assume elected office; others hold leadership positions as media commentators.

In a recent senatorial election campaign in North Carolina, Senator Jesse Helms, widely known for his ardent stance against civil rights legislation, narrowly defeated his black opponent. Part of Helms's campaign strategy apparently was to run a series of racially incendiary commercials on television, one of which showed a pair of white hands crumpling up and throwing away a job rejection letter. The voice-over led viewers of the commercial to assume that the rejection was due to affirmative action policies of the federal government. Helms's contest and subsequent reelection followed the effective use of the infamous Willie Horton commercials by the Bush campaign during the presidential election of 1988. The ubiquitous presence of Horton—a convicted, malicious rapist—in campaign materials probably swayed voters, but it also perpetuated the impression that blacks are inherently violent and should be feared. Some analysts have suggested that if Willie Horton had been white, he probably would not have been used in the commercial.

Politicians tend to elicit a favorable response by couching their racist messages in legitimate issues. Louisiana's David Duke raised this strategy to an art form when

he spoke eloquently about the need to get the federal government off the backs of the people (meaning: end federal
programs that benefit blacks and Latinos) or about our
right to expect a quality education for all our children
(meaning: white children should not have to go to school
with blacks). Concerned about such matters, many Americans might support a candidate who addresses the important issues of the day—even if he or she also happens to
espouse racism.

Duke's recent success in Louisiana politics, and, to a
lesser extent, at the national level only serves to under-
score his former role as a Ku Klux Klan imperial wizard
and the founder of the National Association for the Advancement of White People (NAAWP). In a 1986 fund-
raising letter distributed by the NAAWP, Duke stated:

> [U]nless we act soon, whites will become outnumbered in
> the nation that we created—*within a generation!* No issue is
> more important than our people preserving its identity, cul-
> ture, and rights. An America ruled by a majority of Blacks,
> Mexicans, and other Third World types will not be the
> America of our forefathers, or the kind of nation for which
> they struggled and sacrificed. (11)

Even the most respectable commentators have been
willing to give public voice to their personal biases, without regard for the consequences that their statements
might have on intergroup tensions. Syndicated columnist, CNN celebrity, and presidential candidate Patrick
Buchanan—former aide to the Nixon–Agnew team—
recently suggested that the Anti-Defamation League was
out to smear him. Referring to the Congress of the United
States as "Israeli-occupied," he claimed that the Israeli defense minister and "its [Israel's] amen corner in the United
States" had tried to drag the United States into war against
Iraq because it would serve Israeli interests (he failed to
foresee Baghdad's Scud missiles being aimed at Tel Aviv).

In pleading his case against the Persian Gulf war, he argued that if we went to war, those who fought would have names like "McAllister, Murphy, Gonzales, and Leroy Brown." Even his ally on the right, William F. Buckley, Jr., could see the anti-Semitism in this assertion: "There is no way to read that sentence without concluding that Pat Buchanan was suggesting that American Jews manage to avoid personal military exposure even while advancing military policies they (uniquely?) engender." (12)

Buchanan's remarks regarding the war against Iraq are simply the most recent in a series of anti-Jewish, anti-Israeli statements. He is the same commentator who previously proclaimed his skepticism about whether hundreds of thousands of Jews actually had been executed at Treblinka (like David Duke, he says the estimate of concentration camp deaths has been severely inflated). He is also the individual who defended former President Reagan's visit to a cemetery in Germany where SS troopers had been buried. (Reagan later claimed that he had been misled into believing that German soldiers who had risked their lives to save Jews were buried there.) (13)

Also in the political arena, a growing number of "shock jocks" have emerged as the controversial hosts for popular radio talk shows around the country. To the delight of a national audience of millions, right-wing talk master Rush Limbaugh regularly castigates feminists, animal rights advocates, and gay rights activists. In New York City, Howard Stern's FM talk show makes a fetish of targeting blacks, gays, women, and the disabled. Stern's "satirical" disparagement of minorities—for example, his "shuck-and-jive" imitation of Washington's Marion Barry, Jr., and his impression of "a lisping, mincing" Mr. Blackswell—have propelled the contentious talk show host into the national limelight. He is presently heard on major stations around the country and has appeared in syndicated form on national television. (14)

A particularly appalling version of the culture of hate is the omnipresent portrayal of women being victimized by grotesque forms of sexual violence in motion pictures. Though these films are supposedly made for adults, they actually appeal to teenage audiences. These R-rated "slasher" films—widely available to members of all age groups in theaters as well as on video cassettes—depict the assault, torture, and murder of women, but in erotic and romantic contexts. In *Tool Box Murders*, for example, a "glassy-eyed lunatic" type is shown literally nailing a nude young woman to a wall as romantic music plays softly in the background. In *I Spit on Your Grave*, several men are shown tracking, taunting, and then "playfully" gang raping a terrified young woman whom they have trapped on a desolate island. Such films contain even more sexual violence against women than do their less available X-rated counterparts. The R-rated versions may send a message that sex and violence are inseparable—that you cannot or *should* not have one without the other. Moreover, research indicates that a heavy diet of slasher movies can make some men more accepting of sexual violence against women. (15)

We do not suggest that every promoter of the culture of hate *means* to defame or to injure others. Still, just because something is *intended* to be entertaining doesn't necessarily mean that it's also benign. Because a musician's "heart is in the right place" doesn't always guarantee that his message is without harm. Even when an artist's motive is honorable, his effect on a youthful and unsophisticated audience can be deceptively dangerous. A comic's sexist and racist jokes may be hilarious but, at the same time, perpetuate the nasty stereotypes that many people hold of those who are different. A rap or heavy metal artist may engage in hyperbole only to make a point with his audience, or espouse a philosophical position that only he *really* understands, and still bring a sexist or racist fan to the precipice of violence. Similarly, a particular R-rated film may keep you on the edge of your seat, yet act as a catalyst for violent behavior toward women.

Thinking about ourselves, we would like to presume that hatred reflects a sick, pathological fringe element that has little, if anything, to do with the dominant American culture. We comfort ourselves by believing that vicious acts of bigotry originate outside of mainstream society, that they reside in only the darkest recesses of the marginal or abnormal mind. To the extent that this view is accepted, we see ourselves as innocent, blameless, and clean, whereas *they* are guilty as sin. We are free of prejudice, while *they* are rednecks, racists, and bigots. *We* can continue to go about our business as usual, whereas *they* must change their evil ways.

Yet, the large numbers of people who continue to rent slasher movies and buy tickets to see racist musical groups in concert indicate instead that the threads of a culture of hate are woven into the fabric of American society. Clearly, we are not talking only about the acts of a few entertainers or politicians who operate outside of the mainstream of American culture. If TV audiences were actually repulsed by the humor of Andrew Dice Clay, he would never have been asked to host "Saturday Night Live." If his guest appearances on national talk shows caused their ratings to drop, then he would hardly be asked back. Yet, he is.

The culture of hate is part of a vicious cycle of hate and crime; it both reflects and affects the growth of hate crimes in the United States. As cause, the culture of hate provides support and encouragement to those who seek to express their personal version of bigotry in some form of criminal behavior. As suggested earlier, stereotypes serve an important but dangerous function: they *justify* hate crimes in the mind of the perpetrator by providing him with the essential dehumanized images of vulnerable individuals. It would be difficult, if not impossible, for most people to assault another human being, but it becomes a good deal easier to attack or kill "a urine-colored person with a towel on his head," "a Christ killer," "a whore," "a bitch," "a nigger," "a cracker," or "a rapist."

Young Americans are frequently targeted as the primary audience for the culture of hate, especially for its films, music, and humor. Partially because they are lacking in diverse personal experiences, young people are generally unprepared to reject prejudiced claims coming from sources they regard as credible. Moreover, because they are less likely to handle their frustrations with tolerance and self-control, young Americans are more likely to resort to violence to resolve conflicts. In fact, most hate crimes are committed by offenders under the age of twenty.

The growing presence of a culture of hate reminds us that hate crimes are only the tip of the iceberg of bigotry and prejudice. Popular culture often represents a more pervasive, if less extreme, version of the same underlying hostilities that trigger criminal behavior. There are many members of society who are very angry—if not quite angry enough to vandalize a cemetery or assault someone whose skin color is different. Instead, they might only parrot the racist lyrics of a heavy metal song, shout their agreement with a racist talk show host, laugh at a racist stand-up comic, or vicariously relish the murder spree of a deranged killer depicted in an R-rated slasher film. For a few misguided souls, however, the culture of hate is simply not enough to satisfy their need for malice; their quest is for personal justice.

In the culture of hate, we find the posture that is

politically correct for the social and economic climate of the 1990s—divisiveness and group conflict rather than intergroup harmony and cooperation. Certainly, there was a period in history when nonviolence, egalitarianism, and multiculturalism were actually politically correct. On many college campuses around the nation, baby-boomer college students—wearing bell bottoms and love beads—once protested en masse against racism, war, and sexual harassment. During the 1960s and early 1970s, these boomers were intent on changing the world, or at least the world on their campuses. The culture of that time—its music, films, humor, and politics—often reflected the desire of young people for social change.

Of course, that was more than twenty years ago, and the old egalitarian version of political correctness has since been buried. It went out of fashion just as the Carter administration left office, and Americans began blaming the so-called welfare parasites for everything that had gone wrong with our country.

In the growing culture of hate, liberalism has become about as popular as leprosy. In its place, we find a new brand of political correctness—one that fits better with the prevailing conservative proclivities of the American people and our hard economic times, with the recent influx of newcomers from Eastern Europe, Asia, and Latin America who are blamed for stealing job opportunities. If anything, the rising tide of multiculturalism is being met by growing resentment among native-born white males who believe that their masculine advantage has eroded. Far from being politically correct, anyone in 1992 who dares take a position in favor of diversity and egalitarianism is committing political suicide!

CHAPTER 4

Resentment

At the tender age of four, David Lewis Rice lunged head-first through a sliding glass door, which left him badly scarred and blind in one eye. During his teenage years, the left side of his face was burned in a freak welding accident that only added to his already grotesque appearance. Some of Rice's schoolmates routinely targeted the disfigured and pitifully skinny youngster for their harassment and ridicule; the "nicer" kids simply avoided him.

Depressed by his failure both in and out of the classroom, Rice dropped out after his second year of high school and went to work. But his ill fortune continued. He had a brief and miserable marriage and an extended period of moving in and out of menial jobs. By his twenty-seventh birthday, Rice was destitute and living in a shelter in Seattle, Washington. He held part-time jobs whenever he could get them, which wasn't very often.

Totally down on his luck and unable to function in everyday life, Rice sought aid and comfort. He found both by joining the ranks of the Seattle Duck Club, an organization notorious for its violently antigovernment, anticommunist, and anti-Semitic philosophy, and he gradually developed the belief that his personal problems were a result of some vaguely defined global conspiracy involving Jewish lawyers, communists, the Federal Reserve System, and international bankers.

In line with his friends in the ultraconservative fringe, Rice grew particularly enraged by the presence of a prominent attorney in Seattle, Charles Goldmark. In 1962, Goldmark's father had waged an abortive election campaign for state representative. During this period, he was widely regarded as a communist sympathizer, based only on his membership in the American Civil Liberties Union and his wife's previous association with the Communist party as a young girl in New York City. Following his defeat, Goldmark's father filed and won a libel suit against his detractors that received months of national attention. Because of the publicity, however, he continued to be unfairly linked to communism. And, in later years, so was his wealthy son, Charles.

On Christmas Eve of 1985, in the middle of the night, Rice decided singlehandedly to eliminate the "top communist" and "head Jew" in Washington State. The bearded, anemic-looking vagrant walked into an affluent Seattle neighborhood and, posing as a delivery man, gained entry into the home of the "enemy"—Charles Goldmark. At the point of a realistic-looking toy handgun, he handcuffed Goldmark, his wife, and their two sons and then used chloroform to drug them all into unconsciousness.

Rice slaughtered his victims as they slept. First, he viciously bludgeoned Goldmark to death. Then, taking a carving knife from the kitchen drawer, he fatally stabbed Goldmark's wife and children.

While Rice was repeatedly slashing and bludgeoning the members of the Goldmark family one by one, their

Christmas tree sat conspicuously by the fireplace in the living room, and their Christmas ham baked slowly in the oven. It didn't occur to Rice that Charles Goldmark was neither Jewish nor communist, but a wealthy Protestant capitalist attorney who had attended Quaker schools as a child and later graduated from Harvard Law School. But, then, such "details" are unimportant to someone on a mission. (1)

Whether or not David Lewis Rice was psychotic is beside the point; there are many other just as bitter, indignant, hostile, or irate individuals who are not severely mentally ill. Like Rice, they may feel left out and abused, fearful of becoming so, or convinced beyond a shadow of a doubt that their way of life is being destroyed and that their rights are being eliminated. *They* are the victims, from their distorted perspective, of a society that is out of control, and *they* are looking for someone to blame.

Resentment can be found, at least to some extent, in the personality of most hate crime perpetrators. The interchangeability of victims gives us a clue that this resentment may be immense and that it likely serves a deep-rooted psychological need. Extremely prejudiced individuals are frequently *ethnocentric;* they harbor a generalized hostility toward groups that are different. Thus, one black victim can easily substitute for another; one Jew is as good (or, more precisely, as bad) as the next. But the choice of victim also can cross group lines: if blacks aren't available to victimize, then Latinos will do; if Latinos can't be found, then gays will be targeted, and so on.

Actually, the generalized resentment that often forms the basis for hate crimes is frequently aimed at society as a whole rather than at any particular individual or group. It is the wider society from which a perpetrator is estranged, and it is the wider society that he perceives as having rejected him. He is convinced that the country has changed for the worse, that political leaders are taking us down the road to total ruination, and that people like himself—the "little guys"—have lost all control of their destiny.

At the same time, however, hate crimes have a basis in what the members of a society are *normally* taught when they are growing up. Thus, the perpetrator of hate crimes is socialized in the values and rules of conventional society. He learns to hate in the same way that he learns love of country, motherhood, and church. He may be raised by a set of parents who repeat bigoted jokes at the dinner table, watch stereotyped portrayals of minorities on television, and listen to friends recount their negative experiences with the members of different groups. Every time he passes through the inner city on the way to work, his stereotyped attitudes are reinforced. Every time a news report highlights violence committed by blacks or academic awards achieved by Asians, he feels validated in his fears and concerns. He learns his culture and, as a result, *knows precisely those groups against which he is supposed to vent his anger.* These are the groups that his culture has stereotyped as inferior in either an intellectual or moral sense; these are the people who deserve to be disparaged and belittled in the culture of hate. Thus, by defining the enemy in unmistakable terms, the offender's culture has given him *permission* to attack.

Decades ago, the authors of *The Authoritarian Personality* recognized that prejudice satisfies a deep-rooted psychological need to protect or enhance self-esteem. (2) An authoritarian child is raised with harsh and threatening forms of discipline. He is expected to be weak and to submit to the desires of his parents. In the extreme case, he may be physically assaulted. The parents, in turn, assume a dominant posture in relation to their child. As a result, an authoritarian child makes only a superficial identification with his parents, actually harboring much latent hostility and resentment toward them.

The outcome of such childhood experiences has relevance for an understanding of the psychological roots of hate crimes: authoritarians may finally become hatemongers; they may come to treat others in the manner that their parents treated them. As adults, they identify with power and the powerful—*the aggressor*—and maintain a general contempt for the allegedly inferior and weak members of society. Thus, they come to despise such diverse groups as blacks, foreigners, Hispanics, Jews, and gays. In the process, they are able to bolster and protect their self-esteem whenever it is threatened.

Threat to self-esteem may have a basis in objective reality, not only for a few authoritarian types but for Americans in general. Resentment is a state of mind, but it is also a state of our society. A growing number of observers have applied the term "downward mobility" to characterize the economic plight of an entire generation of middle-class Americans who are slipping and sliding their way down the socioeconomic ladder. According to political analyst Kevin Phillips, the culprit can be located in a long-standing economic trend that began in the 1980s and will probably continue into the indefinite future. (3)

This trend has involved a dramatic shift away from manufacturing and toward services, a shift that has transformed us into a postindustrial society. In 1959, production of goods represented some 60 percent of all employment. By 1985, this figure had dropped to only 26 percent, and the overwhelming majority of Americans were employed in the service sector of the economy. During this transitional period, new jobs were created, but mainly

"bad" jobs that paid poorly and provided few opportunities for upward mobility. Thus, large numbers of
Americans were forced to take a substantial cut in pay
and, therefore, in their way of life.

The rich really have been getting richer . . . and doing so at the expense of poor and middle-income Americans who have seen their achievements evaporate over
time. Through at least the last decade, the biggest losers
have been blacks, Hispanics, young men, female heads of
households, farmers, and steelworkers; but almost everyone else has suffered at least to some extent.

According to Phillips, the widening gap between rich
and poor may have been encouraged by national economic policies of the 1980s—a period during which there was a
strong reversal of almost four decades of downward income redistribution. At the upper end of our class system,
the after-tax proportion of income controlled by the
wealthiest 1 percent of Americans climbed from 7 percent
in 1977 to 11 percent in 1990. Even when adjusted for
inflation, the number of millionaires doubled between the
late seventies and the late eighties, resulting in a record
one and one-quarter million households with a net worth
exceeding $1 million.

For families positioned on lower rungs of the socioeconomic ladder, however, the economic quality of life has
deteriorated. Since 1977, the average after-tax family income of the bottom 10 percent of Americans declined 10.5
percent in 1992 dollars. According to a recent study conducted by Timothy Smeeding of Syracuse University, the
percentage of U.S. children living in poverty rose from
less than 15 percent in 1978 to 20 percent in 1992. Compared with seven other industrial countries (Sweden, West
Germany, Australia, Canada, Britain, France, and the
Netherlands), the United States has the dubious distinc-
tion of having the greatest monetary inequality among

its citizens. That is, we have more poverty and fewer people who are middle class.

In order to maintain their standard of living, larger numbers of middle-class households have become dual-career families. Where family earnings have grown at all, they have increasingly resulted from ". . . greater work effort—from a rise in the number of earners per family and in the average weeks and weekly hours worked per earner. The primary source of the increased work effort has been women, including many with children." (4)

This option for keeping up economically—by increasing the number of people working in a family—is less available to poor Americans than ever before. More and more poor families are headed by a single parent. Indeed, a study by the Center for Social Policy Studies at George Washington University determined that almost 70 percent of all poor families are headed by a single parent. In 1960, just the opposite was true: 70 percent of poor families contained two parents. (5)

Polling data collected in conjunction with the 1990 presidential election reveal a type of watershed in public attitudes. For the first time in this century, most Americans believe that their children will *not* have a better standard of living than they presently enjoy and that there is very little parents can do to ameliorate this situation. This important shift in attitude contradicts a long-held American belief: parents work hard to be able to provide a better quality of life for their children. If people now believe that their personal effort is ineffectual, they may look for an alternative means for improving their economic position. One way is to challenge those who are perceived to be causing their economic difficulties—blacks, Jews, Hispanics, Asians, women, immigrants, and perhaps anyone else who is "different."

Many Americans now feel that their long-term economic condition is being controlled by persons, groups, or forces that they can no longer influence. Again, hard work is not enough. The causal factors are seen as outside of personal control. The traditional American middle-class lifestyle is slipping away, and *somebody somewhere must be responsible.*

Young people have been particularly hard hit by downward mobility. As a result, they are taking longer to finish college, living for a longer period of time with their parents or other relatives, and delaying their plans to marry. Young married couples are today less likely to own their own homes.

Comparing their worsening economic circumstances with those of their parents, millions of teenagers and young adults have begun to experience what sociologists call *relative deprivation*—they question the essential validity of the American Dream and are less optimistic about prospects for their own future. In fact, many of them feel downright deprived and disillusioned in comparison with their parents' generation.

Called "selfish," "passive," and "ultraconservative" by those who remember the liberal activism of the prosperous 1960s, many young Americans are trying merely to maintain or improve their standard of living. In the face of an erosion in their incomes, they frequently regard tax increases as a burden that they cannot afford. Instead of having an altruistic orientation toward those in need, young Americans feel *personally threatened* by the growing presence of newcomers and minorities who compete for diminishing amounts of wealth, status, and power. And, in fact, they are being *challenged*, to an increasing extent, for jobs, power, and prestige by a broad range of "outsiders." The growing presence of women, people of color, and international students has threatened the dominance of white males on college campuses across the country. More and more lesbians and gays have first "come out" to friends and relatives and then expressed their demands in assertive public demonstrations for inclusion in politics, work, education, and the military. Unprecedented numbers of newcomers from Asia, Eastern Europe, and Latin America are competing for jobs with native-born Americans. And affirmative action guidelines and quotas are widely regarded as "reverse discrimination" policies that, at the expense of white males, grant special treatment to undeserving minorities and women. More than just cultural baggage left over from a previous era, bigotry may to some extent also be a reaction to a continuing and objective threat to group position. Thus, racial tolerance drops as the size of the minority population grows enough to challenge the status quo. (6)

Although hatemongers may grow up learning the conventional culture, they are *abnormal* with respect to their lack of power and prestige in mainstream society. According to police officials who specialize in responding to hate offenses, many of the young people who commit hate crimes have been particularly hard hit by economic bad times and, as a result, feel that they are on the margins of society. Bill Johnston, Director of the Boston Police Department's Community Disorders Unit, which investigates hate crimes, suggests that these kids may be in school, but they are not successful in school. They believe that "the system" has failed them, not just the schools or their jobs, but the entire American way of life. Thirty years ago, they would have worked in a factory, where they could have made a decent living. Now there are no jobs they can get that pay well. In the past, these young people used their hands to build things. Now, they are using their hands to destroy things. For them, the American Dream is dead, and whether as a result of the dramatic change from a manufacturing to a service economy or simply the consequence of inept government policies, it really makes no difference to them. They believe they have no future, but they won't blame themselves for their situation. And to some extent they shouldn't. Still, they fail to place the responsibility on large-scale abstract social and economic forces or on the government. They are looking for *someone* to blame, someone who is concrete, visible, and vulnerable. Someone who is different.

Two gays in Boston were recently shot and wounded in an apparent civil rights violation (the assailant was reported to have called his two victims "faggots" and "queers"). Robert Weinerman, victim advocate for the Fenway Community Health Center, tried to explain to members of the press why hate-motivated violence against gays and lesbians in Massachusetts had increased 29 percent in only one year. "It is happening more now than in the past because more and more gay and lesbian people are openly visible and holding positions of power in state and city government," he said. "That increased visibility brings a backlash." (7)

To an increasing extent, then, Americans engage in *zero-sum economic thinking*. They view two or more individuals or groups as striving for the same scarce goals, with the success of one automatically implying a reduced probability that others will also attain their goals—for example, a job, raise, or promotion. If you believe that the "pie" is shrinking, you might not be so willing to give a slice to someone who doesn't have his own piece. In the postindustrial era of the 1990s, the economic pie no longer appears to grow—if anything, it seems to be getting smaller.

But zero-sum thinking is not limited to economics. It can also be applied to relative judgments of moral worth, even to evaluating the basic value of others as human beings. In the same way that an individual feels in competition with others for money or prestige, so he may feel in competition for moral righteousness. That is, he can only feel righteous when he compares himself with someone who is evil; he can only gain in moral worth to the extent that someone else loses in moral worth.

Zero-sum thinking engages the individual in a competitive struggle to upgrade himself and to downgrade others. Respectability demands deviance; good requires bad. Thus, a strong position against Jews, Moslems, or homosexuals can make an individual feel that he is a good Christian; a radical stand in opposition to Christians, Jews, or homosexuals can make an individual feel that he is a good Moslem; and so on. At the extreme, an individual who engages in zero-sum moralistic thinking gives himself a shot of moral adrenalin each and every time he assaults or harasses those he deems deserving of it. (8)

Resentment takes many forms. Some groups are actually *blamed* for the misery of the perpetrator. Throughout history, Jews have been held responsible for just about everything that has gone wrong—the crucifixion of Jesus, the Black Plague, inflation and depression, rampant capitalism, rampant communism, mortgage foreclosures, and the AIDS epidemic, to mention only a few. In Eastern Europe, we are currently witnessing a revival of this kind of anti-Semitic thinking. Jews are being blamed for a host of economic and social problems over which they could not possibly have had control. In the United States, members of organized hate groups have similarly blamed Jews for causing bad economic times and for creating racial antagonism between black and white Americans.

Decisions made in far-off places like Washington, D.C., Moscow, Tel Aviv, or Baghdad can determine whether we place the responsibility for our problems on people who are different from us. Under conditions of war, cold war, or the threat of war, anxious citizens may direct their wrath at members of the local community who are perceived to be in league with the "enemy." Japanese-Americans were cast in this unfortunate role during World War II. Iranians were victimized during the hostage crisis in 1978.

In response to the Iraqi invasion of Kuwait and the American involvement in the Persian Gulf war in 1991, local resentment turned toward Arab-Americans. Dozens received death threats or harassing phone calls. In Detroit, the publisher of the largest Arabic-language newspaper in the United States got an anonymous call warning that he would be killed if Americans in Kuwait were harmed. In Boston, a forty-one-year-old Palestinian-American was forced to move from his apartment after several neighbors called his landlady to demand his eviction. At midnight, he heard a voice outside the front window of his apartment telling him, "You move out or you'll die."

The threat against Arabs was on occasion more than just verbal. In Toledo, Ohio, an Arab-American business-man reported that he had been beaten by members of a white supremacist organization, the National Association for the Advancement of White People, because he refused to sell his business. In San Diego, California, someone tried to bomb a mosque. In Dearborn, Michigan, vandals burned an Iraqi flag on the front lawn of a Lebanese-American family. In nearby Blissfield, "USA No. 1" was spray-painted on the walls of a Dairy Queen owned by a Palestinian-American. The store was later burned to the ground. (9)

Asian-Americans have also served as the convenient targets for the anger of many Americans. During World

War II, hundreds of thousands of Japanese-Americans were rounded up and thrown into camps, their possessions confiscated and their lives profoundly disrupted. Because we were at war with Japan, Americans could easily rationalize their treatment of Japanese-Americans as a defensive strategy necessary to minimize anti-American activities among a population susceptible to divided loyalties. (It is interesting that neither Italian-Americans nor German-Americans were interned, though we were also at war with both Italy and Germany.) The treatment of Chinese-Americans could not be so easily justified, because China was an ally. Yet, the harassment of Chinese-Americans—rocks thrown and racial slurs shouted—became so pervasive that, in 1941, *Life* magazine felt compelled to run a two-page story, instructing its readers as to the particular physical characteristics (higher cheekbones, flatter nose, ruddier complexion, and so on) that would distinguish "friendly Chinese" from "enemy alien Japs." One wouldn't want to throw rocks at the *wrong* United States citizens or visiting dignitaries!

During the 1982 recession, anti-Asian sentiment once again gained momentum when many Americans blamed Japanese car manufacturers for massive layoffs in the automobile industry. Detroit was particularly hard hit, not only by unemployment, but also by hate and violence. Capitalizing on anti-Japanese attitudes, automobile dealers sought publicity by giving angry Americans a chance to get even, if only symbolically, with Japan. They placed a Japanese car in a conspicuous section of their lot and encouraged residents to come in and smash it with a sledgehammer. Incorporating both American capitalism and resentment, the sign on one car lot in Detroit read, "Pay a Dollar—Bash a Toyota."

The bashing of an Asian presence occasionally turned

from cars to human beings. In June 1982, a twenty-seven-year-old Chinese-American, Vincent Chin, was spending his Saturday night drinking in a topless bar located in one of Detroit's many working-class neighborhoods. The young man was enjoying a "final fling" at his bachelor party. Before he could extricate himself, two strangers—a Chrysler autoworker and his stepson—had engaged Chin in a shouting match and then an all-out brawl. Shouting "It's because of you we're out of work," one of the attackers took a baseball bat to the Chinese-American's skull and beat him to death. Apparently, these enraged hate-mongers didn't worry about making fine distinctions between Japanese- and Chinese-Americans. From their point of view, any Asian was the enemy.

In March 1983, after confessing to the murder, Vincent Chin's killers—Ronald Ebens and Michael Nitz—were sentenced. Wayne County Circuit Court judge Charles Kaufman gave the two men three years of probation and fines of $3,780 each. Explaining his lenient ruling, the judge said that the defendants were "not the kind of people you send to prison. . . . These men are not going to go out and harm somebody else." Needless to say, the Asian-American community was furious. (10)

Resentment is a thread that runs through the fabric of society today. In all quarters, Americans take exception to the demands made by those who seek to preserve or increase their own share of economic resources at "our" expense. When a group has suffered some degree of oppression, it becomes easier for its members to blame the advantaged group and justify criminal behavior. In extreme cases, resentment may be translated into brutal acts of violence.

From 1981 to 1987, for example, members of the Temple of Love in Miami, a black separatist cult, plotted fourteen killings and two attempted murders in the name of Old Testament vengeance. Their charismatic leader, Yahweh Ben Yahweh (God, Son of God, in Hebrew), preached that all whites were "serpents" and "demons." He taught that blacks were the only true Jews and that whites who identified themselves with Judaism were actually "false imposter Jews" who worshipped in "the synagogue of Satan."

Under Yahweh's direction, at least six black separatists conspired to kill "white devils" in retribution for the oppression of blacks by whites. As part of the initiation ritual for joining their Temple, recruits had to murder a "white devil" and then bring back the victim's severed ear as proof of the killing. Eight of the victims were white vagrants who just happened to be in the wrong place at the wrong time. But several victims were blacks who had somehow challenged Yahweh's directives. One disobedient "blasphemer" was decapitated; two others were shot to death for failing to vacate an apartment owned by the Temple. A female ex-member had her throat slit. And one black man was killed because he had chased Temple members seeking donations from his home.

In his sermons, Yahweh told his followers, "All hypocrites must die." Before his plan could be carried out, however, the fifty-five-year-old son of a Pentecostal minister was convicted and sent to prison for conspiracy to commit murder. (11)

Following the acquittal of Los Angeles police officers charged in the videotaped beating of Rodney King, another episode of black-on-white violence captured the attention of the country. During the riots in Los Angeles, a white truck driver, Reginald Denny, was literally dragged from the cab of his truck and, as the TV cameras rolled, beaten without mercy by a group of five blacks. The victim, whose only crime was being white, had stopped his truck at a red light during the early hours of the rioting. The five black men beat Denny with the fire extinguisher from his truck and then robbed him of his wallet. One offender shot him with a shotgun, while others hit him with beer bottles and savagely kicked him in the head. The long-haired truckdriver survived perhaps only because four black bystanders were willing to risk their own lives to stop the beating and rush him to a local hospital. (12)

Blame is only one expression of resentment. Other groups are deeply resented but are not necessarily viewed as responsible for the problems suffered by the offender. Instead, they are seen as the *undeserving recipients* of some advantage. At the close of the American Civil War, during the Reconstruction period, ex-slaves were given a series of legally guaranteed opportunities for equal treatment. Unfortunately, the reaction to this promise of equality took the form of increased lynchings of blacks throughout the South. White Americans simply could not accept efforts that would reduce their own advantaged position in society.

At present, blacks and Hispanics may be similarly regarded as receiving preferential (and undeserved) treatment under affirmative action-type programs in schools and companies. Asians may be commonly (and incorrectly) perceived as getting a special government handout in the form of financial assistance when they come to this country. As women continue to earn places in previously all-male occupations, they too are confronted with accusations that they only got their jobs because of their gender.

In the final analysis, many individuals suffer low self-esteem, dislike entire groups of people, and feel profoundly resentful; yet, they would never actually commit a crime motivated by bigotry. But perpetrators of hate crimes in addition feel some *personal threat* originating in the groups they despise: Jews have too much power; they are responsible for our recession and therefore *my* unemployment. Blacks benefit from reverse discrimination; because of affirmative action, *I* can't get into law school. Feminists are taking more than their share of jobs; their presence makes it more and more difficult for *me* to feed *my* family. Asians are grabbing all the college scholarship money; because of them, *my* son might not be able to attend college.

Fed up with "unfair competition" and sick and tired of feeling disadvantaged, what are disgruntled and resentful Americans to do? Ten or fifteen years ago, they might have grabbed a beer from the refrigerator and turned on the reruns of "Leave It to Beaver" or taken a snooze on the couch. They were variously labeled, sometimes unfairly, as the "silent majority" or the "me generation," by reporters and political pundits eager to characterize what they saw as a trend toward indifference.

But Americans are now taking their cues from a new breed of hero: idols of activism who are admired and respected not for their ability to keep us entertained nor for their success in business, but for their courage to take active charge of their own lives and the lives of others. In the face of overwhelming and impersonal social, political, and economic forces, Americans feel increasing admiration for those who come forward from their place among the spectators. Unlike the couch potatoes of the so-called boob tube generation, Americans now make heroes out of the likes of Ross Perot, Bernhard Goetz (the Subway Vigilante), Oliver North, the Guardian Angels, and Sylvester Stallone as Rambo or Rocky. Thus, our choice of idols reflects our growing determination not to stand idly by but to respond to perceived injustice and to act on our important beliefs. At the same time, each and every idol of activism also expresses a growing impatience with legitimate avenues of making it in mainstream society. *You can no longer depend on government or corporate America; it is now entirely up to you.*

Also in the spirit of renewed activism, Americans are generally more willing to express their resentment, even if it means committing acts of discrimination and violence. In his abortive campaign for the governorship of Louisiana and later the presidency, David Duke became an activist voice for white, blue-collar workers who felt that "welfare parasites," corrupt government officials, and civil rights advocates were at the root of America's economic woes. To many of his supporters, Duke was courageous for *daring* to act on beliefs that other politicians shared but presumably were afraid to acknowledge in public, let alone act upon.

At the extreme, members of organized hate groups— Aryan Nations, the White Aryan Resistance, and the Ku Klux Klan—have become increasingly willing to translate their bigoted attitudes into criminal behavior. Militant revolutionaries have taken on new prominence within the white supremacist movement, giving it a broad political and economic activism that incorporates racism among such issues as taxes, foreign aid, immigration, crime, and AIDS. During the 1980s, members of organized hate groups were responsible for committing armed robberies, assaults, and murders across the country. During one eighteen-month period in 1984–85, for example, members of the white supremacist group known as the Order killed two FBI agents, a sheriff, and a state trooper. By late 1985, twenty-three Order members had been convicted of racketeering offenses and sentenced to long terms in prison. (13)

Resentment often gets played out in themes apparent only at the level of motivation. From the viewpoint of the hatemonger, a criminal act may seem perfectly justified, even necessary. He may believe sincerely that his violence is reactive or that he is only getting even with those who have ruined his life, or the country, for that matter. Or, in some cases, the perpetrator may even see his hate crime as recreational sport, in which he gets together with "the boys" for an evening of drinking beer and bashing gays.

CHAPTER 5

For the Thrill of It

In the same way that some young men get together on a Saturday night to play a game of cards, certain hate-mongers gather to destroy property or to bash minorities. They look merely to have some fun and stir up a little excitement . . . at someone else's expense. In a *thrill-seeking hate crime*, there need not be a precipitating incident. The victim does not necessarily "invade" the territory of the assailants by walking through their neighborhood, moving onto their block, or attending their school. On the contrary, in looking to harass those who are different, the assailants search out locations where the members of a particular group regularly congregate. The payoff for the perpetrators is psychological as well as social: they enjoy the exhilaration and the thrill of making someone else suffer. For those with a sadistic streak, inflicting pain and suffering is its own reward. In addition, the youthful perpetrators also receive a stamp of approval from their friends who regard hatred as "cool."

Actually, the leader of a thrill hate crime may be the only member of the group to be motivated by intense hatred of the victim. He manipulates the others by playing on their need to prove their loyalty, by daring them not to back out. Most members merely follow along; they conform, they accept the challenge to avoid being rejected by the people in their lives who mean the most—their good friends. Each one believes that he alone is hesitant to go along and that, should he resist, the others would consider him a coward.

Indeed, many youths who participate in a hate-motivated rampage against gays, blacks, or Asians would probably not engage in such behavior on their own. Groups provide both inspiration and security. For a teenager who is on the verge of flunking out of school and who doesn't get along with his parents, group membership is especially influential. Being accepted by his pals makes him feel special. Indeed, being rejected by them may be tantamount to being given a death sentence, at least in his eyes.

Moreover, an individual in the presence of his friends may take risks that he would otherwise find unacceptable. Under such circumstances, he feels free from accountability—responsibility is shared with his buddies, and so is the blame. In addition, members of the group act within a division of labor and are typically asked to play only specialized roles in the commission of a violent act. One of them selects the victim, another knocks her to the ground, still another tears off her clothing, and so on. According to Robert Panarella, a professor of police science at the John Jay College of Criminal Justice, the result is that "while the action of each individual can seem relatively minor, the action of the whole may be horrific." (1)

Many of the hate crimes directed against property— acts of desecration and vandalism—can be included in the thrill-seeking category. In a recent incident in Wellesley,

Massachusetts, two alienated white youths looking for excitement went on a spree of destruction and defacement that resulted in attacks on twenty-three properties in three different communities. The two went out at night when "there was nothing else to do" and defaced walls, driveways, and automobiles with slurs against Jews, blacks, Greeks, and even skinheads. After their arrest, the two young men claimed that they hadn't intended to hurt anyone and that it happened because they were drunk.

The selection of victims in the Wellesley incident is typical of thrill hate crimes in general—victims are chosen more or less on a random basis. Thus, interchangeability occurs not only within a target group—for example, among blacks, Jews, or women—but across groups as well. Indeed, almost any vulnerable and easily identified victim will do.

Actually, the culture of hate is important for singling out the victims of thrill hate attacks and justifying the violence perpetrated against them. Offenders target the members of certain groups because they regard them as inferior—perhaps even subhuman—and because they are convinced that their criminal behavior will simply not engender the negative sanctions that crimes against more respectable groups might. These youths see gays, blacks, Asians, Jews, and women being the butt of jokes by certain comedians (not to mention members of their audience who repeat the same jokes), being belittled in the lyrics of popular music, and being discredited by thinly disguised political messages. In some cases, young people looking for a thrill learn a dangerously misguided message: nobody will care if we attack the members of this group; in fact, others might applaud us!

The utter randomness of these thrill-seeking hate crimes—especially those aimed at property—makes it particularly difficult to apprehend the perpetrators. Their motives tend to be obscure and their patterns of committing the crime are haphazard at best. But, because they usually do not have an economic motivation—they gain no money, property, or jobs—such hate crimes are relatively easy to deter with the threat of appropriate sanctions. In fact, according to some experts, the offenders get little more than "bragging rights," the ability to tell their friends about how they "trashed that temple" or "beat up that gook." (2)

Thus, the hatred beneath thrill-seeking violence is for most perpetrators actually at a superficial level; perpetrators hold on to their disparaging images essentially to justify victimizing strangers. Consequently, offenders are usually not profoundly convinced of the legitimacy of their criminal acts and can be dissuaded from repeating them. It is important, therefore, to apprehend hate crime perpetrators at this point, especially in light of the possibility that many property offenders who go undetected later graduate to hate crimes directed against people. Because the perpetrators derive minimal reward from committing these crimes, they may be very influenced by a strong statement from society at large that says this type of behavior won't be tolerated.

Not all thrill-seeking hate crimes are so benign, however. Assaultive hate crimes can also occur as a deadly game in which the perpetrators express a need to feel powerful and dominant in destructive behavior. In 1990, for example, unidentified vandals in Madison, Wisconsin, first smashed the windows and then cut the brake lines of a bus that was supposed to take Jewish children to a day camp. Fortunately, the act of sabotage was discovered before the children took their ride, so no one was injured. But the climate of anti-Semitism became so dangerous in

Madison that armed police had to be stationed outside of local synagogues while worshipers inside celebrated the Jewish New Year, Rosh Hashanah. (3)

Thrill hate crimes are occasionally committed by couples—two friends or relatives who share a deep disappointment with life and have enough time on their hands to get into trouble, so they team up to go bashing. In a racially mixed area of Wheaton, Maryland, for example, two young white men—both unable to find work—were recently charged in a particularly bizarre hate crime. The incident occurred in the early-morning hours of March 3, 1992, as two black women—ages twenty-nine and thirty-nine—were walking from their apartment to a pay phone in a nearby shopping center. According to police reports, the two white men—one nineteen, the other twenty-one—stopped their car and then chased their victims on foot. One woman ran toward a house in the neighborhood and was rescued by the occupant, a thirty-year-old man who heard one of the assailants warn, "If you knock on that door again, I'll kill you."

But the other woman tried to escape into the woods, where she fell to the ground. One of the attackers, catching up, beat her around the head and face, ripped off her blouse, and doused her with lighter fluid. While he was attempting to light the fluid, however, police cars arrived on the scene. Before having the chance to burn the victim, both men escaped. They were later apprehended and charged with attempted murder, assault with intent to murder, assault with intent to maim, kidnapping, and attempting to injure a person for racial reasons under a 1988 hate crimes statute. One woman was left hysterical but otherwise unhurt. The other was left naked from the waist up and bleeding from cuts to the head. (4)

When large numbers of teenagers go on a rampage,

they are said to be "wilding." But smaller groups of hatemongers can also go wild, and terrorize innocent people
"for a thrill." In a particularly strange series of incidents,
for example, groups of white teenagers in New York City
have recently attacked younger black children on their
way to school. In January 1992, two black youngsters, a
brother and sister, were roughed up and robbed by four
sixteen-year-old boys shouting racial slurs. One of the attackers told his victims, "You'll turn white today," and
then smeared them with a shoe whitener. When the girl
tried to flee, another attacker cut her hair with scissors. (5)

Gays, who are the most frequent targets of thrill-
motivated attacks, make particularly "good" victims for
groups of bored young men looking for a thrill. First of all,
gays may congregate in certain areas of major cities, which
makes them relatively easy to find. Second, gays may represent a particularly disquieting psychosexual threat to
teenage males who are in the process of establishing their
sexual identity. The members of skinhead gangs frequently
dress to emphasize their toughness and masculinity—for
example, steel-toed boots and motorcycle jackets. Their
exaggerated macho appearance may indicate an underlying confusion and self-doubt as well as a sense of powerlessness associated with adolescence. Finally, gays may
be particularly reluctant to report attacks against them,
even though their injuries are often serious. Those who
have not "come out of the closet" may fear that people
who discover their sexual orientation may use it as a basis
for discrimination. Some gays may be concerned about the
practical problems of possibly losing their apartments or
their jobs. Others may worry that they will be rejected by
disappointed family members or ignored by unsympa-
thetic police. Criminologists Kevin Berrill and Gregory
Herek have labeled this process *secondary victimization*, the

negative response of others to a crime victim because of his or her sexual orientation. (6)

Unlike offenders who bash the members of ethnic and racial groups, those who target gays are more typically "average young men" without criminal records who come from any of a number of different lifestyles, backgrounds, and social classes. Even when they are from economically secure families, however, most gay bashers still suffer from a form of *marginality* stemming from a sense of powerlessness that often accompanies the teenage years. Based solely on their status as adolescents, even those who from an adult perspective appear to be successful and well-adjusted may search for ways to overcome acute feelings of alienation and inferiority. They bash gays for the same reason that other teenagers might steal hubcaps, shoplift, or hold wild parties when their parents are out of town. Young men who have been socialized to be aggressive and to find violent solutions to their problems may end their search for power by physically attacking others who, themselves, lack the power to retaliate. (7)

According to Matt Foreman, executive director of the New York City Gay and Lesbian Anti-Violence Project, gay-bashing ("Let's go beat up some queers") has actually become a fad or sport among certain high school students. In the typical case, two or more young men arm themselves with knives, bottles, hammers, or baseball bats and then target a part of the city in which they suspect that large numbers of gays congregate or reside. The intruders rush in, assault their unsuspecting victim, and rush out again.

This is precisely the sequence of events that transpired during the early-morning hours of July 2, 1990, in a New York City school yard widely known as Vaseline Alley, a homosexual hangout after dark. At 2:00 A.M., Julio

Rivera, a twenty-nine-year-old Puerto Rican, who worked as a bartender in gay bars and as a prostitute, was passing through Vaseline Alley on his way home. He was suddenly surrounded by three young men who, without warning or provocation, literally hammered him with repeated blows in the face and head, viciously kicked him, and then stabbed him in the back. Rivera was still conscious when his assailants left the scene. He managed to stagger from the school yard to get help and was taken by ambulance to a nearby hospital, where he died a few hours later.

In a videotaped confession, Daniel Doyle, a Union College freshman, later implicated two of his friends in the assault on Rivera. Prior to the attack, they had spent four hours guzzling beer, said Doyle. Then, he and his friends had decided to take a little walk. Sure, it was almost two in the morning, but none of them could sleep. So, they walked without purpose or destination. However, according to Doyle, before leaving the house, one of them had slipped a claw hammer into the waistband of his pants. Another had taken along a wrench and a knife, snatched from Doyle's kitchen. But they had had no particular place in mind to go. They just couldn't sleep.

The Bias Review Panel of the New York City police saw the assault somewhat differently. Alleging that the perpetrators despised homosexuals and that they were connected with a gang of skinheads in the neighborhood, the Bias Review Panel concluded that the incident was a vicious hate crime—an attack perpetrated against Rivera because of his sexual orientation. (8)

In November 1991, Daniel Doyle took the stand in a packed Queens, New York, courtroom. He was present not as a defendant, but as the prosecution's star witness against the two defendants, Eric Brown, twenty-one, and

Esat Bici, nineteen. Doyle had previously confessed to having made the fatal wound by plunging his knife into Rivera's back. But in a plea bargain with the prosecuting attorneys, the charges against him had been reduced from second-degree murder to manslaughter. In exchange, Doyle agreed to testify against his two friends.

According to Doyle, he had held a "skinhead" party at his Jackson Heights apartment on the evening that Rivera was slain. As the party was winding down, Doyle suggested to Brown and Bici that they go out and "beat some people up."

Later that night, the trio walked along the Long Island Rail Road tracks, hoping to run into "a drug addict, a homo, or homeless" person to assault. Along the way, they knocked over a temporary shack left vacant by a homeless person and then—for the hell of it—set it on fire. When an appropriate victim failed to appear, the three friends left the tracks and walked toward the Jackson Heights school yard known as an area in which gays congregated. Rivera was just coming around the corner as the trio approached. The attack was swift and deadly. "We stabbed him and killed him," Doyle told the court in a calm tone of voice. "I killed him because he was gay." (9)

It would probably not be an exaggeration to suggest that many teenagers are "temporary sociopaths," generally lacking in either a strong sense of conscience or profound empathy for the problems of others. In psychiatric terms, a sociopath often engages in irresponsible and antisocial behavior such as lying, stealing, vandalism, and fighting. He is typically manipulative, cruel, and reckless. By the time a sociopath reaches middle age, it is highly unlikely that he can be rehabilitated—one does not suddenly develop a conscience at the age of forty.

But teenagers are a different story. Even the brightest

and most popular fourteen-year-old may be searching for guidance and belonging that he simply cannot find at home or in school. During the difficult period between childhood and adulthood, many young people are profoundly confused and easily persuaded. As a society, we expect them to begin their journey toward independence and responsibility, but we also keep them in a dependent and subservient relationship with adults. They come to depend on one another—on their peers—for emotional support and direction. Many teenagers will therefore do things when they are fifteen that they wouldn't dream of doing at the age of twenty-five or thirty-two. Even an act of extreme violence may not be out of the question.

Of course, teenagers are not alone in their ability to commit hate offenses. Adults also attack others based on race, religion, national origin, sexual orientation, or gender. Hate crimes committed by middle-age adults, however, differ in at least one important respect. Adults usually do not regard their hate offense as a game or sport committed for the fun of it. Instead, they sense that a personal threat is being directed against them and are deadly serious in what they consider to be an appropriate reaction.

CHAPTER 6

Reacting to a Personal Threat

Not all hate offenses are motivated by thrill or excitement. In *reactive hate crimes,* hatemongers seize on what they consider to be a precipitating or triggering incident to serve as a catalyst for the expression of their anger. They rationalize that by attacking an outsider they are in fact taking a protective posture, a defensive stance against intruders. Indeed, they often cast the outsiders in the role of those actively threatening them, while they regard themselves as pillars of the community.

Whereas in thrill-motivated hate crimes a group of teenagers travels to another area to find victims, the perpetrators in reactive hate crimes typically never leave their own neighborhood, school, or workplace. Although the members of almost any group of "outsiders" might be targeted, the primary victims of reactive hate crimes are people of color. In the Howard Beach case, for example, three black men drove through an all-white neighborhood and were assaulted because their very presence in the community was seen as an invasion by outsiders. Similarly, in Jersey City, New Jersey, an East Indian chemist was se-

verely beaten with an iron bar in his own apartment by a
racist who resented the presence of "Hindus" in *his* neighborhood. And when a black woman and her young son
moved to a previously all-white block located in the North
End of Boston, they were greeted with the words "No
niggers" spray painted on the front of their brownstone.
When asked about the incident, a longtime resident of the
neighborhood told a reporter, "We don't want them niggers. We never had them, and we never want to see them.
That's true. They're terrible, strange people. I've been
here for thirty-seven years, and I've never seen colored
people here." (1)

From the point of view of the perpetrators, it is their
community, means of livelihood, or way of life that has
been threatened by the mere presence of members of
some other group. The hatemongers therefore feel justified, even obligated, to go on the "defensive." Character-
istically, they feel few, if any, pangs of guilt even if they
savagely attack an outsider.

In thrill hate crimes, almost any member of a vulnerable group will usually do as a target. In contrast, the
perpetrators of reactive hate crimes tend to target a particular individual or set of individuals who are perceived to
constitute a personal threat—the black family that has just
moved into the all-white neighborhood, the white college
student who has begun to date her Asian classmate, or the
Latino who has recently been promoted at work.

Just as in thrill hate crimes, the offenders in reactive
attacks are not necessarily associated with any organized
hate group (although, as we shall see, they may call upon
the members of an organized group to help "repel the
intruders"). The perpetrators usually have no prior history
of either criminal behavior or overt bigotry. Their reaction
may have an economic basis—they fear losing property

value or opportunities for advancement at work. Sometimes they react instead to a symbolic loss of "turf" or "privilege"—for example, as when "our women" begin to date "them" or when "they" come into our neighborhood and begin to "take over."

Thus, reactive hate crimes are intended to send a message—for example, that blacks are not welcome on the block or that Latinos should not apply for a promotion. In their intended effect, these crimes are very much like acts of terrorism, meant to send a signal by means of fear and horror. If the original criminal response fails to elicit the desired retreat on the part of the victim, then the offender frequently escalates the level of property damage or violence. Thus, a black family moving into an all-white neighborhood is first warned; if they don't heed the warning, then their windows are broken; and if they still refuse to move out, their house may be firebombed, or worse.

The victims of reactive hate crimes are typically apprehensive and frustrated. Unlike thrill hate crimes, in which many members of a group feel vulnerable to random attack, reactive hate crime victims are very much aware that their particular situation precipitated the attack and that they could easily be attacked again. The frustration that these victims feel comes from knowing why they were attacked: simply for attempting to take action—move into a new home, date someone, accept a promotion—that everyone else takes for granted as appropriate. The victims of reactive hate offenses were attacked for exercising their constitutional rights—for example, their right to live in a home free from intimidation and harassment or their right to equal opportunity for career advancement.

According to a survey conducted by the Klanwatch Project, a unit of the Southern Poverty Law Center in Montgomery, Alabama, about half of all racially inspired

acts of vandalism and violence are directed at blacks moving into previously all-white neighborhoods. Typical of
these hate crimes is the case of Purnell Daniels, a forty-
one-year-old black engineer whose house was located in a
mostly white section of Newark, Delaware. In May 1989,
he discovered a piece of cardboard inscribed with the
raised letters *KKK* glued to the front door of his home. (2)

Given the competitive nature of the workplace, it
should come as no surprise that many reactive hate crimes
also occur on the job. In their study of "ethnoviolence at
work," sociologists Joan Weiss, Howard Ehrlich, and Barbara Larcom interviewed a national sample of 2,078 Americans. These researchers found that 27 percent of all respondents who reported "prejudice-based" episodes
experienced them while at work. These incidents included
break-ins, property damage, robbery, harassing language,
physical assaults, sexual harassment, and rapes. (3)

Hatred inspired by job competition has occasionally
involved organized hate groups. During the recession of
1981, white fishermen in the Galveston, Texas, area became troubled about the growing presence (and prosperity) of Vietnamese refugees who had settled along the Gulf
Coast and were fishing in Galveston Bay. Complaining
that the Vietnamese newcomers engaged in unfair competition, the white fishermen asked the Ku Klux Klan for
help in driving their Asian competitors out of the area. (4)

The Klan gladly complied. Only a few weeks passed
before thirty-year-old Louis Beam, a longtime KKK leader
and grand titan of the Texas chapter, supervised a Klan
rally in support of the Galveston Bay white fishermen.
Carrying rifles and shotguns, the Klansmen raised their
hands in a Nazi salute and shouted, "White power! We
will fight." They then set fire to a cross. Several weeks
later, a radio station in Houston reported that the Klans-

men, under the direction of Louis Beam, had invited fifty white fishermen to participate with them in military training exercises.

The KKK then waged a vicious campaign of intimidation and violence against the refugees. Several Vietnamese-owned fishing boats were set on fire; crosses were burned in the front yard of a Vietnamese fisherman and near a marina in which the newcomers stored their boats. To the few white residents who had befriended their Asian neighbors, the Klan sent business cards warning: "You have been paid a social visit by the Knights of the Ku Klux Klan—Don't make the next visit a business call." As a final warning, fifteen Klansmen sailed their fishing boat within sight of the marina and the homes of many Vietnamese. Displaying semiautomatic rifles and shotguns, the Klansmen wore robes or battle fatigues. After hanging a human effigy from the craft's rear rigging, the Klansmen paused for a moment, then fired a blank round from a cannon they had brought on board. When they felt sure of having made their point, they returned to shore.

The Klan's threatening gestures toward the Vietnamese refugees continued for months. It took a legal maneuver orchestrated by the Southern Poverty Law Center's Klanwatch Project and its civil rights attorney Morris Dees to end the KKK threat. In the spring of 1982 the Vietnamese Fishermen's Association filed suit in federal court to prohibit the Klan from operating paramilitary training camps in Texas. After three days of testimony by the Vietnamese and a handful of their white friends and business partners, Judge Gabrielle McDonald issued an injunction that barred the Klan's menacing campaign. (5)

New York City has recently been the site of several major reactive hate crimes apparently precipitated by the presence of outsiders in a predominantly white neighborhood. Sociologists note that many of these areas in which blacks have been assaulted are blue-collar communities consisting largely of second- and third-generation families of European immigrants, who were themselves new-comers at one time. Thirty years earlier, many of the white residents had moved out of their neighborhoods to dis-tance themselves from black and Latino newcomers arriv-ing from the South, the Caribbean, and Latin America. From the viewpoint of the remaining white residents, blacks and Latinos had invaded their neighborhoods—now they were doing it again. (6)

According to sociologist Robin M. Williams, Jr., of Cornell University, young men in these lower-middle-class communities must struggle to make a place for them-selves where they feel a sense of power and control. They commit murderous hate crimes when they begin to believe that outsiders are contesting their right to neighborhood, community, or privilege.

On the evening of August 23, 1989, a reactive hate crime in the Bensonhurst section of Brooklyn left the en-tire city of New York shaken to its core. Sixteen-year-old Yusuf Hawkins and three other black teenagers had walked into the mostly white, working-class Bensonhurst neighborhood because they were interested in inspecting a used car they had seen advertised in the newspaper. But they never got to check out the automobile. Instead, they were immediately surrounded and then chased down the street by a gang of local white youths carrying baseball bats and shouting "Let's club the niggers." Provoked by a rumor that one of their former girlfriends had been dating blacks and Hispanics, the white youths were already agi-tated. The sight of blacks in *their* neighborhood, who may have been visiting that local girl, was simply too much to take. The thinking was all too clear: "Here come niggers.

They don't belong here. They are probably here to take *our* women. We must protect our neighborhood, our women, ourselves." One of them yelled, "The hell with beating them up." He pulled out a gun and fired four times. Hit directly in the chest by two shots, Yusuf Hawkins collapsed to the pavement and died a short time later.

In June 1990, two of the defendants were convicted for their part in the Hawkins slaying. Identified as the trigger man, nineteen-year-old Joseph Fama was convicted of second-degree murder and sentenced to a term of thirty-two years to life. His codefendant, Keith Mondello, also age nineteen, was named as the organizer of the gang of white youths who had attacked Yusuf Hawkins and sentenced to five to sixteen years for rioting and discrimination. In a separate trial concluded in December 1990, a third defendant, twenty-two-year-old John Vento, was acquitted of murder and manslaughter but convicted of rioting. His conviction carries a maximum penalty of four years in prison. (7)

Canarsie, New York, has also long been the focal point for crimes designed to protect the neighborhood from an "invasion" by outsiders. Situated in the southeast corner of Brooklyn, Canarsie looks like any other comfortable working-class community. Its streets are lined with two- and three-story brick houses, churches, and small businesses. On a tranquil summer day, residents can be seen sitting on their porches with friends and neighbors, walking to the park with their children, or fishing off Canarsie Pier. But there is another, more disturbing side to Canarsie. The community has erupted in racial turmoil as blacks from surrounding communities, who are seen as invaders, move into the neighborhood.

Racial antagonism is nothing new to the people of Canarsie. The community has a history of racial tensions dating back two decades. In the fall of 1972, the local school board demanded that Canarsie accept into its schools a few dozen black children from neighboring Brownsville. But Canarsie's residents, the majority of whom were lower-middle-class whites, refused to comply. They swiftly mobilized in an effort to protect their community from what they regarded as an invasion by outsiders. A number of Canarsie residents marched through the streets, boycotted the schools, firebombed the home of a black family, and hurled rocks at buses carrying black children into the neighborhood. The rallying cry spread with incredible speed through the community of 70,000 outraged people: "Canarsie schools for Canarsie children." What these residents actually meant, of course, was Canarsie schools for *white* children—no *blacks* allowed. (8)

To be fair, it should be emphasized that the majority of Canarsie residents never participated in the racial incidents protesting busing (this is true in almost every community where racial conflict has occurred). Yet the effect of violent demonstrations by the antibusing forces was probably far greater than their small numbers would suggest. First, such episodes send a message to blacks in surrounding communities who might otherwise consider breaking the racial barrier: "Stay in your own neighborhood, or the same thing will happen to you." Second, the publicity given to violent acts assures that most of the residents of Canarsie, whether or not they participated in demonstrations or illegal behavior, would be labeled as "racists" and "bigots." (9)

The efficacy of violent demonstrations notwithstanding, the "invasion" of Canarsie, which continued in full force, changed the character of the community. The focus of this change was directly on the neighborhoods; an influx of black homeowners between 1980 and 1991 reduced the proportion of Canarsie whites from 90 to 75 percent. Many blocks that had been predominantly Irish, Jewish, or Italian became increasingly populated by newcomers from the Caribbean, East Asia, and Central and South America . . . but not without struggle and conflict. (10)

By 1991, the real estate market had softened, and homeowners in Canarsie—as in countless other communities around the country—saw their property values plummet. As unemployment rates climbed, so did anxiety about the future. Then, the trouble started again.

During a twelve-month period, there were more than fifteen racial incidents in Canarsie. Unknown arsonists burned a Pakistani grocery store and firebombed a black-owned insurance office. A local real estate office was fire-bombed after it showed homes to black families. Then, three black men beat up a twenty-year-old white man after shouting racial slurs at him from their car.

Reactive hate crimes often occur in response to minorities moving into a community or neighborhood. A recent outbreak of racial hostility in the predominantly white city of Dubuque, Iowa, coincided with debate concerning a plan to encourage blacks to move to this city. Recognizing that only 331 of Dubuque's 58,000 residents were black, an official task force decided to design and implement a program for increasing the city's racial diversity. During the spring of 1991, Dubuque city officials approved a plan whereby twenty minority families a year for five years would be recruited to move into the city. The official nine-page report, entitled "We Want to Change," acknowledged the existence of racism in Dubuque and called on local businesses to bring in black families for professional as well as lower-level jobs. To attract blacks to the area, recruits would receive subsidies to rent or own a home and would be guaranteed job security. According to Mayor James Brady, implementation of the plan over a five-year period would increase Dubuque's black representation from 1.2 to 1.8 percent of the population.

Many Dubuque residents endorsed the idea, at least initially. (11) By August 1991, however, the residents of Dubuque found themselves in the grip of a major national recession. The town's factories laid off workers, and jobs became increasingly scarce. Dubuque's unemployment rate soared to 10 percent, and many city residents were questioning the legitimacy of bringing in "outsiders" to compete for jobs at a time when so many longtime residents were out of work. Talking to the Associated Press, for example, a twenty-four-year-old, unemployed construction worker explained: "They want to bring 100 minorities in, and we just don't have the jobs for those people. If they want to move here, they should move here on their own." (11) Another unemployed resident argued that blacks were getting special treatment, a form of reverse discrimination. Calling David Duke a "saint, a white Martin Luther King," he asserted: "Seems like they're getting everything and we're getting trounced on." (12)

The reaction to the city's plan was angry and widespread. Burning crosses were found at homes, in parks, and on school yard playgrounds; the letters KKK were scrawled on a garage door; racist slurs like "No niggers" and "We don't want them" were painted on school buildings; fights between black and white students broke out at Dubuque Senior High School. Some of the town's teenagers attempted to form a chapter of the National Association for the Advancement of White People. Thomas Robb, national director of the Knights of the Ku Klux Klan, traveled from his home in Zinc, Arkansas, to rally the residents of Dubuque in defense of "our heritage." (13) In November 1991, Alice Scott moved her family from Milwaukee to Dubuque to "protect her three children from the hazards of growing up in the inner city." Within a matter of days, the black woman was welcomed by a brick thrown through her living room window and a cross burned on her front lawn. (14) The young granddaughters of another black resident, Hazel O'Neal, walked three blocks to get some ice cream. Along the way, a truckload of white men screaming "Niggers get out" tried to spit on them. O'Neal later told a reporter, "You're afraid to walk in the streets because you're harassed." (15) By December 1991, city leaders were promising that they would not spend tax dollars to implement the diversity plan, and recruitment dropped off.

Asian Indians have also experienced their share of abuse and harassment from those who resent the "invasion of outsiders" into their communities and act to preserve the dominance of the majority. During the last few years, growing numbers of East Indians have moved into the northern section of Edison, New Jersey, and the Iselin section of neighboring Woodbridge, towns located in Middlesex County. In these formerly white-dominated communities, some thirty miles south of New York City, there are now dozens of sari shops, Indian restaurants, and Asian jewelry stores as well as tens of thousands of Indian newcomers. There is also growing hatred.

According to police reports, such vicious anti-Indian gangs as the Dotbusters and the Lost Boys in central New Jersey have targeted their campaign of terror at the Indian outsiders. On many occasions, groups of young white men have driven through local areas populated by Indians, smashing automobile windshields or shouting anti-Indian slurs and threats (for example, "Dotheads come out. We're going to kick your asses"). On New Year's Day 1991, several Indians were accosted by a large group of young white men at a diner in Iselin. More than insults were thrown. They also hurled bottles and their fists, leaving several Indians injured. On May 23, 1991, eight members of the Lost Boys allegedly assaulted a young Indian man behind a local convenience store. Carrying sticks, rocks, and bats, they encircled their victim and repeatedly struck him in the head. He required a two-day stay in the hospital and needed thirty stitches to close the ugly wound in his forehead and four stitches for an injury below his left eyebrow. (16)

In its narrow sense, the term *reactive* means to act in opposition to an attack. Hate crimes perpetrated in Howard Beach, Bensonhurst, central New Jersey, and Dubuque clearly fit this definition in the perpetrators' minds. In each case, the victims were regarded as making some illegitimate move into a community that was dominated by whites. The perpetrators felt that their homes, schools, or neighborhoods were under attack by outsiders. This is typical of the thinking in reactive hate crimes.

The concept of reaction or defense can easily be expanded to include preemptive strikes, terrorist attacks, and even the wholesale slaughter of innocent civilians. The massive displacement of Native Americans by white settlers provides a case in point that is uncomfortably close to home. In some reactive hate attacks, it is similarly the perpetrators who were originally the outsiders. Now, they move in on and attempt to displace their victims. The hatemongers typically possess an inordinate belief in their own *entitlement*. Once they occupy a neighborhood, it belongs to them. Even if blacks or Latinos have lived on the block for decades, they are the "outsiders" who must now move. From the hatemonger's point of view, this is a white country, a white state, and a white community. "White is right; white rules." So, anyone who isn't white is expected to defer to the "ruling elite" . . . or else pay the consequences.

Fostered by cheap real estate and highway construction, the town of Alton, Illinois, has—since the 1970s—attracted a growing white population from nearly St. Louis. The small number of blacks in Alton can trace its presence in the community back at least 125 years, beginning with the days when the New Bethel African Methodist Episcopal Church was founded by former slaves. For most of their history in the town, Alton's blacks lived in peace. But, during the last couple of decades, as more and more whites have moved in, black members of the community have repeatedly come under attack.

Unlike the situation in Howard Beach, Bensonhurst, or Dubuque, it was whites rather than blacks who were the outsiders in Alton. Still, according to Linda Lindsey, a visiting professor of sociology at Washington University in St. Louis, the focal point of the attack was the black church. In 1974, two bombs were detonated inside the church. Throughout the 1980s, vandals broke windows, scrawled racial epithets on the walls ("KKK" and "Die nigger"), and desecrated tombstones in the church cemetery. In 1988, arsonists burned the church to the ground twice. From the viewpoint of some whites wanting to take over the town, says Lindsey, New Bethel was a symbol of the population that should be removed. (17)

Reactive hate crimes are generally aimed against particular outsiders—those who are regarded as posing a personal challenge to a perpetrator's workplace, neighborhood, or physical well-being. The attack tends to be narrowly focused. Once the threat is perceived to subside, so does the criminal behavior.

On occasion, hate crimes go beyond what their perpetrators consider reaction, at least in the narrow sense.

Rather than direct their attack at those individuals involved in a particular event or episode—moving into the neighborhood, taking a job at the next desk, attending the same party—the perpetrators are ready to wage "war" against any and all members of a particular group of people. No precipitating episode occurs; none is necessary. The perpetrator is on a moral mission: his assignment is to make the world a better place to live.

CHAPTER 7

Ridding the World of Evil

The rarest version of hate crimes consists of an attack carried out by individuals with a *mission;* they seek to rid the world of evil by disposing of the members of a despised group. In the hatemonger's view, all outgroup members are subhumans, either animal or demon, who are bent on destroying *his* culture, *his* economy, or the purity of *his* racial heritage. The perpetrator therefore is concerned about much more than simply eliminating a few blacks or Latinos from his job, his neighborhood, or his school. Instead, he believes that he has a higher-order purpose in carrying out his crime. He has been instructed by God or, in a more secular version, by "der Führer," the Imperial Wizard, or the Grand Dragon to rid the world of evil by eliminating *all* blacks, Latinos, Asians, women, gays, or Jews. And he is compelled to act before it is too late.

The perpetrator of a mission hate crime is often psychotic; that is, he suffers from a severe mental illness that may cause hallucinations, impaired ability to reason, and withdrawal from contact with other people. What is more, he believes that he must get even for the misfortunes he has suffered. In his paranoid and delusional way of thinking, he sees a conspiracy of some kind for which he seeks revenge. His mission is in part suicidal. Before taking his own life, however, he must attempt to eliminate an entire category of people he is absolutely convinced is responsible for his personal frustrations.

In 1989, Canadians were made painfully aware of a growing resentment toward all women by an outbreak of sexist acts on college campuses across the country, culminating in the largest mission hate crime in Canada's history. During the year, a female law school professor at the University of Western Ontario claimed sex discrimination; the male students at Wilfrid Laurier University in Waterloo reportedly conducted panty raids in the female dormitories; and the "No means no!" catchphrase of the student council's antirape campaign at Queen's University at Kingston, Ontario, was perverted by some first-year male students who jokingly displayed their own version, which read "No means more beer!"

But all other acts of sexism were immediately overshadowed by the murderous rampage of twenty-five-year-old Marc Lepine. On the rainy afternoon of December 6, 1989, Lepine entered the engineering school at the University of Montreal with a .223-caliber semiautomatic hunting rifle, a hundred rounds of bullets, and a single purpose: to get even with women—especially feminist women—whom he held to be totally responsible for all of his troubles. Weapon in hand, Lepine walked slowly into a classroom crowded with students and, in a calm voice, ordered everyone to stop what they were doing. With a smile on his face, he told the women to move to one side of the room and the men to leave. Firing a shot into the ceiling to move the students along, Lepine shouted: "I want the women. You're all a bunch of feminists. I hate feminists."

And then, Lepine opened fire—in that classroom, in the corridors, and in the cafeteria. He moved quickly from floor to floor, looking only for women. Two hours later, the police tactical squad entered the building. They found the bodies of fourteen women—ages twenty-one to thirty-one—all gunned down by Lepine before he took his own life. Lepine's final words: "Ah, shit." (1)

Upon searching the body of the killer, police found a three-page handwritten suicide note in Lepine's pocket explaining his hideous outburst. "I have been unhappy for the past seven years," he lamented. "And, I will die on December 6, 1989, . . . Feminists have always ruined my life." On page three of his suicide note, Lepine had scribbled the names of fifteen prominent Canadian women, the very "feminists" he so thoroughly despised.

Those who are psychoanalytically inclined might speculate that Lepine's contempt for women was a generalized form of his hatred for his mother. Perhaps she abandoned him at an early age. Or, perhaps he *believed* he was a victim of abusive behavior when he was a young child. Lepine's murderous rampage at the University of Montreal could then be interpreted as a desperate final attempt to get even with his mother; his victims were only surrogates. (2)

The same kind of reasoning is sometimes applied to explain the behavior of serial killers who target female victims. Between 1962 and 1964, for example, the so-called Boston Strangler, Albert Desalvo, brutally raped and murdered thirteen women in the city of Boston. Based on evidence found at the crime scenes as well as theoretical assumptions, psychiatrists developed a profile that pegged the killer as a homosexual man who hated his mother. When Albert Desalvo was finally apprehended, however, he didn't fit the profile. Instead, he respected and admired his mother; it was his father he despised. In addition, he was heterosexual and sexually insatiable, demanding that his wife have sexual intercourse with him several times daily.

There is reason to believe that Marc Lepine's resentment toward women was not a generalization of anger toward his mother. Like Desalvo, Lepine seems to have detested his father, a man who had brutally assaulted both his wife and his children and who showed little interest in his family. At their divorce proceedings in 1970, Marc's mother testified that her husband was very brutal, that he showed little control of his emotions. He had beaten her in front of the children; he had hit her in the face; he had hit Marc so hard that the young boy bled from his nose and his ears. When Marc was only seven, his father threw him, his sister, and his mother out of their apartment. By the time he was fourteen years old, the boy's resentment was so intense that he decided to take his mother's name. It was at that time that Gamil Gharbi, son of Liass Gharbi, became the man known as Marc Lepine.

Life was not easy for Marc. He attempted to join the army but, for reasons that were never clear, was rejected. And his lifelong ambition to become an engineer was thwarted, at least in his mind, when his bid for admission to the engineering school at the University of Montreal failed. By his own twisted logic, women were to blame. They were responsible for his repudiation by the military and for his inability to be educated as an engineer. Indeed, female students had taken his seat at the University of Montreal. Perhaps it would not be too far-fetched to speculate that·Marc Lepine's final assault was an extreme version of his father's behavior toward women. Marc Lepine may have hated his father, but ultimately he identified with the aggressor.

Marc Lepine's rampage was clearly a hate crime. His suicide note and his remarks to his intended victims lead us to conclude that Lepine blamed all women for his personal failures. He looked for "feminists" behind every negative experience that he had.

George Henard was similar in this respect. In October 1991, the thirty-five-year-old unemployed man drove his pickup truck through the plate glass window of Luby's Cafeteria in Killeen, Texas. As frightened customers sat in horror, Henard got out of his truck and opened fire. Aiming his semiautomatic at one victim after another, he mumbled under his breath, "Wait till those fucking women in Belton [Texas] see this! I wonder if they think it was worth it!" (3) Moments later, he had killed twenty-two people—among them fourteen women—in what the press called the largest mass murder in American history. Earlier in the week, Henard had reacted violently to the Clarence Thomas hearings on television. He complained to a convenience store proprietor that Anita Hill's charges of sexual harassment against the soon-to-be Supreme Court Justice were ridiculous and that women were taking over the territory that rightfully belonged to men. He blamed females for causing what he saw as the decline of American civilization. In June 1991, Henard walked into the office of the FBI and attempted to file a civil rights charge against "the white women of the world" but was rebuffed by an agent who explained that his complaint was improper. Just days before his killing spree, Henard wrote in a cryptic letter to a young woman who lived nearby, "Please give me the satisfaction of someday laughing in the face of all those mostly white female vipers from the two towns who tried to destroy me and my family."

Not every mission hate crime is clearly marked as such. Even when the crime is perpetrated exclusively against the members of a particular group, we cannot always be sure that it was motivated by bigotry or bias. Like Marc Lepine, Patrick Purdy was a young man filled with hate who went on a deadly rampage. But unlike Lepine, Purdy never broadcast his intentions, nor did he leave a note explaining his behavior.

Purdy was almost always by himself, had no girlfriends, and seemed to dislike everyone. He was conspiratorial and paranoid in his thinking. In the end, he singled out a particular group as being especially blameworthy.

For some five years, the twenty-four-year-old loner had drifted from place to place. Working as a laborer, a security guard, or a welder, he traveled—to Connecticut, Nevada, Florida, Oregon, Tennessee, and Texas—to any state where his past might not come back to haunt him. But, wherever he went, Purdy argued with his bosses and simply couldn't hold a job for more than a few weeks at a time.

Along the way, Purdy repeatedly got into trouble with the law. In 1980, he was arrested in Los Angeles for soliciting a sex act from a police officer. Two years later, he was arrested on charges of possession of hashish. In 1983, he was convicted of possessing a dangerous weapon. A few months later, he was arrested on a charge of receiving stolen property. In October 1984, he spent thirty days in a Woodland, California, jail for his part in a robbery.

Three years passed and Purdy's behavior became increasingly bizarre. In 1987, he was apprehended in El Dorado, California, for indiscriminately firing a 9-millimeter pistol in the El Dorado National Forest and charged with resisting arrest. He kicked deputies who tried to arrest him, shattered a window of their patrol car, and then told the police that it was his duty "to overthrow the suppressors." While being held in jail, Purdy tried to hang himself and cut his wrists with his fingernails; but, like everything else in his life, even his suicide attempt was a failure.

It was now January 1989. By this time, Purdy despised almost everyone, but especially people in positions of authority and especially his "enemies," the newcomers to America's shores. He had been living for a few weeks in Room 104 of El Rancho Motel on the edge of Stockton, California, a riverfront agricultural city located some 80 miles east of San Francisco, plotting his final assault on those who were to blame for his miserable existence. To develop an effective military strategy, he would spend hours in his room manipulating the hundreds of toy soldiers, tanks, jeeps, and weapons that he had collected in order to simulate an attack. He kept them on the shelves, on the heating grates, even in the refrigerator. He had carved the words "freedom," "victory," and "Hezballah" into the stock of his rifle. And on the camouflage shirt that he wore over his military jacket, he had written "P.L.O.," "Libya," and "Death to the great Satan." He perceived a conspiracy involving people in charge. The symbols on his weapon and jacket were the symbols of anti-Americanism ("The great Satan"). (4)

On Tuesday morning, January 17, Purdy put on his military flak jacket, picked up a handgun and an AK-47 semiautomatic assault rifle, and drove his 1977 Chevrolet station wagon a couple of miles to Cleveland Elementary School in Stockton—the elementary school he had attended from kindergarten to third grade. When he had lived there as a child, the neighborhood was white; now it was predominantly Asian.

Arriving at the Cleveland School just before noon, Purdy could see hundreds of young children—most of them refugees from Cambodia, Vietnam, China, and

Mexico—playing at recess on the blacktop in front of the brown stucco building that housed the school. As a diversion, he immediately parked his car and set it on fire with a Molotov cocktail in a Budweiser bottle. Then, Purdy eased through a gap in the fence surrounding the building and walked onto the crowded school grounds, where he opened fire.

For a period of two minutes, Purdy sprayed sixty rounds of bullets from his AK-47 at screaming children in a sweeping motion across the blacktop. He then took the handgun from his belt and shot himself in the head. Written on the pistol's handle was the word "victory."

Purdy's "victory" toll was high. Five children, all from Southeast Asia, were dead, and thirty more were wounded before the gunman killed himself. (5)

Purdy's attack was based on racial hatred. He had frequently made hostile racial comments to coworkers about the influx of Southeast Asian refugees into the United States and had protested bitterly about the large number of Southeast Asian classmates in industrial arts courses he was taking at the local community college. He complained that the newcomers were taking too many jobs and he resented having to compete with them. In less than eight years, the population of Southeast Asian refugees in Stockton went from fewer than 1,000 to more than 30,000. Just prior to his murderous rampage, Purdy told another resident of El Rancho Motel: "The damn Hindus and boat people own everything."

But why had Purdy chosen this particular set of targets—children in a school yard—to carry out his mission? Purdy hated the newcomers from Vietnam and Cambodia who had taken over his old elementary school, if not the entire community. He was angered by the presence of these foreigners in the school that he had attended

as a child. He believed that Asian-Americans had taken
his place. But Purdy also hated the school and everything
that it symbolized in his mind. He recalled his early years
as a child, a particularly painful period when the shy and
socially inept youngster was apparently rejected by his
classmates. In his warped and delusional way of thinking,
Purdy's victims may have seemed like little more than
the toy soldiers he had manipulated back in Room 104 of
the El Rancho Motel. As a result, five children died at the
hands of a deranged gunman who was full of hate.

* * * * *

Hate crimes represent one endpoint on the continuum of prejudice and bigotry. For economic as well as psychological reasons, there are countless individuals who
feel resentful. They have suffered some loss in self-esteem
or status and are eager to place the blame for their loss
elsewhere—on those groups and individuals portrayed in
the culture of hate as weak, immoral, or uncivilized.

Yet, millions of Americans who have suffered a decline in their standard of living and/or their self-esteem
would never commit a criminal act against individuals
who are different from them. Some people simply do not
buy into the culture of hate; others may possess enough
self-control that they are able to stop themselves from be-
having in a deviant or violent manner, no matter how
great the appeal. For a few, however, the desire to commit
a hate crime is overpowering. In a thrill-seeking hate
crime, an individual joins a group activity so that he will
not be rejected by the people who are most important to
him—his friends. In reactive hate crimes, an individual
believes that he must protect himself from the encroachment of outsiders. And, in mission hate crimes, an indi-

vidual becomes convinced that his personal problems are a result of some conspiracy involving an entire group of people with whom he feels compelled to get even. Like Patrick Purdy, the hatemonger may suffer from an extreme form of mental illness that leaves him paranoid and delusional. As we shall see, however, one does not have to be psychotic in order to commit a mission hate crime. The desire to rid the world of evil also motivates the activities of organized hate groups.

CHAPTER 8

Organized Hate

Life hadn't been easy for twenty-seven-year-old Mulugeta Seraw, but his future looked bright. The dark-skinned young man with a foreign accent and a ready smile lived and worked in the city of Portland, Oregon. Having emigrated from Ethiopia seven years earlier, Seraw was a part-time student while working as an Avis shuttle-bus driver at the airport. He was far from wealthy but hoped eventually to save enough money to finish college and improve his standard of living. As an ambitious newcomer, Seraw was every bit the embodiment of the American Dream.

Early on a Sunday morning, November 13, 1988, Seraw and his two companions, also of Ethiopian descent, were returning home from a nearby party. Before turning in, they stopped their car in the middle of the street to chat awhile, totally unaware that they were being watched by three local skinheads. The three members of a group known as East Side White Pride were returning from an evening of recruiting, drinking, and partying. Wearing military jackets, steel-toed boots, and sporting shaved heads, the racist skinheads—Kenneth Mieske, Steven

Strasser, and Kyle Brewster—stood on a corner about 100 feet from Seraw and his friends. Brewster said, "Hey, I see a nigger. Let's go over there and mess with him."

The skinheads immediately hopped in their car and drove down the block to the car of the three Ethiopians. Mieske got out of the car first and exchanged angry words with Seraw and his companions. Strasser and Brewster joined in and there was a scuffle.

Then Mieske went further. Moving up behind Seraw, he repeatedly struck him in the back of the head with a baseball bat, while Strasser and Brewster kicked all three black men. When it was over, Seraw and his companions were taken to Emmanuel Hospital and Health Center. Two of the Ethiopians were treated and released; Seraw was pronounced dead on arrival. He had died as a result of a fractured skull.

In May 1989, Mieske pleaded guilty to murdering Seraw and admitted that his motivation was racist. He was given a life sentence. The other two skinheads, Strasser and Brewster, were convicted of first-degree manslaughter, for which they are presently serving prison sentences up to twenty years in length.

Despite the convictions, the courtroom battle was far from over. In October 1990, Oregon's Multnomah County courthouse became the scene of a civil action—a wrongful death suit—brought on behalf of the Seraw family by Morris Dees, chief trial counsel of the Southern Poverty Law Center in Montgomery, Alabama, the Anti-Defamation League of B'nai B'rith, and attorney Elden M. Rosenthal.

The lawsuit was aimed not only at two of the skinheads who had attacked Seraw and his Ethiopian companions in 1988, but also at Tom and John Metzger and their White Aryan Resistance (WAR) organization, headquartered in Fallbrook, California. Tom runs WAR—hosts its

long-running cable-access TV program, oversees its newspaper, and is heard on its Washington, D.C., hotline. To
make a living, he repairs TV sets. In the 1960s, Metzger
was a member of the John Birch Society. During the 1970s,
he served as California grand dragon of the Knights of the
Ku Klux Klan. In 1980, he won the Democratic nomination
to the House of Representatives and later ran unsuc-
cessfully for the Senate. Tom Metzger's son John, leader of
the Aryan Youth Movement (formerly the White Student
Union), is responsible for recruiting young people to the
cause.

The Metzgers, both Tom and John, were accused of
being liable for Seraw's murder. The suit claimed that, in
their roles as heads of WAR, the two men had encouraged
and instigated the skinheads, who "conspired to inflict
serious bodily harm" on Seraw.

Writing in *The Nation*, Elinor Langer suggests that the
influence of the Metzgers and the organization WAR on
racial violence in the streets of Portland actually began in
March 1988. An Asian-American man, the white woman
to whom he was married, and their young daughter were
leaving a local restaurant when they were accosted by
three skinheads shouting racial slurs and insults. The publicity surrounding this incident caught the attention of the
Metzgers at their Fallbrook, California, headquarters. During the summer of 1988, John Metzger began writing to
Portland skinheads, including Mieske, Brewster, and
Strasser, urging them to join his cause. By the fall, WAR
organizers had arrived. (1)

Not unlike entire nations, organized hate groups have
broadened the meaning of the term "defense" to include
aggressive behavior toward innocent people. In a recent
issue of his WAR newspaper, for example, Tom Metzger
asserts: "We have every right to use force in self-defense,

in retaliation, and *in preemptive strikes against those who openly threaten our freedom."* (2)

Thus, no pretext of a precipitating event is even required. Blacks need not move into an all-white neighborhood; Jews need not join a "Protestants-only" club. The very *presence* of members of a particular group—no matter where and in what numbers—may be considered enough to call for a group response.

In civil court, Ken Mieske argued self-defense: his lethal attack on Mulugeta Seraw had been part of a spontaneous street fight; he had merely reacted to the Ethiopian man's attempt to strangle one of his skinhead companions. Representing the Seraw family, however, Attorney Dees was able to show that Mieske's notion of defense was absurdly inclusive and out of touch with reality. The Metzgers, through agents they had sent to recruit Portland's skinheads, had aided and encouraged the violent behavior that led to Seraw's death. In their campaign of hate, the Metzgers had conspired to do violence to blacks and had been reckless in sending representatives, including a former vice president of John Metzger's Aryan Youth Movement, Dave Mazzella, to Portland as their agent.

Mazzella's testimony left little to the imagination. Testifying for the plaintiffs, he candidly confessed that he had in fact been sent by WAR for the purpose of recruiting and training Portland skinheads. Tom Metzger had taught him how to assault blacks by provoking them first, attacking them with baseball bats, and then claiming self-defense. According to Mazzella, he would send "report cards" to the Metzgers consisting of newspaper accounts of his beatings. In addition, he had distributed copies of John Metzger's Aryan Youth Movement newspaper as a tool for recruiting skinheads in Portland. In one issue, an article entitled "Clash and Bash" introduced the "sport" of bashing, whereby "hunting parties of white youth seek out non-whites and break their bones." (3)

In court, Tom Metzger attempted to distance himself from the murder. He had never met Mazzella, and, in any event, he claimed he was only exercising his freedom of speech. But Seraw's side produced damaging evidence to implicate the Metzgers in a more direct manner. First, they showed records of numerous telephone calls between Metzger in Fallbrook and Mazzella in Portland. Then, they produced a photograph in which Tom Metzger was holding an assault rifle as he gave paramilitary training to a group of skinheads.

On October 22, 1990, after deliberating for little more than five hours, the jury reached a decision on an eleven to one vote. Tom Metzger was ordered to pay $5 million, his son John was ordered to pay $1 million, their White Aryan Resistance organization was directed to pay $3 million—all in damages to the family of Mulugeta Seraw. In addition, skinheads Kenneth Mieske and Kyle Brewster were ordered to pay $500,000 each. Another $2,500,000 in damages was also awarded. (4)

It took only hours for Tom Metzger to publicize his defiant response to the verdict against him. In a recorded telephone message on his hate-filled hotline, the head of WAR issued a warning to his "new" targets everywhere. In an emotional statement of purpose, he proclaimed that "we will put blood on the streets like you've never seen and advocate more violence than both World Wars put together. . . We have a new set of targets to play with. So if you're white and work for the system, watch your step. Whether you be a system cop, a controlled judge, or a crooked lawyer, your ass is grass." (5)

The vicious murder of twenty-seven-year-old Mulugeta Seraw could easily serve as a textbook illustration of the operations of organized hate groups today. First, we learn that *Metzger's White Aryan Resistance supports and encourages the violence committed by skinhead groups.* Though only about 15 percent of all hate crimes are perpetrated by organized groups such as WAR, their impact is actually much more pervasive. Thousands of racist skinheads rely on such organizations for slogans, mottoes, and guidance. In 1969, Charles Manson apparently did not physically assault actress Sharon Tate and her four companions. He wasn't even at the Tate residence when the massacre occurred—but he ordered the murders. Similarly, Hitler may not have been present at the scene of the Nazi atrocities, but they were orchestrated by him. In the same way, there may be thousands of alienated youngsters looking for a role model who will encourage them to express their profound resentment. Such impressionable youths may not actually join some hate group. They may not be willing to shave their heads and don the uniforms of skinheads, but they are nevertheless *inspired* by the presence of such groups and *intrigued* by the use of their symbols of power. In some cases, they receive their marching orders from the leaders of organized hate.

The marginal teenagers who spray paint racist graffiti on buildings are usually not members of WAR, but they are attracted by its slogans. In the murder of Mulugeta Seraw, the White Aryan Resistance attracted youngsters looking for a thrill and used them as instruments to carry out its group mission of ridding the United States, if not the world, of its "subhuman" residents. In this scenario, we see the potential strength of an organized hate group. It is able to mobilize more than one source of motivation for action. Its leadership may be motivated by missionary zeal. Many of its members may believe that their violence is defensive, aimed at protecting the "American way of life" or their Aryan heritage. Its "field soldiers" may consist of skinheads, or other disgruntled youths, with minimal political consciousness, who are looking for a thrill and, at the same time, a way of seeing themselves as special. They are typically working-class youngsters who have not been successful at school or on the job. They usually don't get along with their parents or other family members. Among fellow skinheads, however, they feel both accepted and important.

Some skinhead groups lack either formal structure or ties to organized hate groups. Their alliance is maintained by little more than common haircuts, shared racism, political alienation, and more-or-less spontaneous outbursts of violence which they direct against blacks or Latinos in their communities. At the other end of the continuum, however, there are thousands of skinheads who have organized for action. They give themselves a name ("Romantic Violence," "American Front Skinheads," "Reich Skins," "Confederate Hammer Skins," or the like), select a leader, hold regular meetings, distribute racist propaganda, and attend rallies sponsored by organized hate groups like the KKK. While there is no single national organization of skinheads, networks of skinhead gangs have been known to exist, over the past five years. For example, the Confederate Hammer Skins, Western Hammer Skins, American Front, National White Resistance, and Old Glory Skins are presently linked together in a loose confederation. Even among skinheads associated with organized hate groups, however, members typically move in and out of different groups and switch their allegiances. (6)

Skinheads with connections to organized hate groups often employ hard rock music as a means of putting forth their racist message and as a tool for recruiting. A number of "white power" rock bands have begun to surface, whose members perform songs containing blatantly racist lyrics and advocating violence against the despised groups. Recognizing the power of a tune to persuade, the White Aryan Resistance has encouraged its members to use racist music as a recruitment tool. In its newsletter, WAR advises: "Music is one of the greatest propaganda tools around. You can influence more people with a song than you can with a speech." (7)

Ken Mieske was the lead singer in the rock band Machine. In 1986, he was convicted of petty theft and served a one-year sentence in the Oregon state penitentiary. Mieske must have been listening carefully to those who advocate mixing music with violence. In heavy metal style, he sang about being consumed with the urge to kill and about the pleasure that he derived from watching his victims suffer and die.

Another important lesson to be learned from the Seraw murder is that *the leaders of organized hate groups have tended to become mainstream rather than fringe, at least in the image they attempt to project.* Tom and John Metzger wear ties, not sheets. Some of the most influential members of WAR are former KKK members who recognize the futility of looking deviant, perhaps even anti-American. They wear suits and ties. Some get face-lifts or don hairpieces. Several have run for public office. Even in their support of bizarre-looking skinhead youths, they themselves are more concerned with projecting a respectable public image. They realize that younger people often reject the robes and ritual in favor of paramilitary dress. Concerned with the reaction of both the public and the police, some skinhead groups have recently taken a cue from their mentors by wearing their hair long and getting rid of their black leather jackets. (8) The new groups talk in code words and phrases about the issues that concern middle

America. They preach that the *heritage* (meaning: race) of white Christians is being eroded by *foreign* (meaning: Jewish/communist) influence; they lament the rise of *government interference* (meaning: Jews in high places who force racial integration down the throats of white Americans) in the lives of *average citizens* (meaning: white Christians); and they condemn *welfare cheating* (meaning: blacks), which they see as being of overwhelming proportions and on the rise.

Even some Klan leaders have changed their tune, at least in the way it is played for recruiting purposes. The leader of the Knights of the Ku Klux Klan in North Carolina barred the participation of violent neo-Nazis from its meetings. The head of the Klan in Florida urged its members to become a group "known for hating evil, instead of being a group known for hating Negroes." And the national leader of the Knights of the Ku Klux Klan has repeatedly suggested that his group does not hate anyone, but "loves the white race."

A third important message derived from the Portland murder is that *organized hate groups are technologically sophisticated*. Metzger's WAR uses computer networking, answering machines that leave hate messages, and public-access cable television. He and his colleagues are seen on nationally syndicated programs like "Geraldo," "Oprah," "Primetime Live," and "20/20."

Since 1984, Metzger's White Aryan Resistance has operated a computerized "bulletin board" that can be accessed by anyone with a personal computer and a modem. WAR uses its computer bulletin board, among other things, to spread propaganda, announce its future meetings, and provide the addresses of various hate organizations around the country.

Metzger's WAR telephone message line offers white

supremacist news and philosophy. It chastises government officials for their economic policies ("All you worth-
less bastards in the House and Senate, what are you up to
now? What's your beloved Pentagon pork barrel going to
do for you now that the phony cold war is being flushed
down the toilet? What other ways are you planning to
destroy white working people in the U.S.?"); for their policies toward immigrants ("Stop bringing in all these Asians
and make room for national parks. Boxcar a few million
Mexicans and Central Americans south of the border and
watch the streets get cleaner overnight"); and for their
treatment of Jews ("Why do you allow the Jew Mossad
secret police full freedom to spy on Americans from the
seventh floor of the Jew anti-defecation league right there
in front of you? You chicken-shits worship the Jews so
much you must have holes in the knees of all your
pants"). (9)

In a hotline message recorded after the Los Angeles
riots in 1992, Tom Metzger explained black violence directed against Korean shopkeepers in the inner city as a
natural response to unscrupulous foreign influences. According to Metzger:

> The blacks burn out the Koreans. That makes sense if
> you're black. It'll probably make sense if you're white pret-
> ty soon. The Mexicans, Nicaraguans, Guatemalans, Salva-
> dorians—illegal aliens for the most part—looted Jew and
> Korean-owned stores, taking inferior quality crap made in
> Hong Kong. I don't see any problem with that.
>
> It's too late for Band-Aids. It's almost time for serious and
> deep surgery. In the meantime, burn baby burn. (10)

According to the Anti-Defamation League, the number of cable television programs devoted to preaching hate
is on the rise. Featuring interviews with skinheads, hate
group leaders, and other hate activists, there are now fifty-

seven such programs being broadcast on public-access channels in twenty-four of the country's top television markets. Most have been found in California, thirty-one of them entitled "Race and Reason" and produced by Tom Metzger's White Aryan Resistance. But programs preaching racial and religious hatred have also turned up in other top markets such as Boston, New Haven, Phoenix, Denver, Tampa, Atlanta, Chicago, St. Paul, Cincinnati, Albuquerque, Pittsburgh, Houston, Richmond, and Seattle. (11)

Concerned citizens in these communities often wonder how the media activities of hate groups like the White Aryan Resistance are financed. Actually, they typically operate on a small budget provided by membership dues and private contributions. The exact amount and sources of their funding are closely kept secrets intended to protect the confidentiality of donors and to create a false impression of widespread support. Moreover, because of public-access laws and technological advances, a minimal budget is probably all that is needed to express bigotry on a widespread basis. Cable-access television provides an effective soapbox at virtually no expense. For the cost of a personal computer, a VCR, and an answering machine, an organization can easily create regional, if not national, exposure for itself.

According to the Southern Poverty Law Center's Klanwatch Project in Montgomery, the number of organized hate groups has grown significantly, perhaps as a result of hard economic times during the last few years. More specifically, Klanwatch estimates there has recently been a 27 percent increase in the number of white supremacist groups, mainly in Georgia, Florida, Southern California, northeastern states, and around Chicago. But numbers alone do not tell the full story. In total, there may be less than 20,000 and almost certainly no more than 50,000 members of white supremacist groups across the country. It is not only their revolutionary activism, however, but the growing sophistication of these organized hate groups in reaching the young people of America, through their finesse and ostensible respectability, that represents the real cause for alarm. It should also be noted that hundreds of thousands of Americans agree to some extent, if not wholeheartedly, with the principles of white supremacy, even if they would never join a hate group. (12)

Most Americans are at least somewhat acquainted with the objectives of white hate groups like the Ku Klux Klan and the neo-Nazis. Those who are familiar with American history know that the Klan has risen and fallen time and time again in response to challenges to the advantaged position of the white majority. During a short period of post–Civil War Reconstruction, for example, many whites were challenged by newly freed slaves who sought some measure of political power and began to compete for jobs with white, working-class Southerners. The Klan, responding with a campaign of terror and violence, lynched many blacks. Klan-initiated violence increased again during the 1920s, as native-born Americans sought "protection" from an unprecedented influx of immigration from Eastern and southern Europe. Those old enough to remember the 1950s and 1960s might recall uniformed members of George Lincoln Rockwell's American Nazi Party giving the Nazi salute and shouting "Heil Hitler," or Klansmen in their sheets and hoods marching in opposition to racial desegregation in schools and public facilities.

By contrast, the newer organized hate groups of the 1980s and 1990s don't always come so easily to mind for their bizarre uniforms or rituals. As noted, followers of

Metzger's White Aryan Resistance have shed their sheets and burning crosses in favor of more conventional attire. They often disavow the Klan and the Nazi movement in favor of a brand of "American patriotism" that plays better among the working people of Peoria (not to mention Rochester, Akron, Burbank, and so forth).

Moreover, white supremacist organizations now often cloak their hatred in the aura and dogma of Christianity. Followers of the religious arm of the hate movement, the Identity Church, are only "doing the work of God." At Sunday services, they preach that white Anglo-Saxons are the true Israelites depicted in the Old Testament, God's chosen people, while Jews are actually the children of Satan. They maintain that Jesus was not a Jew, but an ancestor of the white, northern European peoples. In their view, blacks are "pre-Adamic," a species lower than whites. In fact, they claim that blacks and other nonwhite groups are at the same spiritual level as animals and therefore have no souls.

Members of the movement also believe in the inevitability of a global war between the races that only white people will ultimately survive. The survivalists among Identity followers prepare for war by moving to communes where they can stockpile weapons, provide paramilitary training, and pray. According to a recent Identity directory, there are Identity churches in thirty-three states, Canada, England, South Africa, and Australia. (13)

The Idaho-based Aryan Nations was developed around Rev. Richard Butler's version of the Identity Church, which he calls the "Church of Jesus Christ Christian." Like other organized hate groups, the Aryan Nations is militantly committed to anti-Semitism and racism. Rather than demand that only blacks and Jews be expelled from the United States, however, Butler's group proposes establishing a separate white racist state in the northwest region of the United States and Canada.

Each year, Butler holds an "International Congress of Aryan Nations" at his headquarters in Hayden Lake, Idaho. Attracting as many as 200 racists, the annual festival is meant to bring together white supremacist leaders from around the world who share information, give speeches, and offer courses in guerrilla warfare. (14)

The particularly depressed economic conditions in rural areas of the United States since the early 1980s have provided a fertile breeding ground for organized hate. Playing on a theme that has special appeal to downtrodden farmers and small town residents, members of Posse Comitatus (Latin for "power of the county") argue that all government power should be focused at the county, not the federal, level. From this perspective, IRS agents and federal judges are mortal enemies of the white race, and the county sheriff constitutes the one and only form of legitimate government. Many members of the Posse refuse to pay taxes. They charge that Jews create recessions and depressions and control the Federal Reserve.

Consistent with its emphasis on maintaining local control, Posse Comitatus has no nationally recognized leadership and consists of a number of decentralized and loosely affiliated groups of vigilantes and survivalists. But, from time to time, the Posse has attracted national attention.

In February 1983, for example, Posse member and farmer Gordon Kahl murdered two federal marshals in Medina, North Dakota, who had come to arrest him for a parole violation. The sixty-three-year-old Kahl evaded apprehension for almost four months. While a fugitive, he wrote a letter to James Wickstrom, leader of the Wisconsin chapter of the Posse Comitatus, describing the shoot-out with federal marshals as an early response to a prophecy from God to eliminate from the United States all Jews and communists. "We are a conquered and occupied nation," Kahl wrote, "conquered and occupied by the Jews who plan to rule the world by destroying Christianity and the white race." (15) In June, federal agents located the small farmhouse in the Ozark Mountains of Arkansas where Kahl was hiding out. They fired a volley of gunfire and tear gas through the windows of the house, igniting the ammunition stored inside. Kahl was killed in the fiery explosion.

Like the Posse, members of the Populist Party also take a conservative political position with an anti-Semitic twist. They claim that Jews are running the media as well as the federal government, and they oppose the United States' alliance with the state of Israel. Before being elected to the Louisiana State House as a Democrat, David Duke was an unsuccessful Populist candidate for President. (16)

The agenda of the Populist Party seems, on the surface, to be responsible and patriotic. Its platform calls for "a respect for racial and cultural diversity." By means of code words understood by its members, however, the Party actually expresses a covert anti-Semitic theme. For example, alleged respect for diversity is twisted into the message, "The Populist Party will not permit any racial minority, through control of the media, cultural distortion or revolutionary political activity, to divide or factionalize the majority of the society–nation in which the minority lives." The term "racial minority" refers specifically to Jews, while "cultural distortion" refers to the allegedly corrupting Jewish influence in American life. (17)

White supremacist groups represent a fringe element among those who commit hate crimes. In statistical terms alone, the membership of all organized hate groups combined constitutes a tiny fraction of American citizens, most of whom wouldn't consider burning a cross or wearing a swastika. Even so, the influence of white supremacist groups like Posse Comitatus, White Aryan Resistance, Aryan Nations, and the Klan may be considerably greater than their numbers suggest. It takes only a small band of dedicated extremists to make trouble for a large number of apathetic middle-of-the-roaders. Even in this age of activism, there are many solid citizens who have neither the time nor the inclination for political action.

It is of even greater concern that the bigotry espoused by white supremacists has moved into the mainstream of American society, even if in more subtle terms. No longer can we point an accusatory finger only at hooded Klansmen or at uniformed Nazis. On the contrary, we must now turn to examine our young, our own schools, and perhaps even ourselves.

CHAPTER 9

Hate Goes to School

Students on the Amherst campus of the University of Massachusetts sat glued to the tube. This was the final game of the 1986 World Series—a championship contest between the New York Mets and the Boston Red Sox that had raised the collective level of excitement to a feverish pitch. Watching TV in residence halls around the campus, groups of undergraduates rooted their approval, booed the opposition, and drank in excess. Having sat through a lengthy rain delay and a frustrating loss for the Red Sox the night before, the majority of them were eager to see the "hometown boys finally make good." Surely, this would be the night when the Red Sox—widely regarded as the "white team"—would put to rest their reputation for choking in the clutch, for never being able to win the Big Game (the Red Sox had not won a World Series since 1914).

When the contest ended, however, it was the much despised Mets—commonly considered the "black team" —and not the Red Sox who had come out on top. Thousands of disappointed Sox fans on campus—many of them drunk and angered by their team's defeat—poured out of the dorms to gather in the courtyard in front. They were immediately confronted by a few hundred euphoric Mets supporters, loudly celebrating their team's triumph and unsparingly taunting their losing rivals. In response, some of the Red Sox fans concocted homemade firebombs and found bottles to throw; others armed themselves with sticks. Sporadic fighting broke out between the two sides, and a few students were injured. (1)

At the beginning, confrontations involved only white Mets fans against white Red Sox fans. But the focus of the assault quickly turned racial when a particularly loud and unruly white student decided to attack one of the black students in the courtyard. As though looking for a target to blame for the Red Sox's loss, the crowd of whites moved menacingly in the direction of the fifteen to twenty blacks.

In an instant, the melee between Mets and Red Sox supporters had evolved into a shoving and pushing match based on race alone. A white football player threw a punch. A black student began swinging a stick after being jumped from behind and punched to the ground. Shouting racial insults, groups of white students chased the black students as they attempted to escape. Some of the whites broke windows and hurled rocks; others yelled racial slurs. Many attempted to force their way into a building where some of the black students had gathered to hide. One black attempted to defend himself with a golf club, but was tackled to the ground, kicked, and then beaten into unconsciousness. The crowd finally dispersed, but only in reaction to prodding by the Amherst police and the University of Massachusetts security police. (2)

*   *   *   *   *

Between August 31 and September 18, 1990, pollster Louis Harris set out to determine the views of students across the nation regarding the state of racial and ethnic tensions in America. Working on behalf of the Reebok Foundation and Northeastern University's Center for the Study of Sport in Society, Harris's staff talked with a cross section of 1,865 high school students attending the tenth, eleventh, and twelfth grades in public, parochial, and private schools around the country.

The pollster's findings paint a rather bleak picture of race relations among American youths of the 1990s. Apparently, confrontations between individuals of different races and religions have become "commonplace" in the nation's high schools. More than half of the students interviewed claimed that they had witnessed racial confrontations either "very often" or "once in awhile." One in four reported having personally been a target of such an incident. Yet, only 30 percent of all students said that they were prepared to intervene in or even to condemn a confrontation based on racial hatred. On the contrary, almost half either admitted that they would join in the attack or, at the very least, agreed that the group being attacked was getting what it deserved. (3)

The findings of a recent survey of all 1,570 elementary, middle, and secondary public schools in Los Angeles County also support the view that youthful hatred is on the rise. Thirty-seven percent of these schools had encountered incidents of hate-motivated violence during a school year. As expected, students in middle and high schools were particularly likely to have experienced hate violence, with a response rate of 47 percent and 42 percent, respectively. Somewhat more surprising was the finding that 34 percent of the elementary schools had also had violent episodes based on hate.

The Los Angeles County survey also determined that no one group had been singled out as a target for violence. Schools reported hate incidents against black, Latino, white, Asian, Pacific Islander, and Arab students, as well as incidents directed against Jewish students, gay and lesbian students, and immigrant students. As found in hate crimes generally, most students who engaged in forms of hate-motivated violence were not involved in any organized hate groups. In fact, only 5 percent of the incidents reported in the Los Angeles survey were committed by students with links to white supremacist organizations. (4)

Perhaps some part of the dramatic increase in youthful bigotry is a reflection of the latest version of an age-old conflict between the generations: an adolescent counterculture designed to attract teenagers to one another and, at the same time, to freak out older individuals, especially parents. At the extreme, rebellious members of the baby-boom generation of the 1960s expressed their independence by espousing "love," tripping on LSD, smoking dope, and voicing political dissent through demonstrations. Their behavior was at times so outrageous that it really left little for the next generation of youthful rebels to outdo. However, members of the punk counterculture of the 1970s and early 1980s made their own statement by emphasizing violence rather than peace, as well as drinking to excess, inventing slam dancing, dying their hair bright purple, and retreating from politics altogether.

Alas, what have we left for contemporary youths who wish to make a statement to their parents as well as their peers? Never fear. In their own version of a collective quest for independence, some youngsters have gone one more step by embracing out-and-out evil. At the extreme, there is now a growing interest in the darker side of life, a concern with Satanism, murder, and nihilism, in the service of racism. Alienated teenagers around the country have increasingly experimented with bizarre cult rituals. In the name of Satan, some have met clandestinely together to cut off the heads of pigs, dogs, and cats, and then drink their blood. Others have held secret "hell parties" where they listen to heavy metal music, ingest mescaline and LSD, and then sacrifice animals. At the extreme, a few have even committed ritualized murder. For example, a fifteen-year-old girl from Daytona, Florida, was recently sentenced to fifty years in prison after pleading "no contest" to the kidnapping and Satanic slaying of a Vietnamese immigrant, Ngoc Van Dang. The young devil worshiper, a ninth-grade dropout, had allegedly gotten the idea to commit a human sacrifice from reading *The Satanic Bible* and participating in a satanic ritual with the use of a Ouija board. Along with three friends, she abducted Dang after hitching a ride with him in Orlando. At gunpoint, she forced him into the woods and shot him seven times, killing him. She then carved a large inverted cross on her victim's chest. (5)

As in previous generations, these latest incarnations of the generation gap have succeeded in transforming themselves enough to become marketable to the middle-of-the-road American teenagers. Just as the hippies of the 1960s formed the basis for the music, dress, hairstyles, and politics of the so-called hip generation, just as punk culture was later incorporated into "New Wave" music, art, and fashion, so a softened version of extremist cultural and political themes has been absorbed into conventional culture. For example, whereas they were earlier denied access to the commercial mainstream, a few heavy metal bands espousing nihilism, violence, and bigotry are now positioned at the top of the popular music charts, finding a responsive audience on "contemporary hit" radio stations. Heavy metal's pounding rhythm and painful noise level may differ only subtly from the hard rock of previous generations, but its lyrics speak to a new genre of adolescent concerns, including oral sex at gunpoint, murder by ice pick, anal penetration, necrophilia, physical abuse of women, and satanic sacrifice. (6)

As a youth-oriented counterculture that appeals to alienated teenagers, the skinhead movement has grown in dramatic fashion as well. Across the country, disillusioned youths—especially those who aren't getting along with their families, teachers, and classmates—have shed their hair as well as their humanitarian values to revel in the limelight of the latest version of a racial superiority complex. In 1990, there were some 3,000 racist skinheads operating in thirty-four states. According to the Anti-Defamation League of B'nai B'rith, this figure represents some leveling off in a longer-term trend that began much earlier in the last decade. Overall, the Southern Poverty Law Center reports that whereas membership in adult racist organizations such as the Klan or the Aryan Nations has remained relatively stable, membership in skinhead groups increased dramatically throughout the 1980s. In England, where they began in the late 1970s, skinheads now number as many as 10,000. There are some 30,000 in Germany, where they have spearheaded hundreds of violent attacks on foreigners during the last few years. Skinheads are also found in all European countries, Canada, Australia, New Zealand, South Africa, and in several Latin American nations. (7)

Of course, only a tiny proportion—far fewer than 1 percent—of all American teenagers can be characterized as racist skinheads. The progress of these groups should, however, be measured not in terms of numbers alone, but also by their increasing dangerousness. There is a growing pattern of recruitment and activity across the country. As we have noted, skinheads have tried to enlist students in high schools from a number of states including Arizona,

Texas, Pennsylvania, New York, Oregon, Michigan, California, Colorado, and Florida. Their efforts at the college level have been less effective, being largely confined to a few campuses in the state of Ohio. In junior high and high schools, however, the skinheads have found a more receptive audience. In fact, skinhead gangs seem to be drawing their recruits from younger and younger age groups, some no older than thirteen years of age. (8)

To examine an all-too-typical example, consider the series of events that transpired recently in Glendale, California, a medium-size, blue-collar industrial city situated in the San Fernando Valley, about eight miles northeast of Los Angeles. Rosemont Junior High School in Glendale was the scene of repeated skinhead activity. In February 1989, a thirteen-year-old skinhead, after being refused permission to wear his "white power" T-shirt for his yearbook photo, threatened his teacher with a loaded .357 Magnum. The student pleaded guilty to three felony and two misdemeanor charges. In May of the same year, a Rosemont administrator ejected a skinhead who was not a student at the school. The reprisal took only a few days to occur. At first, it was directed solely at the administrator; he became the target of threatening phone calls and obscenities written on the door of his office. Several days later, however, the counterattack was generalized: The words "Jew bitch," "No Jews," "Happy birthday Hitler," and "We are back in town" were discovered etched, along with SS symbols and swastikas, into the classroom doors of Jewish teachers. The words "fuck Jews" were found scrawled across students' lockers throughout the school. (9)

Skinheads have participated in a variety of racially inspired acts in high schools across the country. At Groves High School in Birmingham, Michigan, skinheads reportedly defaced school property with swastikas and the

words "nigger," "white power," and "skins." At Spray-
berry High School in Cobb County, Georgia, a group of
skinheads purportedly gave Nazi salutes and shouted
"heil Hitler" while reciting the Pledge of Allegiance. At
Oak Ridge High School in Orlando, Florida, skinheads
apparently were responsible for raising a "white power"
flag above the school and spray painting swastikas on the
walls of temporary classrooms . . . and so on. (10)

Hundreds of skinhead attacks have been directed
against persons as well as property. At Shawnee High
School in Medford, New Jersey, for example, a white female student was threatened with death at the hands of a
local skinhead group because she had talked to a black
classmate. In school, she was told by another female student, "I'll have my skinhead friends kill you." Death
threats were also repeatedly made to her over the phone
by the members of a skinhead gang. The female student
who made the original threat, along with Joseph Cotton,
eighteen, and Brian Riccobene, nineteen, was later arrested and charged with making terrorist threats.

In Tulsa, Oklahoma, a group of skinheads recently
harassed and attacked the owner and customers of a mul-
tiracial nightclub. In an attempt to put the establishment
out of business, the skinheads first posted racist leaflets
around the local community, then firebombed the club
with a Molotov cocktail. When the club still refused to
close, the skinheads began to assault its customers and
then attacked its owner by hitting him in the head with a
brick. Then the skinheads knocked down and kicked a
patron in the head until he was unconscious. The club
remained open, however. The four youths involved in this
assault are presently under indictment by a federal grand
jury in Tulsa.

Though often taking a more sophisticated form than

the "in your face" skinhead version, intergroup hostility is also occurring on college campuses. At colleges and universities, acts of hatred directed against individuals perceived to be different have occurred with alarming frequency.

The National Institute Against Prejudice and Violence in Baltimore reports a dramatic upsurge in racial and anti-Semitic incidents on college campuses. At more than 160 colleges around the country, there has been at least a single "intergroup" episode during a three-year period, ranging from acts of insensitivity to episodes of open warfare. The Institute estimates that 20 percent of all minority college students are either physically or verbally harassed. Over a one-year period, the rise in anti-Semitic incidents alone has approached 30 percent. (11)

Toward the more benign end of the continuum of hate incidents, college students make jokes about the ethnicity of their classmates. For example, sociologist Gary Spencer studied the growth of JAP ("Jewish-American Princess") baiting on his campus, Syracuse University, as well as on other campuses around the country. He concluded that these jokes clearly contain a major element of both anti-Semitism as well as sexism.

The predominant theme of JAP jokes has recently become more overtly anti-Semitic in scope. And the people who relate them are increasingly non-Jews. These jokes are a new variation on an old theme—that Jews have too much money for their own good and that Jews have a belief in their own entitlement, going far beyond what is reasonable or healthy for society. In this view, espoused to an increasing extent by non-Jewish students, Jews continue to enjoy illegitimate power and wealth. This idea has been found on campus after campus, in graffiti, anti-Semitic slurs, and sexual harassment of Jewish women.

More insidious versions of JAP jokes on campus have also surfaced during recent years. Rather than emphasize the alleged ostentatiousness of Jews, they suggest in no uncertain terms that the world would be better off if all Jewish women were eliminated. Joke: A solution to the JAP problem. When they go to get nose jobs, tie their tubes as well. Another joke: What do you call 49 JAPs face down in deep water? A good beginning! (12)

Apparently, some college students have taken their bigoted jokes to heart by translating their hatred into action. At the University of Arizona, the windows of the Jewish Student Center were shattered one evening in a burst of gunfire by unidentified assailants. At Dartmouth College, the *Dartmouth Review* recently published alongside its logo an anti-Semitic statement taken from Hitler's *Mein Kampf. Review* staffers claimed that the incident was a hoax perpetrated by an impostor in an effort to discredit the publication. At the University of Wisconsin, an unknown hatemonger spray painted "Think extinction" on the walls of the Jewish Student Center. Then, two Phi Gamma Delta fraternity students at the University of Wisconsin entered a predominantly Jewish fraternity without permission and pelted its members with punches and anti-Semitic slurs. The two Phi Gamma Delta brothers were arrested for battery. At Rutgers University, unidentified vandals defaced the Hillel Foundation building with anti-Semitic graffiti including swastikas.

Acts of intolerance on college campuses have frequently also involved racial or ethnic differences. At Yale University, unknown vandals spray painted a red swastika and the words "white power" on the walls of the Afro-American cultural center. At the University of Michigan, a disc jockey on the campus radio station aired racist jokes and then played a song entitled, "Run Nigger, Run."

He was later suspended indefinitely. At Dartmouth College, four *Dartmouth Review* staffers repeatedly harassed a black professor whose teaching methods had been criticized by their newspaper. Charged with disorderly conduct, injurious behavior, abuse, and invasion of privacy, all four students were subsequently expelled. At Brown University, racist graffiti ("Niggers go home") were found scribbled in elevators, on restroom doors, on posters, and on the doors of black students' dormitory rooms. At Stanford University, unknown students drew thick lips on Beethoven's image on a poster and then hung it on a black student's door in a large residence hall . . . and so on. (13)

Most perpetrators of hate crimes perpetrated against college students are themselves college students. However, an especially hideous exception can be found in an incident that occurred on the evening of August 18, 1992, in Coral Springs, Florida, when several young white men shouted racial insults at Luyen Phan Nguyen, as he left a party. When the 19-year-old premed student from the University of Miami objected to the slurs and then tried to escape, the men chased him down "like an injured deer," according to Coral Springs Police Chief Roy A. Arigo, throwing him to the ground and then repeatedly punching and kicking him in the head until he was dead. Eight men ranging in ages from eighteen to twenty-two were later arrested for the fatal beating and charged with murder. None of the defendants were students; most worked in the area and had no record of criminal violence. (14)

The targets of campus hate crimes encompass a broad range of students aside from blacks and Jews, including whites, Asians, Latinos, Native Americans, and women. Moreover, during the war in the Persian Gulf, dark-skinned students with foreign accents—especially those coming from Middle Eastern nations—were frequently re-

garded as the "enemy" by American college students looking for someone, perhaps anyone, to blame. While the
Gulf war continued, both Arab and Jewish students were
at heightened risk of victimization.

The most persecuted students on college campuses do
not, however, necessarily differ from their assailants with
respect to race, religion, national origin, or even gender;
they differ in terms of sexual orientation. According to
many university officials, lesbian and gay students have
been most frequently targeted for victimization. The Governor's Task Force on Bias-Related Violence in New York
reached the same conclusion: "While evidence shows serious problems for many groups (on New York State campuses), the most severe hostilities are directed at lesbians
and gay men." (15)

On campuses around the country, lesbians and gays
have been threatened with violence. During Gay Pride
Week at the University of Oregon, a number of men burst
into a movie being watched by a gay group on campus and
then blocked the exits to the room. When the intruders
tired of holding the gay students hostage, they surrounded a shuttle van carrying female students and shouted antilesbian remarks at them. Although never identified, the threatening group was believed to consist of
campus fraternity members. At the University of Alaska,
several students wearing sweatshirts bearing the logo
"Anti-fag society" shouted insults at gays and defaced the
books and clothing of gays on campus. After a dance mar-
athon at Northwestern University, the gay couple sponsored by the Gay and Lesbian Alliance on campus received anonymous death threats on their answering
machine. At the University of Delaware, forty antigay
slurs, such as "A warrior needs to kill homos badly" and
"Fags are going to die from AIDS," were scrawled on side-

walks on the central campus. A group calling itself the Anti-Homosexual Federation signed some of the graffiti, which were strategically placed where members of the gay students' organization had earlier written messages of support for National Coming Out Day.

But one does not have to *be* gay to be victimized—one only has to "look" gay. Thus, male students who appear to be effeminate with regard to their body language or speech may be regularly harassed by their peers in college dormitories or campus centers.

The inability of hatemongers to identify gays and lesbians on the basis of appearance alone is a major reason why attacks against them are so often targeted at their campus offices and organizational meetings. Frequently, flyers announcing gay and lesbian meetings are torn down or defaced. At one university recently, campus bigots scribbled their message, "All faggots must die," across the announcements. At the same university, an anonymous caller phoned the office of the campus Gay and Lesbian Coalition to say, "I'm a Nazi skinhead . . . . I'm going to bomb your office and blow you up."

On many college campuses, student organizations tend to be divided along racial, religious, or gender lines and therefore emphasize the *differences* that separate students from one another. Such associations frequently organize around the problems or concerns experienced in common by the members of their group. Hence, the proliferation of such minority student organizations as the Black Student Union and the Gay and Lesbian Alliance.

Organizations based on shared racial identity, religion, or sexual orientation probably provide much-needed support for minority students who would otherwise feel totally out of place in a predominantly white or majority institution. In this sense, then, such organizations may be absolutely essential to the academic survival of minority students in what they perceive to be a hostile, or at best uncomfortable, environment.

Unfortunately, however, many white students apparently misunderstand the defensive objectives of segregated organizations on campus. Thus, whatever the benefits they have for their members, such organizations are used by bigots for reinforcing the notion already prevalent among majority students that minority students *think they are special*, that minority students *want nothing to do with majority students*, that minority students *desire separation*. It is not surprising that white students on about twelve campuses have established White Student Unions to protest what they regard as oppression directed against them. (16)

On the West Coast, White Student Unions were initiated by Tom and John Metzger's White Aryan Resistance as an element of its outreach program aimed at young people. In its publication, *The White Student*, the Metzgers' White Student Unions disseminate a virulent form of anti-Semitism. Specifically, they spread the word that "Communism is Jewish! Boycott Jew stores. Drive the rats out of town!" In hundreds of thousands of flyers distributed to California college students, the organization also declared the Nazi extermination of Jews a total hoax. (17)

Organizations whose memberships are limited to specific groups are nothing new on college campuses—and they didn't begin with minority students. College fraternities and sororities have long deserved a reputation for encouraging racial separation and elitism. Donald E. Muir's recent study at the University of Alabama suggests that fraternities and sororities may continue, at least on that campus, to serve as a sanctuary for traditional forms of racism. Based on the questionnaire responses of some 1,166 University of Alabama undergraduates, Muir found that the white fraternities and sororities on campus tend to recruit students who already dislike blacks and to support racial discrimination on the part of their members. (18)

It is true, of course, that what happens at the University of Alabama does not necessarily apply to all of the thousands of campuses across the country. Indeed, there are more than a few universities at which fraternities promote diversity rather than divisiveness among students. At Northeastern University in Boston, for example, students recently organized a fraternity around the theme of diversity. Rather than emphasize exclusivity, founders of this fraternity actively recruit members representing the full range of racial, religious, and national backgrounds of students on the campus.

Still, too many fraternities on too many campuses continue blatantly to transmit their bigoted theme. At the University of Wisconsin, for example, members of the Zeta Beta Tau fraternity conducted a mock slave auction for which they painted their faces black, wore Afro wigs, and lip-synched Jackson Five songs. At Oklahoma State University, fraternity brothers costumed as black slaves serenaded their sorority sisters as part of a campus "plantation party." At the University of Cincinnati, fraternity members held a Martin Luther King "trash" party, where invited guests were asked to bring Ku Klux Klan hoods, welfare checks, large radios, and "your father if you know who he is." At Brown University, fraternity members printed party invitations announcing that only heterosexuals would be welcome. At Arizona State University, fraternity brothers forced Jewish pledges to say: "My number is 6 million. That's how many Jews were killed and I should have been one of them, sir." (19) At Syracuse University, fraternity members distributed T-shirts reading "Homophobic and proud of it!" and "Club faggots not seals!" (20) At the University of Mississippi, an all-white fraternity left two of its members stranded, bound, and nude at a predominantly black school twenty-seven miles to the north. Racial slurs and KKK had been written across their chests with a Magic Marker. (21)

According to research conducted by Andrew Merton, Professor of English at the University of New Hampshire, college fraternities also serve as a refuge for the worst sorts of sexism. The overwhelmingly macho milieu of the typical all-male fraternity—as expressed collectively in everything from sexist jokes and language to harassment and violence—only reinforces and amplifies stereotyped thinking about women. Rather than regard women as their equals, fraternity brothers typically engage in activities in which females are treated as objects of conquest. Fraternity members build a snow sculpture bearing the image of a woman's breast pierced with a sword . . . pledges approach a woman and bite her on the breast or on the buttocks . . . brothers run through a sorority house wearing only jockstraps and black greasepaint . . . fraternity members congregate in front of a sorority house to sing an obscene tune and to browbeat a young woman who had accused a brother of rape . . . members of a fraternity share a record of how many beers it should take to seduce certain women on campus. (22)

During the 1960s, college students seemed eager to share their good fortune with such nontraditional classmates as people of color, women, and students from other lands. Many young people regarded college not just as a means to a job, but as a place to pursue lofty ideals such as beauty, truth, and love. They gladly embraced the "other," donning East Indian and Native American beads and dabbling in Buddhism and other Eastern religions as well as Transcendental Meditation. By the early 1970s, Yale University's Charles Reich had written his counterculture manual, *The Greening of America,* in which he predicted that it was only a matter of time before America became a nation of hippies. The catchwords of the day included *love, peace,* and *tolerance.* Reflecting the culture on many college campuses, rock idol Neil Young sang "Southern Man," in which he took Southerners to task for discriminating against blacks. College students from around the country marched on the capital to voice their support for civil rights, the women's movement, and the antiwar effort.

And then Americans experienced the energy crisis of 1973. Without warning, millions of motorists were forced to wait in long lines to get their gas tanks filled; for the first time, they worried whether they would be able to buy enough oil to heat their homes during the cold winter months. They were concerned about the spiral of double-digit inflation that threatened to destroy the American economy. Interest rates skyrocketed to the vicinity of 21 percent.

So long as prosperity prevailed and the economy was healthy, white male students gladly accepted the increasing enrollment of blacks and women on their campuses. In fact, white men felt a certain unity with these other groups, insofar as they were, like minorities and women, at risk. White men were draftable and therefore in fear of being sent to a war that many felt was inappropriate, if not immoral. As soon as the economic pie shrank, however, increasing numbers of students began to regard civil rights and feminism with doubt and suspicion.

The campus has changed dramatically since the hip era of the 1960s and 1970s: it now represents an exaggerated version of the zero-sum game that we normally expect to find elsewhere. On campus, the competition is fierce . . . and getting fiercer all the time. As the cost of tuition goes up every year and job opportunities tighten, students increasingly see themselves as soldiers on the field of battle who must fight for their small share of the economic pie. As a result, students do not always view one another as allies or friends, but as opponents or enemies with whom they must vie for scarce amounts of success both in and out of the classroom. Increasingly, white students regard their minority classmates as the undeserving recipients of financial aid and compensatory programs —what they believe to be special attention and special treatment. Similarly, some black and Hispanic students expect to find a racist behind every obstacle to their academic advancement. Moreover, male students resent the challenge posed by a growing presence of successful female students and gay students who have come out of the closet. And students of many different backgrounds take exception to the increasing number of Asian-American students—all Merit scholarship winners in high school, at least according to the stereotype. If there is one sociological law, it is that "competition breeds hostility between groups," especially when the economy is unhealthy.

On the college campus, this law operates in its purest, most dangerous form. Some of the hate incidents at colleges and universities consist of relatively minor pranks— thrill offenses—perpetrated by students with time on their hands and insensitive minds. For example, several Kappa Kappa Gamma sorority members at Stanford University dressed in Native American costumes and parodied "Indian hollers" outside the Native American Center on campus. Or, seven white students at Brown shouted "chink, ching, chong! chink, ching, chong!" at two Asian-American students as they passed on a street near the campus. But, to an increasing extent, campus hate attacks have become more reactive; that is, they are committed by students in response to a particular student or campus event that they feel threatened by—Gay Pride Week, the first black student in a dormitory, hostilities in the Middle East, and so on. For example, at the University of California at Davis, after an unsuccessful attempt by some members of the student government to reduce funding for a minority-oriented campus newspaper, *The Third World Forum*, two of its Chinese-American reporters received threatening phone calls. Identifying himself only as a member of the Ku Klux Klan, the caller suggested that "something drastic" would happen to them if they did not stop writing for the newspaper. Similarly, a first-year Latin-American student at Bryn Mawr College found the following anonymous note slipped under her dormitory door after she had complained about her test grade: "Hey Spic. If you and your kind can't handle the work here at Bryn Mawr, don't blame it on this racial thing. You are just making our school look bad to everyone else. If you can't handle it, why don't you just get out. We'd all be a lot happier."

Ironically, intergroup conflict also reflects growing diversity among students. Over the past three decades, there have been growing numbers of women, blacks, Hispanics, Asians, the disabled, as well as the avowedly gay on campuses around the country. In a situation where everyone has more or less the same background—where almost all students are white, straight, able-bodied, male, and Protestant—intergroup relations does not become an issue. Under conditions of increasing cultural diversity, however, the differences between groups become salient on an everyday basis. For the first time, students must learn to deal with classmates and roommates who are *different*.

For most students, whatever their racial identity, college is the first occasion to have extensive contacts with individuals who differ from them in socially significant ways. Because of the pervasive racial segregation that characterizes our communities, most students grow up going to school among only "their own kind." Then, they go off to college, where they might meet a broader range of humanity.

The first few months of college are a particularly stressful and threatening period. It is often the first time away from home, and students are in an environment where they could fail and be forced to leave. It may be difficult for them to make friends with someone who is different when they are terrified of being rejected themselves. Many students therefore react to this stressful situation by seeking companions who are very much like themselves.

The process whereby students, fearing rejection, befriend other students with similar attitudes and similar previous life experiences can have another, more negative consequence. A small number of such students may make themselves feel more secure by attacking, either verbally or physically, those classmates they see as inferior by virtue of that group's background, race, or creed. The very presence of minority students on a campus may provide just such an opportunity. At the Citadel, a military college in Charleston, South Carolina, for example, five white cadets wearing sheets and hoods burned a five-foot paper cross in the dormitory room of a black classmate. One of the first black students to attend the Citadel, the victim of this prank withdrew from school due in part to the harassment he had received from his peers. The five cadets were later indicted by a Charleston County grand jury under a

"Klan statute" for wearing hoods when they entered the black student's room.

Harassment is more than an isolated event at a single university. Minority student–athletes across the country are frequently faced with racial epithets shouted by opposing fans. This practice became so offensive during a basketball game at a small New England college that the opposing coach pulled his team from the floor and forfeited the game rather than have his players subjected to further abuse.

Among students who attend college to pursue lofty goals and embrace the finest ideals of the mind, going to school with different kinds of people may be regarded as a benefit, even a privilege. In an environment fraught with fierce competition, however, the presence of diversity can represent a *personal threat*. The following flyer discovered hanging on the campus of Brown University epitomizes how some white students now perceive cultural diversity on their campus: "Once upon a time, Brown was a place where a white man could go to class without having to look at little black faces, or little yellow faces, or little brown faces, except when he went to take his meals. Things have been going downhill since the kitchen help moved into the classroom. Keep white supremacy alive!" (23)

CHAPTER 10

Minority against Minority

On Friday, February 7, 1992, some 4,000 grieving and incensed people attended the funeral of Phyliss LaPine, a thirty-eight-year-old Hasidic Jewish woman who had been brutally murdered by a burglar inside her Crown Heights, New York, apartment. She and her husband had recently moved with their four young children to this beleaguered Brooklyn neighborhood—home to thousands in the ultra-Orthodox Lubavitcher sect—in order to live in peace and to strengthen their religious ties. (1)

According to the police, the killer had followed LaPine into her home, where he stabbed her dozens of times in the chest and neck and then left her to die. When the police arrived at the scene of the crime, they found LaPine's blood-soaked body on the living-room floor. Her clothing had been pushed up over her waist in an apparent act of sexual assault.

Though the only eyewitness told police he had seen a white man running from the scene of the crime, members of the Hasidic community were convinced that the culprit was black, and they were enraged. Religious leaders pleaded with the Hasidic community for restraint, but to no avail. Three hundred black-hatted and bearded men assembled in front of the local police station to express their outrage and demand an arrest. As a bottle was hurled in the direction of the demonstrators, they shouted "Go back to Africa" and "No more welfare." Three days later, after an intensive investigation, the police arrested Romane Lafond, a twenty-three-year-old black, unemployed handyman who lived only a half mile away, and charged him with the murder of Phyliss LaPine.

The hostility between blacks and Jews in the Crown Heights section of Brooklyn has a long history. But the precipitating event for open warfare occurred in August 1991, after a seven-year-old black child, Gavin Cato, was accidentally killed and his seven-year-old cousin injured by an Orthodox Jewish motorist, whose car jumped a curb, pinning the children to the wall of an apartment building.

False rumors spread quickly through the black community that a Hasidic-sponsored ambulance had refused to attend to the injured black children and instead had sped away with the three Hasidim involved in the accident. Unknown to witnesses at the scene, the police had given orders to the ambulance driver to remove the Jewish motorist from the scene in order to protect him from the anger of the crowd. Acting on rumors, a mob of black youths rampaged through neighborhood streets, shouting racial slogans ("Kill the Jews"). Some of them later retaliated by stabbing to death a twenty-nine-year-old rabbinical student from Australia, who was chosen entirely at random and had no connection to the accident. During three days and nights of confrontations between blacks and Jews, homes were damaged, cars were vandalized, and dozens of people were injured. For one week, blacks and Jews exchanged racial epithets and hurled bottles and rocks. (2)

The presence of black leader Rev. Al Sharpton on the following Tuesday added fuel to the fires of dissatisfaction. Sharpton claimed that Hasidim in the Crown Heights neighborhood had long enjoyed special treatment from the police—immunity from being targeted for investigation and arrest—and that the incident in which young Gavin Cato was killed was just another in a long series. At 6:00 P.M., Sharpton led a rally near the site of Gavin Cato's death. Within minutes, however, the angry crowd dispersed. There was widespread looting; the windows of nearby stores were shattered. Bottles and rocks were hurled, and youthful demonstrators pounded on the doors of the homes of frightened Jewish residents.

The history of relations between blacks and Jews illustrates more generally factors in the development of minority-against-minority hate crimes. Jews in the neighborhood are often regarded by local black residents not as another oppressed minority, but as representatives of the white power structure. The visibility of Jewish wealth on the block—the presence, for example, of stores and shops owned by Jews—only supports the view that Jews get special breaks from local government not enjoyed by black Americans in the same community.

Perhaps out of a growing impatience with racial inequality, some black leaders have promoted hostility between blacks and Jews. In a recent book, *The Secret Relationship between Blacks and Jews,* commissioned by Louis Farrakhan, leader of the Nation of Islam, Jews were singled out as responsible for exploiting blacks during the centuries of the slave trade. Yet, according to Henry Louis Gates, Jr., director of Harvard University's Afro-American Studies Program, American Jewish merchants were actually responsible for less than 2 percent of the slaves brought to the New World. (3) Gates contends instead that such "pseudo-scholarship" only undermines the historical alliance between blacks and Jews and, at the same time, weakens the moral credibility of black Americans' struggle against racism.

Although possibly self-defeating, black anti-Semitism may give us a clue as to the depth of discontent among black Americans vis-à-vis other groups. Don Muhammad, head of the Nation of Islam in Boston, recently called for a restructuring of black–Jewish relations: "Our relationship to Jews has historically been one of tenant to landlord. We don't always want to be the tenant. We want to be the landlord." (4)

But Jews aren't the only minority in occasional confrontations with black Americans. Since the 1970s, conflicts between blacks and Asians have erupted in major cities across the United States. From Washington, D.C., to Philadelphia to Los Angeles, growing numbers of Koreans have taken over retail stores in areas populated by blacks, who often charge that the Asian shopkeepers do not treat them with respect. Likening the Asian newcomers to Jewish merchants of the 1950s and 1960s, some blacks similarly resent the fact that Korean immigrants have achieved success so rapidly after arriving on the scene.

Important differences between blacks and Koreans account for much of the conflict that separates them. In the first place, Koreans enjoy a considerable economic advantage because of their middle-class status in the "old country." Long before coming to America, they had already developed the managerial skills, through formal education and family guidance, that are necessary for effective entrepreneurism. To make matters worse, cultural differences make communication all but impossible.

In January 1990, the Flatbush section of Brooklyn exploded with racial hatred. Blacks boycotted two Korean grocery stores after an argument between a Korean merchant and a black customer from the neighborhood. According to protesters, the Creole-speaking Haitian woman was unfairly accused of shoplifting and then struck by a Korean shopkeeper when she refused to open her bag for inspection. The Korean merchant told a different story. He admitted yelling at the woman but maintained that he had not hit her. Instead, he accused her of underpaying her bill at the checkout counter and then shouting, "You Chinese, Korean motherfucker. Go back to your country."

For months, the boycott continued, and so did black rage. Some demonstrators spat on customers as they broke the picket lines and entered the Korean markets. Other demonstrators only cursed.

In May 1990, it was widely reported that only a few blocks from the two Korean-American grocery stores under attack, three Vietnamese men were assaulted by a group of black youths carrying knives, bottles, and a claw hammer. One Vietnamese, Cao-Ahn Tuan, was sent to the hospital with a fractured skull. A twelfth grader at Boys and Girls High School in Brooklyn was later arrested and charged with assault, aggressive harassment, and criminal possession of a deadly weapon. (5)

According to the Vietnamese men, Tuan was attacked by two black men. One held a knife with a blade about a foot in length. The other hit Tuan on the forehead with a baseball bat, breaking his glasses and dropping him to the ground. Amid a stream of anti-Korean slurs and obscenities, one black teenager shouted, "Koreans, what are you doing here?" Another yelled, "Koreans go home."

Neighbors gave a slightly different account. They claimed that both sides—the Vietnamese as well as the black youths—wielded knives and shouted insults. According to the police, Tuan was struck on the head with a carpenter's hammer. But as ugly as the incident turned out to be, officials concluded that it was a spontaneous confrontation rather than a planned attack. (6)

Blacks are also increasingly at odds with segments of the rapidly growing Latino community. Formerly staunch allies in the battle for equality, these two minorities now more often see one another as opponents whose members must compete for jobs and political clout. One side charges that Latino immigrants are stealing jobs from low-income black Americans. The other side contends that immigration laws discriminate against Latino workers. Blacks argue that Latinos are receiving benefits from civil rights victories that were largely won without Latinos' help. Latinos respond that African-Americans refuse to treat them like equals in the fight for equality. To make matters worse, U.S. immigration policy has in certain instances favored Latinos. Whereas most of the would-be newcomers from Haiti have been regarded as economic refugees and repatriated, most Cubans are treated as political refugees and allowed to stay in the United States. (7)

In cities like Miami, Houston, Los Angeles, Washington, D.C., and New York, ongoing tension between blacks and Latinos has often provided the basis for political contests at the local level. On occasion, however, the intergroup rivalry has erupted into violent confrontations. Since 1981, at least six different riots have occurred because of black–Latino tensions in the city of Miami. In January 1989, for example, two unarmed black motorcyclists were killed by a Colombia-born police officer who had pursued the pair for a minor traffic violation. Shot in the head, one cyclist died at the scene. His passenger died the next day of injuries suffered when the motorcycle crashed. In response to this incident, black neighborhoods throughout Miami turned violent. More than 200 people were arrested as blacks burned automobiles, looted stores, and threw bottles at the police. At least six people were shot and wounded, two by police officers, as the police returned sniper fire. (8)

In June 1991, blacks rioted again upon learning that the conviction of the Hispanic police officer responsible for the death of the black motorcyclists had been overturned by the courts. The antagonism between Miami's blacks and Hispanics is deeply rooted in economic competition. (9) Cuban immigrants have taken many of the menial jobs—particularly in the tourist-hotel business—that had formerly gone to poor blacks. (10)

In Washington, D.C., the gulf between blacks and Hispanics has sometimes widened dangerously. In May 1991, a thirty-year-old Salvadoran immigrant, Daniel Enrique Gomez, was shot by a black police officer. The policewoman claimed that Gomez had lunged at her with a knife while she was attempting to arrest him. But the word on the streets was that Gomez was handcuffed when he was shot. For two consecutive nights, the streets of Washington, D.C., were filled with angry blacks and Hispanics who set fire to buses and cars, hurled bricks, threw Molotov cocktails, and looted stores in the area. The rioting resulted in 225 arrests and $2 million in property damage. Twelve police were injured. Nothing that the rioters did, however, could possibly alleviate the fundamental cause of racial tension in D.C.—namely, that growing numbers of poor Hispanics are competing with inner-city blacks for jobs and housing. (11)

It should not shock anyone that a minority itself might perpetrate reactive hate crimes on members of another group. First, minorities are socialized within the framework of the dominant culture and, just like every-body else in a society, learn the dominant values, norms, and stereotypes. Second, though oppressed groups might be expected in general to express less ethnocentrism, compassion for others actually tends to remain within each individual's group; that is, whether majority or minority in status, individuals generally have a great deal of sympathy for the plight of *members of their own group*. For anyone eager to reduce intergroup tensions, the trick is to get those same individuals somehow to transfer their sympathy and understanding in the direction of the experiences of outsiders. A first step might be to help the representatives of competing groups recognize important areas of commonality between insiders and outsiders—to realize that problems that might be associated with their own group are actually *universals* or nearly so.

Even within the same racial, religious, or ethnic groups, animosity has often arisen on the basis of criteria that, to the outside observer, might appear inconsequential or even nonexistent. Among the members of that particular group, however, the differences may be regarded as essential. Thus, West Indian versus American blacks, Ashkenazic versus Sephardic Jews, Japanese versus Chinese versus Koreans all represent *intra*group conflict that is not always obvious to the outsider, yet very real to insiders. Not unlike those that emerge between groups, stereotyped distinctions often develop within a group, sometimes purporting to explain the economic superiority of one segment over another. Thus, the more successful members might be stereotyped as "arrogant" and "aloof," while the less successful members might be regarded as "lazy" and "stupid."

Such stereotyped thinking occasionally becomes translated into heinous acts of discrimination. During

World War II, for example, tens of thousands of Korean women were literally dragged from their homes and forced to act as prostitutes for the occupying Japanese soldiers. In addition, thousands of Korean men were kidnapped to serve in the Japanese army or to become slave laborers for the Japanese war machine.

In a local community, the animosity may deepen when members of different minority groups compete head on with one another for the same jobs, to live in the same neighborhoods, and to send their children to the same schools. As they struggle to improve their social status, minorities may find themselves in fierce competition with the members of other groups who struggle with equal desire toward the same goals. Other minorities may be viewed as enemies rather than as allies, as opponents in the contest for scarce resources. Hence, the groundwork for intergroup hostility is laid.

Social scientists used to believe that intergroup contact almost inevitably promotes tolerance and harmony, that prejudice is literally a *prejudgment* used by the members of one group to characterize another in the absence of firsthand information. In this way of thinking, people from different backgrounds would like one another were they to get to know one another as individuals rather than as stereotypes.

Sadly, however, the conditions for enhancing intergroup relations are far more complex than was earlier believed. In some cases, groups whose members get to know one another better also get to despise one another more. Mutual admiration is usually not promoted by connecting the lower-class members of one group together with the middle-class members of another. More often, the two groups will come to believe that they share little if anything in common and that their differences are irreconcilable. It should come as no surprise then that middle-class Koreans or Jews in a squalid inner-city neighborhood may not be universally loved by their black neighbors.

But even when the members of two groups possess equal status and income, whether they live in peace and harmony or go to war depends very much on the circumstances under which they interact. If one group is perceived as *challenging* the goals of the other, confrontation rather than peace may prevail. If the members of a group are seen as *threatening* the position of another group, then conflict may replace cooperation.

Psychologists Muzafer and Carolyn Sherif long ago demonstrated the link between competition and intergroup hostility in a series of experiments that took place in an isolated summer camp for eleven- and twelve-year-old boys. After a period of time together, the boys attending the camp were separated into two groups and placed in different cabins. When each group of boys had developed a strong sense of group spirit and identity, the Sherifs arranged for a number of intergroup encounters—a tournament of competitive games such as football, baseball, tug-of-war, and a treasure hunt—in which one group could fulfill its goals only at the expense of the other group. Though the tournament had begun in a spirit of good-natured rivalry, it soon became apparent that negative intergroup feelings were emerging on a large scale. The members of each group began to name-call their rivals, completely turning against members of the opposing group, even boys whom they had selected as "best friends" upon first arriving at camp.

The Sherifs' experiment didn't end after the competitive tournament that had turned former friends into arch enemies. Instead, the researchers staged a simple situation to make a point—a situation that required the two groups of campers to *cooperate* in order to achieve a common objective. The boys loved going into the nearby town on Saturday nights. But, on this particular evening, the bus carrying all of them "got stuck" in the mud. In order to have a little fun in town, the boys from both groups were forced to put aside their differences and to pile out of the bus and push together to get it going again. Not only did the campers make it into town, but their intergroup hostility subsided as well. Their cooperation toward what the Sherifs call a *superordinate goal*—that is, a common objective—helped reestablish friendships between former enemies. In the Sherifs' classic experiment, we find a ray of hope for the future: human beings like one another more when they need one another to achieve a common goal. (12)

Competition between economically disadvantaged groups for status, power, and wealth is nothing new. Indeed, America's minorities have historically fought to climb the ladder of success while pushing their rivals off at every rung. At the turn of the century, the conflict grew between Irish and Italian immigrants; during the forties and fifties, it was between Puerto Ricans and blacks.

Unfortunately, however, blacks have become the focal point of the largest number of minority-against-minority confrontations in cities across the country. In almost every violent encounter, it turns out to be blacks who have had unfortunate confrontations with other groups—Latinos, Asians, or Jews.

It has been accurately observed that the historical experience of blacks in the United States is qualitatively different from the experiences of almost every other minority group. Only blacks came to America in chains; only blacks suffered the indignities of a legal system which forbade them to marry, own books, inherit money, or learn to read and write. Into the twentieth century, blacks have been stigmatized by a society that uses skin color and racial physiognomy as a basis for awarding educational and economic opportunities. Now blacks watch in horror as newcomers from Asia, Europe, and Latin America too often go around blacks on their way up the ladder of success. In a radio interview recently, Nation of Islam leader Don Muhammad summarized the feelings of millions of black Americans when he suggested that "blacks have been in America 437 years, and people who have been here 437 days have walked past us." (13)

CHAPTER 11

Hate around the World

The voices of xenophobia and racism are once again reverberating throughout German society. The resentment associated with hate crimes can be clearly seen in a sweeping new wave of violence—the largest spree of racial violence in Germany since the early days of Nazism.

Recent changes in what used to be East Germany as it struggles to make the transition from a communist to a free-market economy have set the stage for violent attacks on refugees and workers from Eastern European and Third World countries. Unemployment has approached 50 percent in some eastern cities, and the collapse of the once tightly controlled communist economic system has made living conditions deplorable. There is a housing shortfall in the major cities. Young Germans watch as their parents lose their jobs, their teachers are replaced, and their old political heroes are arrested. According to Heinrich Sosalla, director of social services in Magdeburg, "young people are desperate for some sort of new authority." Some find it in a revised version of Nazi activism; they work out their frustrations on a new scapegoat—the hundreds of thousands of foreign refugees who struggle to gain a foothold in their host country.

Five million foreigners reside in Germany, including hundreds of thousands who seek political asylum and almost three million "guest workers"—émigrés who are permitted to reside in Germany because they are needed to fill a particular job—and their families, most of whom are permanently excluded from citizenship. In addition, about 400,000 ethnic Germans in the Soviet Union—persons of German ancestry—who return to the fatherland are automatically granted citizenship. (1)

The contributions of newcomers to a thriving German economy should not be underestimated. They provide a cheap source of labor that keeps industry competitive, spurs investments, and revitalizes decaying communities. Many of them perform jobs that native-born Germans see as simply beneath them. Moreover, the population of Western Europe is waning and aging rapidly. The presence of large numbers of immigrants assures that Germany will be able to maintain its current labor force. (2)

All of this is lost on the hordes of out-of-work neo-Nazi German youths who regard newcomers as little more than insects to be crushed under foot. During 1991 alone, there were almost 1,500 attacks against foreigners in Germany, but only a handful of convictions. In April 1991, a twenty-eight-year-old Mozambican was killed by a gang of East German neo-Nazi youths who pushed him from a moving trolley in the city of Dresden. In September 1991, 600 right-wing German youths firebombed a home for foreigners and then physically assaulted 200 Vietnamese and Mozambicans in the streets of Hoyerswerde.

More recently, normal tranquility in the East German seaport town of Rostock was shattered by seven nights of organized violence in the streets. Armed with gasoline bombs and stones, a thousand Nazi youths attempted to force out foreigners seeking asylum in Germany. First, the mob firebombed a ten-story hostel in which Romanian gypsies were housed. Then, they stormed the building next door, a residence for Vietnamese "guest workers," and set it on fire. Some 600 police officers in riot gear used water cannons and tear gas to subdue the crowd. At least 195 Nazi youths were arrested. One hundred and fifteen Vietnamese and 200 Romanians were evacuated by police and relocated to a former East German army barracks under heavy guard. Within days, the attacks in Rostock had touched off a massive wave of antiforeign violence in at least twenty cities around eastern Germany. (3)

Much of the violence in Germany is perpetrated by a relatively small number of extremists—an estimated 5,000 hard-core neo-Nazis and another 30,000 racist skinheads out of a total German population of almost 78 million. In East Berlin, a chapter of neo-Nazis recruited only a few hundred unemployed and alienated young men who give expression to bigotry and racism as a way of "fighting back." Several hundred neo-Nazis from former East German towns recently met to commemorate the death of Hitler's deputy Rudolf Hess. (4)

Yet, the degree of resentment can be easily underestimated. There are actually millions of "silent sympathizers." In a recent national poll, up to 40 percent of all Germans expressed some sympathy for the issues— "Germany for Germans," "racial purity," and "foreigners out"—espoused by right-wing extremists. Moreover, 15 percent of Germany's youth said they now consider Adolf Hitler to have been a great man. In Germany and surrounding European countries, violence is taught by means of underground Nazi computer games, which have recently circulated among high school students there. In the game "Aryan Test," players are asked to indicate the most effective method for exterminating Jews. The winning answer is to kill them in gas chambers. In the game "Concentration Camp Manager," the objective is to kill as many Turks with as little gas as possible. (5)

Even in China, where foreigners have long enjoyed deferential treatment, there are signs that resentment against the 1,500 African students who study there has been on the rise. (6) Former minor points of contention have become major points of conflict. In 1989, two black African students showed up with their Chinese dates to attend a Christmas Eve dance in the city of Nanjing. Word of this incident spread quickly, precipitating several racially motivated confrontations between college students. Hearing about the demonstrations in Nanjing, young people in several other Chinese cities met en masse to express their collective displeasure with the foreigners. Thousands of demonstrators screamed racial slogans like "Beat the blacks." Rather than deal harshly with the local students who rioted, the police in Nanjing instead beat the African students, held them incommunicado, and even tortured them by shocking them on the genitals with cattle prods. (7)

The Chinese are apparently resentful of a historical tendency, probably motivated by politics, for foreigners to be given special treatment by China's government. On trains, for example, Chinese passengers travel "hard class," while foreigners and high officials ride in the "soft class" cars. Similarly, Chinese students on university campuses see their government furnishing African students with special dormitories, cafeterias, and scholarships. Thus, African students are particularly resented not only because of simple racism, but because these foreigners are seen as getting preferential treatment. (8)

In France, mounting resentment against its three million Muslim Arab immigrants has provoked the government to tighten controls against illegal immigration. Public opinion pollsters report that 76 percent of all French citizens now believe that there are too many Arabs in their country. Jean-Marie Le Pen's extreme right-wing National Front, a powerful political force in some regions of France, has called for the eviction of all immigrants. Le Pen has made his greatest inroads in areas of France having high unemployment and large immigrant communities. In the port city of Marseilles, the home of many North African newcomers, for example, the sixty-three-year-old Le Pen recently won 25 percent of the vote. In some cases, anti-immigrant sentiment has been transformed into ugly acts of violence. In March 1990, three men of North African origin were viciously murdered in separate racially motivated attacks. (9)

Le Pen's anti-immigrant position is matched in fervor only by his anti-Semitism. He has openly disputed the authenticity of the Holocaust, dismissing stories of Nazi gas chambers as "historical detail," and has often raised the issue of national loyalty among French Jews. In a widely shown television debate, Le Pen repeatedly asked Lionel Stoleru, a Jewish government minister, whether he held both Israeli and French citizenship. "We have the right to know who you are," Le Pen told Stoleru. (10)

Perhaps inspired by its right-wing political movement, France has also been forced to deal with a rising tide of crimes against Jews. Through the 1980s and into the 1990s, numerous Jewish cemeteries have been vandalized. In May 1990, a particularly grisly series of desecrations occurred. At the cemetery in Carpentras, situated in southern France, vandals shattered thirty-four tombstones with sledgehammers and iron bars. They then dragged one woman's body halfway out of her grave and exhumed the body of an eighty-one-year-old man buried only two weeks earlier. As an expression of their disdain, the vandals impaled the man in the middle of his chest with an umbrella to hold in place a Star of David. (11)

In Italy, a traditional haven for newcomers, hospitality has similarly turned cold, as the Italian economy worsens, unemployment grows, and the influx of newcomers remains unchecked. Hardly a week passes without some episode of conflict between immigrants and Italians. In March 1990, for example, a large gang of Florentine youths battered their way into an immigrant dormitory and beat up immigrant workers. In May 1991, a crowd of Italians cheered as the police arrested a group of Albanians who were demonstrating in the city of Asti to protest the living conditions in their refugee camp. Also in May 1991, two Italian workers placed a high-powered air-compression hose into a Moroccan coworker's anus, destroying his intestines and killing him. (12)

There are some 800,000 legal immigrants in Italy, many of whom hold jobs as domestics and physical laborers. Some Italians argue that, given their country's very low birth rate, immigrants are necessary to the vitality of the economy. But most Italians see the high unemployment rate and argue instead that immigrants are taking their jobs. In fact, 75 percent of all Italians now favor closing the borders to all new immigration. (13)

As the economic woes in Eastern Europe have worsened, racism and anti-Semitism have resurged. In Moscow, twenty-five-year-old Zimbabwean student Gideon Chimusoro was fatally shot in the neck by police after he kicked a dog belonging to the owner of a kiosk. When Chimusoro's classmates marched in protest, riot troops clubbed and kicked them to the ground. Some of the Afri-

can students were pinned against walls and pounded viciously with clubs. Dozens of Russian onlookers, dis-
gusted by the sight of protesting Africans, made obscene
gestures at the demonstrators. All of the students attended classes at Moscow's Patrice Lumumba People's
Friendship University, once a showcase of communist propaganda but now a run-down institution beset with
charges of neglect and racism. (14)

In what was formerly the Soviet Union, political factions have focused their assault on the small Jewish minority in an effort to force Jews to give up good jobs or to
leave the country. Hundreds of thousands have already
left; millions more are on their way out. Procommunist
groups have used Jews as scapegoats to explain the de-
mise of Soviet Marxism; anticommunists have blamed
Jews for the current state of economic misery. In February
1992, anti-Semites marched through the streets of Moscow, shouting "Beat the Yids and save Russia" and demanding the dismissal of Jews from important public positions. (15)

Given the minuscule number of its Jewish citizens,
the growing anti-Semitic impulse in Poland seems particularly absurd. In a country of 38 million, there are now
fewer than 10,000 Jews, most of whom are in their
eighties. Yet, this fact hasn't diminished the public debate
concerning whether or not public officials ought to be required to reveal their Jewish ancestry. Scrawled across
Jewish monuments, graffiti hoping to discredit popular
Polish figures make false claims that they are actually secret Jews. (16)

The 80,000 Jews in Hungary have similarly experienced a revival of anti-Semitic sentiment, at the same time
that they benefit from a rising tide of democracy. Just as in
other countries of Eastern Europe, the demolition of the

Soviet Union has made possible a new degree of Jewish practice unthinkable under the communist order. Hungary has resumed relations with Israel. The central synagogue in Budapest is now filled to capacity on religious holidays. An official memorial to the country's Holocaust victims was recently dedicated. And the first Jewish secular school is in full operation. (17)

Yet, because some Jews held party positions under the communist system, the new Hungarian version of anti-Semitism is being merged with anticommunism. During the national election in 1990, for example, Miklos Tamas, an important member of the Hungarian Parliament, was singled out for harassment. While Tamas's political party is avowedly anticommunist, it appeals to a broad constituency, including many intellectuals, former communists, and Jews. A practicing Protestant whose mother was Jewish, Tamas received at least thirty anti-Semitic death threats by mail and telephone. In one letter, the anonymous bigot wrote, "The place for the Jews is Israel; the place for Dr. Tamas is the cemetery."

During the election campaign, one Hungarian political party sought to exploit anti-Semitism by making veiled references in its radio broadcasts to the "dwarfish minority" that was stealing Hungarian culture from its people. In an article published in the Hungarian socialist press, Jews were told that they must limit their presence in visible occupations—for example, in radio, TV, and newspapers—in order to assure that anti-Semitism would not increase. The socialist columnist Gyorgy Domokos wrote, "They must be careful that the number of Jews does not dominate." (18)

Paul Bookbinder, Professor of History at the University of Massachusetts in Boston, suggests that the old Soviet regime—by means of police state tactics and extremely tight controls—had long suppressed overt expressions of anti-Semitism. According to Bookbinder, "anti-Semitism had no place officially in communist ideology and, in fact, was specifically opposed by early creators of the communist movement. From 1919 through the 1930s, anti-Semitism was against the law in the Soviet Union, and people were prosecuted for distributing anti-Semitic propaganda or committing acts of violence against Jews." (19)

Bookbinder contends that the Russian government was generally passive in its reaction to bigotry. If it seldom singled out Jews for harassment, then the Soviet system did even less to attack the centuries-long underlying roots of anti-Semitism. Under communism, bigotry lay dormant but never disappeared, instead festering among many elements of the population. In the wake of the disintegration of the Soviet Union, Eastern Europeans were free for the first time since the Russian Revolution to express their beliefs and feelings openly. Thus, when the tight controls were lifted, anti-Semitism burst loose with a vengeance.

To some extent, violence directed against newcomers may reflect an almost constant mixture of such irrational factors as racism, ethnocentrism, and xenophobia. Regardless of the state of the economy at any given point in history, certain members of society—especially those who can trace their own ancestry in a country back several generations—are bound to be offended by, and seek to remove, the strange customs, rituals, and appearance of "inferior outsiders."

At the same time, however, anti-immigrant and anti-Semitic violence also may have a more "rational" political and economic basis. During periods of economic retrenchment, it sends a powerful message to foreigners and minorities from those who seek to reduce competition for jobs. Hate violence says to anyone considering emigrating for the sake of a better standard of living: "Your kind is not welcome in *our* country. Don't bother to come. If you do, the same thing will happen to *you*." And to minorities, it says loud and clear: "Go back where you came from . . . or else."

As a form of collective scapegoating, hate violence serves a purpose for the rulers of a nation as well. Sociologist Lewis Coser once referred to this phenomenon as a "safety valve." He suggested that when times are bad, hostility that might otherwise be directed at the leaders of a society is instead aimed squarely at its marginal members, those located along the bottom-most rungs of the socioeconomic ladder. Thus, by focusing blame on the "outsiders," the rulers of a society are able to preserve their positions of power, even if their policies and programs are in fact responsible for pervasive economic hardships.

Not unlike other countries around the world, the United States has been guilty of using hate violence as a "safety valve" when times are tough. According to Jorge Bustamante, the president of El Colegio de la Frontera Norte in Tijuana, Mexico, it invariably becomes politically correct to capitalize on anti-immigrant sentiments whenever the U.S. unemployment rate rises above politically acceptable levels. When Americans are out of work, we can expect to hear our public officials call for repatriating recent arrivals, establishing more stringent criteria for accepting refugees, and closing the borders with Mexico. This is when immigrants are routinely blamed for Americans being out of work, for trafficking in drugs, for increasing the cost of social services, and for committing violent crime.

CHAPTER 12

Police Response

A swastika is spray painted on a synagogue; a rock is hurled through the window of a black family that recently moved into an all-white neighborhood; a man perceived to be gay is assaulted. When a hate crime occurs, the local police department is generally the first governmental agency to be notified. The victims of the hate crime, most often members of a minority group, call the police because they are afraid and because they hope that local law enforcement officials can do something to prevent future threats to their well-being. The police, on the other hand, often find themselves in an awkward position. In the minority community, *they* are frequently perceived not as allies or protectors, but as major violators of civil rights.

Not without some justification, minority communities across the United States have long viewed the police as oppressors. During the era of "Jim Crow," it was the local police who enforced the rigid segregation laws in the South, who prevented blacks from sitting at "whites only" lunch counters or from riding in the "whites only" front section of the bus. In the North, the police also played a major role in supporting segregation, if not as openly as in the South. Apparently in the interest of keeping the peace, they enforced unwritten rules of conduct that kept black youths out of white neighborhoods, except in the role of servants. Of course, the police never attempted to keep white shopkeepers from doing business in black neighborhoods. Most importantly, the preferred method of enforcing this segregation on the minority community was through the use of violence. Black youngsters who "didn't understand" were frequently taken to the local police station and "taught a lesson," a lesson most often driven home by a beating. The attitude of local law enforcement officials during this period of oppression may best be summed up in the words of a white local sheriff who, in the film *Eyes on the Prize*, spoke to a member of the black community about violence as follows: "Son, it's mind over matter. I don't mind and you don't matter."

Minority hostility toward the police peaked during the mid-1960s, when a number of cities erupted in violence. In August 1965, a white California patrol officer stopped a young black motorist for an equipment problem in the Watts section of Los Angeles. The young man appeared to be drunk, and the officer arrested him. Jaded by years of police hostility toward the black community, black onlookers misperceived this incident as biased. When the police left the scene, members of the crowd began throwing rocks at cars and setting them on fire. A few white drivers were pulled from their automobiles and beaten. Before the force of the riot could be blunted some thirty-six hours later, there had been 34 deaths, hundreds more injured, $35 million in property damage, and 4,000 arrests. (1)

The disorder in Watts marked the beginning of a period of burning and looting that swept across the country. (2) By the end of 1967, riots had ignited in many urban minority neighborhoods, including Jersey City, Atlanta, Philadelphia, Los Angeles, Cleveland, Newark, Boston, and Detroit. The majority of these violent outbursts were ignited by police incidents, frequently routine arrests of blacks for minor offenses by white police officers. In July 1967, for example, the police in Newark arrested a black cab driver whose license had been revoked for several previous accidents. At 9:30 P.M., residents of a high-rise public housing project watched as the cab driver was dragged kicking and screaming from a police car into the front door of the police station across the street. Rumors spread quickly that he had been a victim of police brutality and that he was either injured or dead. Hundreds of people gathered in front of the station house to protest. By midnight, the crowd grew unruly. Several Molotov cocktails were thrown at the station. When the police attempted to disperse the crowd, hundreds rampaged through the streets, breaking the windows of shops and stores and looting their contents. The Newark riots resulted in twenty-three deaths and some $10 million in property damage.

As a result of this wave of urban unrest, President Lyndon Johnson formed The National Advisory Commission on Civil Disorders to study the causes of violence in the major cities and to make recommendations for changes that would reduce the likelihood that such violence would recur. The Commission confirmed that one major factor contributing to urban violence was the deep hostility between the police and inner-city residents. (3)

An important area of tension between the police and the minority community concerns police use of excessive force against minorities under questionable circumstances. Serving as a catalyst to unprecedented rioting on the streets of Los Angeles, the case of Rodney King is only the most recent example. On March 3, 1991, the twenty-five-year-old black motorist was stopped by Los Angeles police officers, taken from his car, and beaten. A two-minute videotape secretly shot by an amateur photographer showed King lying on the ground as officers took turns swinging their nightsticks at him and kicking him in the head. King sustained extensive injuries including skull fractures, a broken cheekbone, a shattered eye socket, and a broken leg.

Though the officers who participated in Rodney King's beating were later acquitted, the Christopher Commission, an independent panel headed by former Undersecretary of State Warren Christopher, determined that racism and excessive force were a major problem within the Los Angeles Police Department. Some officers in patrol cars, the Commission discovered, sent racist and sexist messages over police computers to describe their encounters with black residents: for example, "Don't cry Buckwheat, or is it Willie Lunch Meat" and "Sounds like monkey-slapping time." In an exchange occurring on the same evening that King was stopped, two of the officers later indicted for the beating of the black motorist sent a message referring to a domestic argument in a black household as "right out of *Gorillas in the Mist*." (4)

Clearly, charges of racism and excessive violence in police response are not confined to Los Angeles, or America, for that matter. In Toronto, recently, the local police slaying of a young black Canadian man, Raymond Lawrence, precipitated a spree of window smashing and looting. (5) Lawrence was shot twice in the chest by a white police officer after a lengthy chase through the downtown area of Toronto. According to police reports, the twenty-two-year-old black man had threatened the officer with a knife so the policeman had no choice but to protect himself; black leaders argued instead that excessive and unnecessary force was used. What began as a protest against racism was transformed quickly into a riot. Some 400 young people, black and white, paraded down the city's main thoroughfare, breaking hundreds of store windows and then snatching the merchandise. Similarly, in Vineland, New Jersey, scores of black and Latino protestors engaged in a night of rioting and looting after a local black man was fatally shot by a white police officer who attempted to arrest him on outstanding warrants for possession of a handgun and assault. The twenty-four-year-old shooting victim, Samuel Williams, had tried to outrun the officer on foot, but was chased down in a gravel pit. According to the police, Williams still refused to surrender, instead attacking the officer with a heavy metal bar. At this point, the policeman fired his weapon and Williams dropped to the ground. (6) Critics argued that excessive force had been used and pointed out that only one officer of the 100-member Vineland police force was black. (7) In Teaneck, New Jersey, a sixteen-year-old black youth was shot to death by a white policeman, touching off a candlelight vigil and a night of violence involving local teenagers who charged police harassment. Two police officers had responded to a 911 call which reported that a youth holding a handgun was seen hanging out with his friends in a school yard in a predominantly black section of the town. When the police arrived on the scene and attempted to search him, the teenager suddenly bolted by running down a driveway behind the school and hopping a hedge. One of the policemen shot him in the back. (8) In New York City, four black family members claimed they had been brutalized in an unprovoked attack by as many as twenty-five police officers, most of whom were white.

The incident apparently occurred when a police dispatcher mistakenly sent out an emergency distress call for immediate assistance. Thinking they were aiding a colleague in danger, the officers rushed to an apartment in the South Jamaica section of Queens and, without waiting for an explanation, clubbed the four occupants with their nightsticks. (9) In Long Beach, California, a black civil rights advocate claimed that a white officer beat him and then slammed his head through a window in a routine traffic stop. Adding to the credibility of the victim's account, the entire encounter was secretly recorded by a local television news team and played on national television. (10)

A number of recent studies have documented the discriminatory use of deadly force against minorities both nationally and in selected cities. A national review of citizens killed by police from 1965 through 1969 found that 42 percent were black, 13 percent Latino, and 2 percent Asian or Native American, numbers much higher than would be expected by either population rates *or* arrest rates. (11) In Miami, a study of citizens killed by police between 1956 and 1983 revealed that the majority of the victims were black, at a time when the black population of Miami never exceeded 20 percent. (12) Racism and violence have historically combined to produce feelings of distrust and suspicion of the police on the part of the minority community. These perceptions, in turn, may prevent victims of bias-motivated violence from coming forward to report these crimes.

A recent United States Supreme Court decision has increased the suspicion that the criminal justice system is not on the side of the minority community in its struggle against bias-motivated violence. In a landmark Minnesota case, the Court ruled that burning a cross on a black family's lawn was an expression of a constitutional right protected by the First Amendment. The Court declared null and void a Minnesota statute which sought to prohibit the display of symbols of hate, including burning crosses and the Nazi swastika. The Court ruled that these symbols are mere expressions of free speech and as such are guaranteed protection under the First Amendment. In the wake of the decision regarding the Minnesota cross burning, the Ohio Supreme Court recently voided a five-year-old hate crime law that rendered more severe penalties in cases where intimidation could be shown to have a basis in the race, religion, or ethnic identity of a victim. (13)

Because the police themselves are already suspected of being prejudiced, it is essential that police departments develop policies and procedures for handling bias-motivated violence as part of an overall effort to be responsive to victims of hate crimes. Unfortunately, however, most police agencies around the country do not treat hate crimes as seriously as they deserve to be treated. A recent survey conducted for the Fraternal Order of Police reported that most police agencies still do not include hate crime training as a normal part of their recruit training programs. The most significant reason for this apparent lack of interest on the part of most police agencies is that they believe that hate crimes are not a problem in their communities.

In contrast, progressive police departments across the United States, although admittedly few in number, have recognized the harm that hate crimes can cause in their communities. These departments have taken a number of steps to improve the identification and investigation of hate offenses. Indeed, some have developed a specific departmental policy for handling all hate crimes that are reported to them, have assigned specialized units to investigate these crimes, and have developed training programs for all officers in techniques for the proper identification of hate crimes.

In departments that have developed hate crime investigation policies, their procedures specify the steps that must be taken by all police personnel under their jurisdiction, whenever a possible bias-motivated crime is committed. The key elements of such policies include (1) designating who within the police department should be notified and when, (2) requiring officers to complete and maintain certain records, and (3) outlining procedures to be followed with the victim.

In the Baltimore County Police Department, for example, the official hate crime policy requires that the responding officers notify their immediate supervisor first and their second-level supervisor before the end of his or her shift. This policy also requires that a formal police report be filled out in all cases which could be bias-motivated. This report must then be reviewed by the supervisor and forwarded to the hate crime investigating unit of the department. In most police departments with such a policy, the initial Incident Report must be submitted by the responding officer within twenty-four hours of receiving the call from the victim. Finally, these policies require that a supervisor contact the victim, in person, shortly after the incident has occurred. Moreover, in such departments, the supervisor is required to take all precautions necessary to protect the victim from further harassment.

Hate crime policies are important to the extent that they send a strong message both to the victim and to the officers in the department. By requiring that a report be written and that a supervisor play a personal role, the department gives notice that these are indeed serious crimes and that they expect them to be treated as a high priority. In addition, by requiring a supervisor to contact the victim to follow-up on the investigation, the department communicates to the victim that it understands that these crimes are serious and that the local police cares about the victims and the difficulties that they may be experiencing.

As with all governmental policies, a hate crime procedure is only as good as the department's overall commitment to fighting hate crimes. If a department develops a hate crime policy but does not take steps to assure that it is implemented in good faith, the policy will be meaningless. To date, only a few police agencies have adopted a hate crime policy. But as more police departments develop such formal procedures, it will be up to community residents to assure that they are being fully implemented.

A recent analysis by the Uniform Crime Reporting (UCR) Section of the FBI concluded that the most successful strategy for investigating a hate crime is to employ what the FBI calls a two-tier investigation process. (14) This procedure involves two levels of response by the local police department to a crime that may be motivated by prejudice. The first response is by the officer who receives the initial call for assistance from the victim. The second, or follow-up, response comes from a specialized unit or officer who has responsibility for investigating all hate crimes in that particular jurisdiction and has been trained to properly identify them. The FBI now recommends this two-tier response strategy to all law enforcement agencies, regardless of their size, for investigating any crime that may be motivated by bias or bigotry occurring in their jurisdiction.

In departments which do not have such a specialized officer, the victims of bias-motivated violence are too often overlooked when they ask police for help. Previous research in Boston indicates that nonspecialized officers, for a number of reasons, fail to properly identify hate crimes. Some blunder because of their own bigotry, others because they are not trained to ask the appropriate questions. Being inexperienced and untrained, for example, officers may not think to ask whether the black family that has just had a rock thrown through its window has also been the recipient of any bigoted threats or racial slurs. In Boston, a group of officers refused to identify certain offenses as hate crimes because they felt it was in the victim's best interest not to do so. As one officer explained it, "I know we have a strong case of assault here, but if I bring up civil rights, the case will get bogged down and we might lose it, because it is harder to prove a hate crime." (15) Actually, one accusation does not preclude another. Trained officers would understand that both charges—assault *and* a civil rights violation—could be brought, leaving the court with the responsibility for determining the guilt on both counts.

One type of evidence that should be collected but is frequently missed is the offender's use of language. If a prosecutor is to convince a jury that the incident was motivated by bias, then the exact language used by the offenders must be included in the original police report. Sometimes officers are reluctant to include certain racial slurs in their formal written report. One Massachusetts police officer wrote when describing an attack on a black man, "during the course of the attack the perpetrators called the victim the 'N' word." This may seem like a small error, but it hampers the prosecutor's case. However, once the officers are told that it is acceptable, in fact important, to record the exact language used in the attack, they have done so.

In addition to specialized units, if the police are to

deal effectively with bias-motivated violence, then *all* officers must be trained in the proper methods to identify
hate crimes. The failure of an officer to properly identify
an incident as hate motivated sometimes results in esca-
lated violence and additional harm to the victim. Say, for
example, that someone slashes the tires on an automobile
belonging to an Asian family that recently moved into an
all-white neighborhood and that the police treat it as a
prank that doesn't warrant investigation. Because the police don't know to ask whether there have been prior incidents of harassment, the offender might easily be convinced that the police will look the other way. This belief
may empower the offender to escalate the violence against
the victim, under the assumption that "the police don't
care about those people any more than I do."

A number of model hate crime training programs are
already in place across the country. Three of the best
known are the FBI's Hate Crime Training program, the
Boston Police Department and Northeastern University's
Hate Crime Certificate Program, and the Montgomery
County Maryland Human Rights Commission Hate Violence Workshop. The curriculum and target audiences for
these training programs are very similar. All are directed
at local police officers and first-line supervisors who may
come in contact with victims of hate violence. And all
include sessions aimed at understanding prejudice and
increasing police awareness of the cultural differences
within the minority populations of the local community.

Most training programs begin with a session that at-
tempts to explain to the officers how prejudiced attitudes
are formed, how stereotypes are used to bolster prejudice,
and how prejudiced attitudes and discriminatory actions
are interrelated. These sessions, which are frequently
taught by a local university professor, are in many cases

the first time the officers, many of whom lack any postsecondary education, have been exposed to formal instruction in the socio- and psychodynamics of prejudice and discrimination.

Such training programs also deal with cultural differences, specifically, with the way of life of the minorities who live in the local area. In these sessions, such differences are often discussed by members of the minority community. In the Boston Police Department program, for example, members of the Southeast Asian community presented problems they had encountered in interacting with the police in the past. One common complaint was based on a cultural difference in expressing deference and honesty. Strictly as a sign of respect, a particular Southeast Asian victim of violence—while in the process of reporting a hate crime—refused to look the police officer directly in the eye. By drawing on American cultural norms, traditional police investigation manuals cite a victim's inability to look an officer in the eye as an indicator that the victim may not be telling the truth. The officer in question therefore assumed that his Asian victim might have lied. Once this cultural difference was explained to police officers, they understood that the interviewed Southeast Asian victim had attempted to give the officer a certain amount of respect (it also turned out that he was telling the truth).

Another problem in dealing with Asian minorities arises from the vastly different nature of the criminal justice system in their country of origin. As some Asian hate crime victims have explained, when the police in Cambodia or Vietnam came calling, it was invariably to report bad news. In addition, corruption was rampant in some Southeast Asian countries, where offenders routinely escaped punishment by paying off local officials. When Asian victims see the American system of bail, where money is exchanged to guarantee the defendant's return to court, they frequently think that they are again witnessing the corruption encountered in their homeland, where the police sided with the offender. As a result, many Asian victims are reluctant to assist the police in their investigation of hate crimes, believing the police corrupt.

A number of training sessions bring victims of hate crimes in to meet the officers. Having victims of bias-motivated violence speak to the officers about the impact of the crime on their lives can be a powerful technique in helping police understand the importance of the role they play in protecting hate crime victims. In the Boston police program, for example, a panel of victims relate the experiences they had both during their victimization and subsequently, when they sought the assistance of the police. Lt. Bill Johnston, director of the Boston police program, believes that this component is essential. He argues: "We may not be able to change an officer's bias in the course of a single training session. But these individuals got into policing to help people who were victims of crime; and if you can show them that hate crime victims need their help, that might make the difference the next time a victim comes forward."

Identifying a hate crime is an issue that all hate crime training sessions for police must tackle. Traditionally, many hate crimes have gone uninvestigated, simply because the police officer responding to the crime did not think of bias as a possible motive for the incident. In learning how to identify a hate crime, the police must also come to understand that the victim is not always a reliable indicator of whether or not any particular offense is motivated by bigotry. Discussions with victims have indicated that many of them look for reasons other than their group membership to explain their victimization, because if people are attacked because they are black or Asian, then there is nothing they can do to reduce the likelihood of an attack happening again. Whatever they do and however they behave, they will obviously always be black or Asian. Training sessions stress that the investigation by the hate crime unit or officer should be the determinant of whether a crime is in fact motivated by bias.

The FBI training sessions list a number of indicators that responding officers should consider in determining whether or not an incident is bias motivated. These factors do not by themselves, however, indicate that any given episode was a hate offense, only that additional investigation may be necessary. For example,

- that the offender and the victim were of different racial, religious, ethnic/national origin, or sexual orientation groups.
- that bias-related oral comments, written statements, or gestures were made by the offender which indicate his/her bias.
- that bias-related drawings, markings, symbols, or graffiti were left at the crime scene.
- that the victim is a member of a racial, religious, ethnic/national origin, or sexual orientation group which is overwhelmingly outnumbered by members of another group in the neighborhood where the victim lives and the incident took place.
- that the victim was visiting a neighborhood where other hate crimes had taken place or where tensions are high against his/her group.
- that a substantial number of people in the community where the crime occurred perceived that the incident was motivated by bias.

- that the incident coincided with a holiday relating to, or a date of particular significance to, a racial, religious, or ethnic/national origin group.
- that the offender was previously involved in a similar hate crime or is a member of a hate group. (16)

The final sessions of most hate crime training programs for police generally include strategies of how to investigate this type of offense. These sessions stress that most of the victims of hate crimes do not know the identity of their attackers. At least in this respect, therefore, hate crimes differ from many other crimes of violence where there is some prior relationship between offender and victim.

It is important that police officers be made aware in training sessions that the motivation for all hate offenses is not the same and that the investigation will differ depending on the type of hate crime being probed. If, for example, investigating officers suspect that a thrill hate crime has been committed, they should anticipate that the perpetrators are *likely* to be a group of males in their teens or early twenties, probably without a criminal record, who live some distance from the immediate crime scene. If, however, the police suspect that a reactive hate crime has been perpetrated, they might instead anticipate that the offenders are *likely* to be adults who live or work close to the crime scene—for example, in the same neighborhood or company as the victim. Also in a reactive offense, the police should recognize that the offender's bigotry may be widely shared by other residents of the neighborhood (or by co-workers), many of whom may see the victim as threatening their property values or their chances of being promoted. Thus, information about the circumstances of the crime may be unusually difficult to obtain by normal interviewing procedures. Finally, if the police encounter what they believe to be a mission hate crime, they should anticipate that members of organized hate groups—for example, White Aryan Resistance or the Klan—may be involved or that the offender may have a history of severe mental illness and may very well consider taking his own life.

The most essential lesson for police officers is that in order to be effective, they must put increased effort into hate crime investigations. (17) If the police are to resolve these incidents by arresting the offenders, they will need to conduct a complete investigation, such as is done in a homicide or a rape, and they will need the continued support of the victim. This latter element, continued victim support, is frequently a major stumbling block in hate crime investigations. Research in Boston indicates that many victims ultimately withdrew their cooperation during the course of the police investigation. (18) Some misunderstood the way the American criminal justice system operates; others were reacting to threats from the offenders or from the offenders' friends. Therefore, the police are encouraged to offer victims substantial support to increase the likelihood of their continued participation in the case. This support could include giving a precinct phone number to the victim in case of any further incidents, placing the victim's home on a regular patrol route, and stopping by the victim's home once a week to update him or her on the progress of the case.

Recognizing that many members of the minority community distrust or fear the police, some local police agencies have begun to work with existing advocacy organizations in their communities to present programs that emphasize the rights of minority citizens and the steps that the police can take to protect these rights.

The Japanese-American Citizens League has outlined a series of strategies that can be effective in community outreach programs generally. (19) The League suggests that such programs should distribute pamphlets or educational videos that explain to community members what their rights are and the police role in guaranteeing these rights. The police should also organize community forums in minority neighborhoods to explain what they will do for victims of hate-inspired violence. All too often, the police will offer a program on the rights of citizens held at police headquarters, then complain when attendance is low. If the police want these programs to work, they must go to the neighborhoods where minorities live in order to make clear to potential victims that the police are committed to protecting their rights. Other outreach components recommended by the League include establishing a program in civil rights at local schools. The Boston Police Department currently presents a program to all fifth graders in Boston public schools in which a hate crime investigating officer discusses the constitutional rights of students and their families. A final suggestion from the Japanese-American Citizens League for outreach activities is to have police representatives participate in the ethnic or religious celebrations of local minority groups. This gives the police and minority group members an opportunity to see each other enjoying themselves, something that rarely, if ever, happens in the course of normal interaction between the two groups.

It is particularly important that the police reach out to members of the gay and lesbian communities. Because many victims of gay bashing have not revealed their gay lifestyle to their friends and family, they are extremely reluctant to come forward and report the violence against them to the police. In addition, the police have traditionally been some of the major violators of the civil rights of gay and lesbian victims. A gay victim of a hate crime in a Massachusetts suburb who was dressed in drag when he was attacked was forced to wait in a cell before being sent to a hospital, while the officers who were out on patrol got a chance to come in to the station and "take a peek." For gay and lesbian victims to feel comfortable enough to approach officials, the police must first go to members of the gay and lesbian communities to explain that they will no longer condone offensive conduct and to discuss what protection the police can provide. Gay hate crime victims have long been among the most difficult groups for the police to understand. Possibly because the stereotype of the gay man is antithetical to the macho image that many police officials project, the latter have trouble dealing with the gay community.

One final component in an integrated approach to dealing with hate crimes is a continued commitment to affirmative action programs. The single most significant policy the police can adopt over the long term to combat hate crimes is to bring into their ranks more women and minority officers. It is generally more difficult to harbor prejudice against individuals who are different when one finds oneself working side by side with them toward a common goal. This is not to say that today's affirmative action programs are working well or that they are without costs. It is, however, clearly in the long-term interest of all police agencies to represent the communities they serve more adequately than they presently do.

A 1989 Department of Labor study found that the police were doing better in recruiting minorities than the civilian labor force generally. In fact, 13.5 percent of police forces are black compared to 10.1 percent of the labor force nationally and 12 percent of the population. (20) In addition, the diversity within police agencies has increased rapidly in recent years, with the percentage of black officers growing from 9.5 percent in 1983 to 13.5 percent in 1989, and the percentage of female officers rising from 5.7 percent in 1983 to 8.2 percent in 1989. (21)

Bringing minority officers into the force has an additional benefit, according to a recent study. An analysis of the 1981 Miami riot found that black officers felt far less alienated from the minority community than their fellow white or Latino officers. (22) If the police departments are to be believed when they say they want to help victims of bias-motivated violence, their staff must be representative of all the groups found in their local community. As we have noted, rioting has often been precipitated by a confrontation between a white officer and minority youths. The possibility of such an incident erupting into violence may be reduced by stationing *pairs* of white and minority officers in tense inner-city areas.

Frequently scared and angry, the victims of hate crimes are typically in need of help. In the past, the police have too often regarded calls for help from members of their community as mere nuisances to be disposed of with the least possible effort or to be ignored altogether. Some police responded out of bigotry; others lacked knowledge or sensitivity. In addition, the appropriate organizational supports for dealing with hate offenses were often missing from police procedures.

To an increasing extent, however, police departments around the country have enlarged and modified their procedures for dealing with hate crimes. In response to a growing demand for their services, some police agencies have provided training in the area of hate crimes and have charged particular members of their staff with the specialized role of responding to hate offenses. Moreover, as a result of affirmative action legislation, larger numbers of minorities and women have been hired by police departments in many jurisdictions.

Conflict between the police and minorities will probably never be eliminated, but it can be be reduced to a considerable extent. Although still far from ideal, the part played by police officers in responding to hate crimes has improved over the past few years. It is true that many police agencies continue to ignore attacks motivated by bias or perhaps even play an obstructionist role. But increasing numbers of police departments have chosen to move in another direction—they have risen to the challenge posed by a rising tide of hate crimes around the nation. We hope to see much more of the same in the years to come, when it will be sorely needed.

CHAPTER 13

The Law

When the police are fortunate enough to make an arrest in a hate crime case, the next decision concerns how the offender will be charged. This judgment is most often made by the prosecutor with jurisdiction over the crime, the United States Attorney for violations of federal law, and the local prosecutor for violations of state law. The decision about which criminal violation to charge can drastically affect the processing of a case by increasing the potential penalties and thus raising the stakes for the offender. The decision to charge a crime as a hate offense will also raise the interest of local advocacy groups and the media. For example, if a fight occurs between two groups of teenagers in a local community, the crime—assault—is generally not considered newsworthy. If however, the two groups are different races, one white and the other black, the decision about whether to charge the crime as a hate offense *is* news and will involve not only the prosecutor and the victims but the local office of the NAACP and other area human rights groups as well. What is more, the crime will likely be reported as the lead story on the eleven o'clock news.

Legislation intended to punish acts of hate violence can be either federal (dealing with violations of constitutional rights) or state (resulting from violations of a particular state law). Conducted by the National Institute Against Prejudice and Violence in Baltimore, an analysis of laws dealing with bias-motivated violence concluded that there are four main categories of federal remedies for crimes motivated by bigotry. (1) Passed by the U.S. Congress, the first federal statute regulating bias-motivated behavior forbids conspiracies intended to interfere with an individual's enjoyment of his or her civil rights. This statute has been used, for example, in cases where a group of white neighbors conspired together to prevent a black family from moving into their community.

Such an incident occurred in an apartment complex during the summer of 1989 in Coon Rapids, Minnesota. On the morning of August 11, several of the white residents of the complex, a group of close friends and neighbors, gathered as they often did at a picnic table outside the home of Bruce Roy Lee. Over beer and pretzels, they discussed what ought to be done about fighting that had recently erupted between black and white children in the apartment complex. At about three o'clock in the afternoon, one of the residents, Werner Jahr, mentioned that he had read an article recently about the Ku Klux Klan's methods of dealing with blacks who live where they are not wanted. Just as the Klan would have a cross burning, so, he said, should the white residents of their apartment complex. Bruce Roy Lee took his neighbor's advice to heart. At about ten o'clock that night, he put on dark clothes and crept out to a small hill about 400 feet from the apartment complex. There, he placed a wooden cross he had fashioned earlier in the day and set it ablaze.

Although Lee was upset that his cross burned only for

a few minutes, it stayed lit long enough to be seen by its intended victims, the Wilsons, a black family that lived in the apartment above Lee's. Telling her husband, "I hope they don't come up here and burn us up," Mrs. Wilson became extremely agitated and upset.

Lee later talked about the incident with a neighbor, explaining that he felt compelled to take a stand. From his point of view, the cross burning was a warning "that would get rid of some of the bad blacks that were there. They would take the message seriously and leave." (2) After a thorough police investigation, however, the Wilsons remained in their apartment. Both Lee and Jahr were arrested and eventually convicted in federal court of conspiracy to deny civil rights.

In response to a series of violent attacks on civil rights workers in the South, the second federal statute, "Forcible Interference with Civil Rights," was enacted in 1968. (3) This statute prohibits individuals from interfering with anyone who is exercising his or her constitutionally guaranteed rights, and it has been used to prosecute individuals who by force or threat of force interfere with such public rights as enrolling in a public school or eating in a public restaurant.

Known as "Deprivation of Civil Rights under Cover of Law," the third federal statute concerns actions committed by public officials—most often the police—who intend to deprive an individual of his or her constitutional rights. It is this statute that the U.S. attorney in Los Angeles County employed to prosecute the police officers who beat black motorist Rodney King. These officers were acquitted of assault charges in California state court, after the trial had been moved to the predominantly white community of Simi Valley. Following their acquittal on state charges, however, the accused officers were then indicted by a

grand jury in federal court, not for assault, but for violating the civil rights of Rodney King while the officers were
acting under the color of law.

The final federal civil rights statute, "Willful Interference with Civil Rights under the Fair Housing Act,"
prohibits any interference with an individual's right to
buy, rent, or live in his or her home. This act has been
applied in cases of firebombing and shots being fired into
a home where these actions were motivated by prejudice.

Although such federal statutes seem to cover a broad
range of behavior motivated by bigotry, they are rarely
applied. A study by the Southern Poverty Law Center
found that between 1987 and 1989, the entire U.S. Department of Justice had prosecuted only thirty-one federal
cases of racial violence, most of which involved housing
discrimination. (4)

One reason for this small number of prosecutions has
been the reduced emphasis on civil rights during the Reagan and Bush administrations. As evidenced by the recent
nominees to the Supreme Court and by the lack of funding
for civil rights enforcement activity, these two Republican
administrations have sent a message throughout the federal system that laws protecting the civil rights of all citizens
are no longer necessary. Arguing that no further government effort is therefore required in the area of civil rights,
these administrations have instead directed federal law
enforcement to focus their attention to other areas, the
chief one of which is drugs.

Another reason for the small number of federal prosecutions in the area of hate crimes is that, in practice, the
federal remedies are extremely limited. They only protect
citizens who are threatened or attacked while they are
exercising a federally protected right, such as buying a

home, renting an apartment, eating in a restaurant, or riding public transportation. Unfortunately, many of the activities that victims are engaged in when they are attacked are not included among these federally protected rights.

An additional limitation of federal statutes at present concerns the variety of groups protected by the remedy. Most federal statutes apply only to actions motivated by racial or religious prejudice, thus excluding from protection a number of victims' groups, including those attacked because they are perceived to be gay or lesbian.

As noted earlier, the United States Supreme Court recently ruled on the constitutionality of one type of hate crime legislation. On June 22, 1992, the Court struck down a St. Paul, Minnesota, hate crime ordinance on the grounds that it singled out certain topics of expression for prohibition while leaving other topics of expression legal.

Two years earlier, a black couple from St. Paul, Russell and Laura Jones, awoke to discover that someone had burned a two-foot cross in the front yard of the single-family home they had recently purchased. Within a few weeks of the cross burning, authorities in St. Paul had charged two white teenage boys, one of whom lived across the street from the Joneses, in connection with the incident. According to the police, one of the boys had asked a group of his friends "if they wanted to cause some skinhead trouble" and "burn some niggers." He explained that "lighting a cross has been passed down [as a tradition]. If it's lit in somebody's yard, they're doing something you don't like or that you want stopped—like living in your neighborhood." (5)

One of the defendants pleaded guilty and received a sentence of thirty days in jail. The second defendant pleaded not guilty and then challenged the St. Paul statute under which he had been charged as being unconstitutionally broad. This statute provides that

> Whoever places on public or private property a symbol, object, appellation, characterization, or graffiti, including but not limited to a burning cross or Nazi swastika, which one knows or has reasonable ground to know arouses anger, alarm, or resentment in others on the basis of race, color, creed, religion, or gender, commits disorderly conduct and shall be guilty of a misdemeanor.

The court agreed with the defendant and dismissed the complaint against him, saying that the St. Paul statute was overly broad and that it could infringe on free speech rights. The state then appealed the ruling to the Minnesota Supreme Court, which reversed the lower court decision. The state supreme court ruled instead that the statute in question may have been constructed in an overly broad fashion, but that a narrow interpretation was still possible. It recommended that such a narrow interpretation be applied in the St. Paul case as follows:

> Although the St. Paul Ordinance could have been more carefully drafted, it can be interpreted so as to reach only those expressions of hatred and resorts to bias-motivated personal abuse that the first amendment does not protect. (6)

The Minnesota cross-burning case didn't end at the state level. The decision was appealed to the U.S. Supreme Court, which accepted the case for its 1992 term. As we noted earlier, the Court decided that the Minnesota statute was unconstitutional because it protected only a limited set of intolerant expressions. For example, the Court pointed out that actions intended to arouse anger, alarm, or resentment based on sexual orientation were not covered by the ordinance. (7)

The Supreme Court decision suggested as well that existing vandalism and malicious destruction of property statutes provided enough protection for the Jones family, making the Minnesota ordinance unnecessary. Unfortunately, this ruling fails to recognize that crimes motivated by bias differ considerably from other offenses in terms of their impact on the victim as well as the community.

The Supreme Court decision notwithstanding, the St. Paul cross-burning episode emphasizes the need to recognize the particularly harassing nature of hate crimes. Like acts of terrorism, they send a message not only to the particular victims of an incident, but to all members of the victims' group. To burn garbage in a neighbor's front yard may involve vandalism, trespassing, or both. But burning a cross can easily be interpreted as much worse: its symbolic association in the past with organized hate gives it the status of a widely recognized sign of violence and brutality—an intention to do harm to its victims. In response to the St. Paul incident, Russell Jones told his wife, "We are being told we had better get out of here or something bad is going to happen." This is precisely the message that the teenagers who burned the cross were attempting to send.

The Court's decision applies only to the St. Paul ordinance, which has now been declared null and void. As of this writing, no other state or federal statutes have been challenged by this ruling, although the Ohio Supreme Court recently overturned its hate crimes intimidation statute. It is not at all clear, however, in which direction the Supreme Court will proceed in the future. The Minnesota statute was widely believed to be unconstitutional because it was too broad. In fact, a number of Supreme Court justices who concurred in the judgment argued that the overly broad nature of the statute, and not its selectivity, should have been the basis for striking it down. In this view, the St. Paul statute could have been invoked to prohibit a broad range of activities historically protected by our first amendment right to free speech. However, the majority on the court chose to challenge the law based on the fact that it singled out some minority groups for protection and not others. In the future, if the same standard should be applied to other types of hate crime legislation, many other state and federal statutes will be in jeopardy.

The largest number of criminal prosecutions by far occurs at the state level. According to Bureau of Justice statistics, only 4 percent of all offenders convicted and sentenced to prison in 1985 came from the federal court system. (8) Similarly, most hate crime prosecutions occur at the state rather than the federal level. More progressive and dynamic than its federal counterpart, state legislation has been changing at almost monthly intervals in response to the growing number of hate attacks that continue to come to the attention of authorities. According to a review of hate crime statutes by the Anti-Defamation League of B'nai B'rith, forty-seven states currently have some sort of hate crime legislation. Only Nebraska, Utah, and Wyoming do not. (9)

The most common type of hate crime statutes in place at the state level deals with "institutional vandalism." Such laws prohibit vandalism and defacement of a variety of locations and institutions, including houses of worship, cemeteries, schools, public monuments, and community centers.

The following cases are examples of the crimes prohibited by institutional vandalism statutes:

- In August 1988, a building which was to house the first African-American fraternity at the University of Mississippi was destroyed by arson. (10)

- In Dayton, Ohio, on January 14, 1991, two individuals threatened to shoot worshippers at a local Islamic center. Later that night, several windows at the mosque were broken. (11)
- In San Francisco, on January 24, 1991, the front windows of four Arab-American–owned food stores were smashed. The vandals hurled flashlight batteries and a fire extinguisher through the plate glass window. (12)
- In Denver, Colorado, on February 5, 1991, gunshots were fired at a grocery store owned by a Libyan-American. Previous to this incident, someone had thrown a box through the store window. The owner has since taken down an Arabic sign and a sign that read "Middle East Grocery Store." (13)
- The home of a black family in Bucks County, Pennsylvania was firebombed twice during July 1986. The second bombing destroyed everything the family owned; they barely escaped with their lives. The bombings were preceded by vandalism and harassment incidents. (14)
- In May 1985, a Catholic church, a Catholic cemetery, and three homes of Catholic families were vandalized in Corry, Pennsylvania. More anti-Catholic vandalism incidents were reported in the town in September. (15)

Institutional vandalism statutes are in place in thirty-six of the forty-seven states (77 percent) with hate crime legislation. There is a broad range of penalties attached to these statutes, with some states designating these crimes as misdemeanors and several others designating them as felonies.

The second most common type of state hate crime statutes across the country covers "bias-motivated violence and intimidation." These laws, in effect in twenty-nine states, make it illegal to intimidate, harass, trespass on the property of, or assault an individual because of that person's race, religion, national origin, or (in several states) sexual orientation.

These statutes are intended to prohibit the most violent hate crimes, some examples of which include the following:

- In March 1989, in Temperance, Michigan, after an African-American family received numerous threatening telephone calls, their thirteen-year-old son was chased down the road by white youths wielding car jacks, and their nine-year-old daughter was chased into a ditch by a car also driven by white youths. (16)
- In March 1988, an African-American woman was injured as she and her two children fled the path of a pickup truck in Taylorsville, North Carolina. Three white males in the truck yelled racial slurs and swerved the truck toward the family. On the third pass, the truck cut off the woman's path of escape, then left the scene when another vehicle approached. The woman fell twice, sustaining injuries to her elbow that required surgery to reset the bone and repair arteries. (17)
- In April 1988, an African-American man died in Halifax County, North Carolina, after being terrorized with a six-foot-long boa constrictor, beaten with a stick, and punched and stabbed by a white male and female. (18)
- In the Crown Heights section of Brooklyn, New York, following the death of a young black child and the murder of a twenty-nine-year-old Jewish schol-

ar, a series of incidents occurred, including the following series of attacks on Jewish residents:

Two men received serious slash wounds. Another man beaten by a crowd of youths suffered a broken collarbone and a concussion. (19)

A man was pulled from his car and beaten; another car was surrounded by a mob that smashed the windshield with a concrete block, injuring one passenger. (20)

An individual was severely slashed in the face with a broken bottle, requiring reconstructive surgery. (21)

- In Denver, Colorado, on February 1, 1991, an Arab student leaving a store was beaten up for his appearance. As a result he dropped out of school and returned home to the United Arab Emirates. (22)
- In Philadelphia during November 1985, a mob of nearly 100 whites gathered at the home of the Williams/Bloxom family. The black family had moved into a white neighborhood. The family subsequently left Philadelphia, and one month later, four white arsonists destroyed their vacant home. (23)
- In 1981, a black teacher in Federal Way, Washington, reported that, since 1978, he had received 150 hand-delivered racist notes, had twice had his classroom vandalized, and had been sent two fake bombs through the mail. (24)

Recent developments in intimidation law are occurring on two fronts: first, in states that are passing such statutes for the first time, and second, in states with existing intimidation statutes that are attaching sentence enhancements—additions to the existing sentences that can be applied to certain specific cases—to their existing penalties. Already employed in cases of gun crime or in crimes committed by "career criminals," sentence enhancement statutes work by allowing the sentencing judge to increase the penalty that he or she would impose under specified conditions. In Michigan's firearm enhancement statute, for example, if a felony is committed with a gun, the judge is allowed to increase the penalty up to two additional years. In Oregon, if intimidation is motivated by prejudice or bigotry, the severity of the offense is increased from a class B to a class A misdemeanor.

An additional characteristic of enhancement statutes is that the legislation frequently specifies that the additional penalty cannot be served until the original sentence has been completed. These "on and after" provisions effectively guarantee that the offender will actually serve additional time for violating the sentence enhancement provision.

New Jersey has a typical enhancement provision. In its sentencing structure, crimes are grouped together by degree: first-degree crimes, second-degree crimes, etc. But if a crime is bias motivated, the next-highest-level sentencing provision becomes available to the judge. For example, if a fourth-degree crime is committed and it is determined that the crime was motivated by bigotry, a judge may sentence the crime as if it were a third-degree offense.

Most states that employ bias-motivated violence and intimidation statutes cover hate crimes based on religion, race, or ethnicity. At present, fewer than half of the states with these statutes extend their protection to victims of violence based on their sexual orientation. More specifically, only thirteen states include violence against individuals perceived to be gay or lesbian under their bias violence and intimidation laws.

An increasing number of states are extending the protection provided by these statutes to individuals attacked on the basis of their gender. Ten states now offer such protection, and a number of others are considering expanding the scope of their statutes to include gender hate offenses. Senator Joseph Biden, who chaired the proceedings investigating Anita Hill's allegations against Clarence Thomas, has recently held U.S. Senate hearings to consider the use of hate crime statutes as a further protection for female victims of violence. Other groups specified in the legislation in various states include attacks against disabled individuals, attacks based on political affiliation, and attacks on members of labor unions.

A third category of state statutes prohibits interference with religious worship. These laws, in place in eighteen states, make it punishable to disrupt an ongoing religious service or to steal a scroll, a religious vestment, or other object normally used in a religious service.

Crimes covered by these statutes include the following:

- In April 1988, and again in October 1988, the New Bethel African Methodist Episcopal Church in Alton, Illinois, was burned down by arsonists. (25)
- In November 1991, two synagogues in Dayton, Ohio, were desecrated with spray-painted swastikas. (26)
- Also in November 1991, a Frederica store being converted into a church by a Puerto Rican group was damaged by fire believed to be arson. A few days afterward, the words "KKK, We're going to burn it down, be careful" were spray painted on the storefront. (27)
- In Spokane, Washington, in 1981, the Christ Holy Sanctified Church was bombed. In the wreckage, literature from the Aryan Nations was found. (28)

Sixteen states have statutes that make it a criminal offense to burn a cross or other religious symbols. These laws differ according to whether the cross is burned on public or private property. In some states, a cross may be burned on private property with the owner's permission. In these states, it is permissible to burn a cross on your own property or on a neighbor's property if you have that neighbor's permission. These states view burning a cross as a protected first amendment right of free speech. And our present Supreme Court agrees.

Cross-burning statutes developed as one of a series of measures designed to disrupt Ku Klux Klan activities. For the members of this organized hate group, the burning cross historically served two purposes: one, to send a message to the members of a minority family (most often black) that they were not wanted in a town or neighborhood; and second, to be used as a ceremonial initiation as part of a ritual of violence, just prior to a Klan-committed lynching. As a result, the burning cross continues to strike fear in the hearts of many minority victims. It was, in many instances, a sign that an innocent black man was about to be murdered. Many fear that it still is.

In general, cross-burning statutes are designed to counteract situations like the following:

- In March 1989, a six-foot cross was burned in the backyard of an African-American man and his three young children in Temperance, Michigan, after he had received numerous threatening telephone calls. (29)
- In August 1988, in North Carolina, a wooden cross was wrapped with rags, laid on a hatchback window of an African-American family's car, and ignited. The burning cross destroyed the car at the

family's home in Gastonia, North Carolina, where the family had recently moved into a mostly white neighborhood. (30)

- In August 1984, a cross was burned at the Carr home in Daytona Beach, Florida. The Carrs were the only black family in the neighborhood. (31)
- In December 1982, a cross was burned at St. Mary's Abbey in Wrentham, Rhode Island. On the next night, forty windows were smashed at a Cumberland school, which also was vandalized with anti-Semitic graffiti. (32)
- In Grand Prairie, Texas, in 1984, men dressed in KKK-type robes or army fatigues harassed the worshipers in a Buddhist temple by burning a cross in full view of them. (33)

With the single exception of Minnesota, no state cross-burning statutes have yet been invalidated by the recent U.S. Supreme Court decision concerning the St. Paul ordinance. According to the reasoning of the Court in that case, however, cross-burning statutes would seem to be in the most serious jeopardy of all hate crime legislation. If the logic in the Minnesota case is applied to cross-burning state statutes, only those few laws that do not list a particular set of "protected groups" (for example, blacks) will withstand constitutional scrutiny. Because the vast majority of state cross-burning statutes do identify a set of protected victims, they are potentially vulnerable to future challenges.

In many Southern states, another type of anti-Klan statute prohibits wearing hoods, masks, and disguises. On the books in fourteen states, these laws seek to limit the activities of the Klan by requiring that members of organized hate groups not hide from prosecution behind their hoods.

In theory, hate crime statutes provide a legal remedy for victims of bias-motivated violence. For such laws to be constructive, however, prosecutors must effectively charge defendants, juries must convict them, and judges must sentence offenders to an appropriate punishment. Little systematic research has been done on how hate crime cases have been processed through the courts. Unfortunately, according to the research that does exist, the present system for processing hate crime cases frequently breaks down. The arrestees may not be charged under hate crime statutes and, even when they are, may never be convicted in a court of law. Moreover, where the prosecution is able to obtain a conviction, judges often do not know what to do with the offenders. Should they serve additional time? Provide restitution to the victims? Be forced to take cultural diversity courses?

One study that addressed court processing of hate violence reviewed 452 hate crimes reported to the Boston police between 1983 and 1987 (34) and followed these cases through the criminal justice system to their final resolution. Results obtained in the research indicated that few cases ever got to court and fewer still were sentenced to a prison term.

Out of the 452 cases reported to the police, 60 resulted in arrest (some of these remained under active investigation at the time of the report), representing an arrest rate of 15.4 percent. It should be noted that the Community Disorders Unit of the Boston Police Department has been cited as a national model of hate crime investigations, so the arrest rates elsewhere are frequently lower.

Of these sixty cases that ended in arrest, thirty-eight resulted in formal charges being filed. Several of the twenty-two cases not charged were dropped by the prosecutor's office because it felt the evidence was insufficient to sustain a conviction as a hate crime. Several other cases were diverted by the prosecutor's office by means of an agreement with offenders that they would do a certain amount of community service or attend a particular program.

Of the thirty-eight cases formally charged in court, thirty resulted in convictions, a rate slightly lower than in comparable cases. Finally, of those thirty convictions, only five resulted in an individual being sentenced to a term of incarceration. The Boston experience seems to demonstrate that hate crime offenders are very unlikely to face punishment. Out of 452 incidents over a five-year period, only five individuals went to prison!

One reason for the low percentage of punished offenders is the tendency for prosecutors to look for a "perfect" case when a new statute is enacted. Specifically, they seek an incident in which clear references about the motivation for the crime are made in front of reliable witnesses and in which the offender has previously engaged in a pattern of bias-motivated violence. The reason for this is that even among those prosecutors who are strongly committed to eliminating hate violence, there is the fear that if they lose the first case brought under a new statute, they will render the law ineffective for future prosecutions. In an effort to prevent losing the first case, then, a prosecutor may reject a series of cases because they are not strong enough to guarantee a conviction. During this transitional period, a large number of victims who have good, but not the strongest, cases may be turned away. In Massachusetts, where a state civil rights act was passed in 1979, the first case was not brought under the statute until more than one year later.

The same sort of reluctance to prosecute can develop when a statute is applied in a new way to a previously unprotected group. In a number of states, for example, prosecutors are presently looking to extend the protection of hate crime legislation to women who are attacked because of their gender. Not unlike their response in the case of new statutes, many of these prosecutors seek the perfect case of gender bias, one they are sure they can win. This leaves women whose cases are not "perfect"—where there are no eyewitnesses to the crime and the offender doesn't make his motivation clear—without the protection of hate crime legislation.

One of the most common misconceptions about hate crimes is their frequency. A comparison of the incidence of reported crime from various jurisdictions reveals that hate offenses are relatively rare. In New York City during 1990, for example, there were 530 hate crimes (referred to as bias crimes in New York City) (35), while during the same period there were 2,245 homicides, 3,126 rapes, 68,891 aggravated assaults, and 100,280 robberies. (36) In fact, hate offenses made up only .003 percent of the personal crimes of violence reported to the New York City Police Department in 1990. In Boston, a similar pattern emerges. In 1990, there were 273 hate crimes (37) compared to 143 homicides, 539 rapes, 6,960 aggravated assaults, and 6,022 robberies. (38) The proportion of hate crimes compared to all crimes of violence reported to the Boston police was much higher than in New York City, but remained a relatively low 2 percent of the total.

Looking at the situation at a state rather than city level, we see a similar pattern. In Florida during 1990, there were 250 reported hate crimes (39) compared to 160,990 crimes of violence reported to the police. Thus, hate offenses comprised merely .002 percent of all violent crime.

We make this point to demonstrate an additional problem in the prosecution of hate crimes, namely, how unusual it is for a particular prosecutor or judge ever to see a bias-motivated offense. The small number of reported crimes is exacerbated by a low arrest rate as well. Because most hate crimes are committed by offenders who are strangers to their victims, (40) these are among the most difficult crimes for the police to solve. In 1990, the arrest rate for bias crimes in New York City was 23.9 percent. (41) In Boston, it was a similar 21 percent. (42) Over a twelve-month period, this meant that 261 individuals were arrested in New York City and 62 individuals were arrested in Boston. Thus, when a judge is deciding on the appropriate sentence for a hate crime offender, he or she probably has very little prior experience on which to base a decision. Facing uncommon territory and being aware that America's prisons are dangerously overcrowded, judges may decide to take the easy route—give the offender probation and let the probation officer decide what to do with him.

Sentencing decisions in hate crime cases are also frequently influenced by media attention, though this has not always been true. During the early part of the century, black rape victims in Southern states were publicly ignored as well as ignored by the police and courts in those states. By contrast, a crime which is motivated by bigotry is currently considered "big news." Local as well as national media will frequently follow all aspects of a hate crime case. Indeed, even the demonstrations and rallies convened by hate organizations are often deemed newsworthy. On August 16, 1992, for example, a KKK rally in the streets of Janesville, Wisconsin—a blue-collar town of some 50,000 situated on the Illinois border—attracted no more than 100 white power advocates and a similar number of anti-Klan counterdemonstrators. But local television stations and newspapers from both Milwaukee and Madison were interested enough to send reporters to the scene. On the national level, Geraldo Rivera was there as well. When Geraldo punched a Klansman who had harassed and assaulted him, virtually every TV station around the country aired the tape. So did CNN and "Entertainment Tonight." Even the *National Enquirer* ran a cover story. According to "Geraldo" producer Bill Lancaster, "the hate groups represented at the rally in Janesville usually don't get along. The significance of this meeting was that they set aside their differences in order to unite in a common cause: an ethnic cleansing of America."

By placing an incident like a Klan rally in the spotlight, the media may influence the decisions of judges and prosecutors who are sensitive to public opinion. A local prosecutor may think twice about dropping charges if that action will result in adverse publicity. A judge who is coming up for reelection may feel pressured to impose a severe sentence so as to avoid being attacked as "insensitive." The net effect of media exposure may be to push public officials to treat hate offenses in a more serious manner and, consequently, to apply more severe sanctions to perpetrators.

Media attention may also have educated a growing number of people about the occurrence and character of hate crimes. Currently, the most common hate crime laws consist of statutes requiring the collection of data about hate-motivated incidents. According to the Anti-Defamation League, as of 1991, seventeen states had data collection statutes in place.

While an important goal, obtaining data on hate crimes shares problems with any nationwide attempt to collect information on criminal activities—inconsistencies between states. Because each state has developed its own hate crime reporting system to conform to its particular state laws and mandates, the systems vary widely from one state to the next. An analysis of ten states with data collection procedures in place in 1990 revealed that data were collected on more than thirty-five different variables, but that only data on the same eight variables were collected by all ten states. The most common information obtained in these states concerned bias motivation (racial or religious), type of offense (against person or property), the race and sex of the victim, and, when the perpetrator is known, the race and sex of the offender. Other data collected in at least some of the ten states included location of the incident, number of offenders, weapon use, extent of damage or injury, victim–offender relationship, and evidence of involvement by an organized hate group.

During the spring of 1990, in an attempt to remedy the problem of inconsistent reporting by individual states, the United States Congress passed and President Bush signed into law the Hate Crime Statistics Act (see Appendix B). Supported by a bipartisan coalition in Congress, this law calls on the U.S. Attorney General to acquire data "about crimes that manifest evidence of prejudice based on race, religion, sexual orientation, or ethnicity, including where appropriate the crimes of murder, nonnegligent manslaughter, forcible rape, aggravated assault, simple assault, intimidation, arson, and destruction, damage, or vandalism of property." The act also requires that the attorney general publish an annual summary of the data acquired under the provisions of the Act.

The Hate Crime Statistics Act does not criminalize any bias-motivated behavior or increase penalties for such offenses. It requires only that the attorney general obtain data on crimes motivated by bigotry. From the point of view of a number of the advocacy groups that sponsored the legislation, the goal of the act was to set the stage for beefing up both state and federal legislation by collecting more and better information on bias-motivated activity across the United States.

Before passage of the Hate Crime Statistics Act, there was no national public data source on the extent or characteristics of hate crimes. The two major national crime data collection sources, The FBI's *Uniform Crime Report* and the Bureau of Justice Statistics' *National Crime Survey* did not include hate crimes among those criminal incidents on which they collected information.

There are some private organizations that have collected hate crime information in past years and continue to do so today. Nationally, the Anti-Defamation League has conducted an *Audit of Anti-Semitic Incidents* since 1979, in which it records information on all anti-Semitic attacks and vandalisms reported to regional ADL offices. In addition, the National Gay and Lesbian Task Force Policy Institute has issued an annual national report since 1985, *Anti-Gay/Lesbian Violence, Victimization & Defamation*, detailing instances of antigay violence in major U.S. cities. A third organization, the Southern Poverty Law Center in Montgomery, Alabama, has collected information on the activities of organized hate groups and reported this information in its publication *Klanwatch*.

Before the passage of the Hate Crime Statistics Act, these alternative sources of information on bias-motivated violence constituted the only national reservoir of information on hate crimes. Their effectiveness was limited by the fact that each group collected information only on a particular area of bias-motivated violence; for example, the ADL collects information only on anti-Semitic incidents, whereas the National Gay and Lesbian Task Force collects information exclusively on antigay/lesbian violence. A second limitation involves the consistency and reliability of the data across groups. Each organization has its own particular data collection regulations and procedures that do not necessarily conform with those of the other organizations. As a result, there are significant areas of inconsistency when comparing information from different sources. For example, the National Gay and Lesbian Task Force accepts reports of antigay hate crimes from anonymous sources, while the ADL does not.

The Hate Crime Statistics Act seeks to reduce issues related to coverage, consistency, and reliability, by having all hate crime information collected in a single format by a single agency: the Uniform Crime Reporting Section of the Federal Bureau of Investigation. The U.S. attorney general designated the FBI as the agency responsible for collecting hate crime data and, following the model in effect in the *Uniform Crime Report*, the local police agencies as the data providers.

The FBI was a controversial choice as the federal agency designated to implement a civil rights act. After all, it was pointed out, the FBI itself has been associated in the past with major violations of civil rights. Even as recently as 1991, for example, the agency came under fire for discriminatory treatment of its Hispanic agents, a charge which culminated in a class-action lawsuit. Despite its checkered history with respect to civil rights, however, two years after the passage of the act, members of the FBI directed to implement it have received high praise for their efforts from advocacy groups such as the NAACP, the ADL, and the National Gay and Lesbian Task Force.

In August 1992, Senator Paul Simon of the Senate Judiciary Committee held hearings on the implementation of the Hate Crime Statistics Act. As the original sponsor of the legislation in the Senate, Simon wished to learn how the national data collection effort was going. He was told by a number of witnesses that the implementation was going well but that the undertaking was more complicated than originally anticipated and thus would take longer to complete. Because the Hate Crime Statistics Act did not require local police agencies to submit their hate crime data, many agencies were slow to comply. The major reasons for this reluctance were budgetary constraints and a lack of awareness about hate crimes in general. It should be noted that no funds were provided by the Hate Crime Statistics Act either to the FBI or to local police agencies.

While the FBI couldn't do anything about the financial burden on the local police, they could at least attempt to increase awareness about hate crimes on the part of many in law enforcement. In training sessions for representatives of all fifty states and from the 200 largest U.S. cities, FBI staffers taught how to identify, investigate, and report hate crimes. Trainers also sought to sensitize police officials to the importance of taking seriously all hate crimes in their community. Senator Simon's committee was surprised to learn that increased awareness on the part of local police as a result of FBI training, rather than the actual collection of data about hate crimes, has thus far been the most significant contribution of the Hate Crime Statistics Act.

Throughout the country, laws are being modified and local prosecutors and judges are becoming more responsive to the victims of hate violence. Yet, in terms of embracing all victims of bias-motivated crime and providing appropriate sentencing, change continues to be very slow and uneven. Some groups in need of protection, for example, women and gays, are left out of many state statutes, and offenders are too often permitted to go free with a slap on the wrist. Most frightening is the potential retreat by the Supreme Court from its role as a protector of civil rights. Government officials, advocacy groups, and citizens themselves must keep the pressure on legislatures and courts to prevent a withdrawal from the goal of protecting all victims of hate crimes everywhere.

CHAPTER 14

Rehab

Local officials and community residents around the country are just beginning to view hate crimes as serious offenses that can tear a community apart, pitting neighbor against neighbor in acts of vandalism and violence. Moreover, as we have seen, hate crimes often have a profound impact on their victims, making them feel fearful and vulnerable. Public officials are consequently being encouraged by local residents and advocacy groups to take a strong public stand against all crimes motivated by bigotry as part of a response to prevent future hate crimes. State legislatures, as noted earlier, have also responded by passing laws that increase the penalties for crimes that are bias motivated.

In more and more communities, once a hate crime is committed, citizens are coming forth to pressure local police to make an arrest, local prosecutors to get a conviction, and local judges to sentence the offenders harshly. This pressure on local law enforcement to deal with hate crimes is generated from communities that realize the severity of these offenses and their impact on victims. But there is often a more practical reason as well. Citizens are becoming increasingly aware that there may be significant negative economic repercussions on communities that are labeled as racist. In one small bedroom community west of Boston, for example, a police officer arrested a black man for suspicious activity. It was later learned that the man was only waiting for his daughter, who was late leaving a sleep-over party at the home of her girlfriend. In a successful lawsuit, the court awarded the man $600,000 in damages that the town was forced to pay.

For reasons both moral and practical, local law enforcement personnel in a number of communities are intent on communicating a strong message that hate crimes will not be tolerated. Yet, they do not always carry through on their intention. Although hate crimes may have severe consequences, they are not typically committed by the most seasoned offenders. The first characteristic which distinguishes hate crime offenders from other serious offenders is their age. Most research to date indicates that the vast majority of perpetrators are very young males, often juveniles. Several studies have uncovered this characteristic of offenders, including a recent Anti-Defamation League report which found that 70–80 percent of the hate crime offenders in anti-Semitic crimes are under twenty-one, a large proportion of whom are much younger. (1)

A second characteristic of the hate crime offenders, which mediates against harsh sentencing, is the lack of a long history of prior criminal activity. Most prosecutors and judges believe that youthful first- or second-time offenders charged with almost any crime should be given another chance. The fear of labeling and stigmatizing a basically good youth "who just made a mistake" leads many in the criminal justice system to look for alternatives to incarceration for first- or second-time offenders.

The present level of overcrowding in our jails and prisons is another factor in judges' decisions as to whether to incarcerate these youths. At present, the U.S. prison population is at an all time high. By 1985, the prison population exceeded 500,000, up from 200,000 in 1970, and was growing at a rate of 750 new prisoners a day. (2) This trend places additional pressure on judges to use incarceration as a sanction for only those offenders considered the most dangerous.

A fourth factor leading judges to consider alternative sentences is the group nature of hate crimes. Research indicates that most crimes motivated by bias are committed by groups of offenders, not single individuals acting alone. Although judges may want to impose a harsh sentence in order to send a message to their community, hate incidents frequently involve a "ringleader" and two or more youths who are present at the scene but who do not play an active part in committing the crime. A judge may believe that incarceration is the appropriate sentence for the ringleader but not for the others involved, especially for those who did not participate actively in the attack.

A case that illustrates this factor is that of Rodney King. Much of America saw the videotape showing four Los Angeles police officers beating King senseless, while twenty-one officers stood by and observed. The Los Angeles Police Department took action against the four officers who engaged in the beating by firing them. But the department decided to take no action at all against those officers who watched, even though they did nothing to stop King's victimization.

Prosecutors who are responsible for charging and judges who are responsible for sentencing are often placed in a difficult position. While many may want to send a strong message that bias-motivated violence will not be tolerated, they are faced with other considerations—overcrowded courts and prisons as well as the youth and inexperience of many hate crime offenders—which undercut the call for the harshest sentences.

Judges have expressed another concern about imprisonment: the increasing presence of gangs behind bars. In prisons around the country, gangs have formed primarily along racial and ethnic lines. They often espouse racist beliefs and maintain connections with organized hate groups outside of the prison setting. Such gangs have become so prevalent that, according to the U.S. Circuit Court of Appeals in Illinois, 90 percent of the inmates in one state prison are members of one gang or another. While little information has been collected about the extent of gang involvement nationally, correctional administrators often cite the activities of gangs as a major cause of inmate violence.

Among the most popular gangs in American prisons is the Mexican Mafia, formed in the late 1960s at San Quentin by a group of Latino inmates from Los Angeles. Also a Latino gang, La Nuestra Familia is a chief rival of the Mexican Mafia, but its members are mainly from Texas or from areas of California outside of Los Angeles. For black inmates, there is the Black Guerrilla Family and for white inmates, the Aryan Brotherhood.

Prison gangs like the Mexican Mafia, La Nuestra Familia, the Black Guerrilla Family, and the Aryan Brotherhood offer their members protection from antagonistic inmates and a certain amount of prestige within the prison. And for hate crime offenders in particular, protection may be essential. After all, many of them have been incarcerated for assaulting individuals from the racial groups to which their fellow inmates belong.

Because gangs are typically organized along racial or

ethnic lines and often espouse racist beliefs, their members tend to develop or intensify biased feelings toward other races or ethnic groups. Once judges realize this, they may resist sending young hate crime offenders to prison—an environment which all too often intensifies prejudiced feelings and beliefs. A young white man serving time for committing a hate crime against blacks will be recruited by gangs like the Aryan Brotherhood, who will regard him as a prime candidate for membership. On his part, the hate crime offender will be drawn to white supremacist gangs for protection. As much as he may be admired and respected by the Aryan Brotherhood, he will be despised and threatened by the black and Latino gangs. It should come as no surprise, therefore, that hate crime offenders may be released from prison having more profoundly bigoted attitudes than they held when they committed the original offense.

The reticence of some judges to imprison hate crime offenders is therefore not without reason. Rather than rehabilitate, the prison experience may instead harden the views of hatemongers and bigots. Moreover, after being released, they may become more zealous than ever about expressing their hatred in violence. According to Daniel Weiss, a counseling psychologist at the Massachusetts State Prison at Cedar Junction, an inmate who serves time for a racially inspired crime wears a symbolic badge that shows in dramatic fashion that "the man" is after him. He means that *he* was "a victim of the system, that he was down for the cause. After all, he was willing to serve time for his beliefs. As a result, the hate crime offender is likely to become a legendary figure so long as he remains behind bars." (3)

Judges have attempted to resolve this problem by employing a form of "alternative sentences." Initially, some judges assigned book reports as a part of the sentence to certain youths convicted of bias-motivated crime. In the case of an anti-Semitic attack, for example, a teenage offender might be required to read a book that describes the atrocities of the Holocaust. The hope, of course, is that exposure to such information will increase the youthful perpetrator's sensitivity to the horror and revulsion that the swastika represents to the Jewish community.

Although appealing in theory, the educational approach has limited effectiveness. First, there is a paucity of effective reading materials designed to counteract hatred, especially materials geared to the reading level of youthful offenders. Consequently, sentenced youths frequently return to the courtroom with a book they cannot read or understand and ask the judge to suggest something more appropriate. Most judges are simply not aware of age-suitable reading alternatives.

A second problem with this approach is the court's inability to enforce it; in some cases, the parents or a friend of an offender actually writes the book report, which becomes apparent, in certain cases, when the judge asks a youth to describe what he has learned from the book and the youth can't recall anything contained in it. Another problem faced by judges employing this approach is what to do when they are presented with a bad or inaccurate book report. Several judges received reports that they felt were unsatisfactory due to the grammar, the conclusions, or both. In at least one case, a judge received a summary of a book that suggested that the Holocaust was a hoax, a finding with which the offender wholeheartedly agreed. In such instances, judges are faced with a very real problem: do they incarcerate a youth basically for writing a bad book report? Many judges therefore find this approach unsatisfactory.

In dealing with first-time youthful hate crime offenders, some judges have chosen a community service sentence. Through volunteer service at a local advocacy organization, it is hoped that offenders will learn about the community they harmed while repaying some of the damage they caused. A common example of this kind of sentence consists of six months' probation including, as a condition of probation, 100 hours of community service to a local advocacy group such as the office of the Anti-Defamation League of B'nai B'rith (ADL).

As with book reports, the community service option appears to be a creative approach until one examines it closely. In one case, a Massachusetts judge was faced with two youths convicted of defacing a Jewish temple with Nazi swastikas. The offenders had no prior criminal history but were loosely tied to a local skinhead group. The judge believed that if these youths could understand the harm they had caused, they might be deterred from future racist and anti-Semitic activity. He therefore required the offenders to work with a group whose main function is to fight anti-Semitism, the ADL. Specifically, they were sentenced to perform 100 hours of community service at its New England office.

The judge didn't know much about the ADL except that it was a strong force against bigotry in the community. He reasoned that this would be the kind of group that might be able to teach offenders the harm of anti-Semitic crime. Unfortunately, the local ADL office was not, at that time, providing service to the court on an ongoing basis and had not been notified that it was to play a role in the sentence that had been imposed.

Without warning, therefore, two anti-Semitic skinheads simply showed up at the local ADL office one day reporting that a judge had sent them to do community service and asking for an assignment. Their presence caused a great deal of consternation among the ADL staff, who had no programming in place to deal with convicted offenders and were not at all accustomed to having skinheads in their offices.

In this case, the situation was resolved successfully when the local director of the ADL's "World of Difference Program," a successful bias sensitivity program for school-age children, decided to develop a program for these and other youths. Still, when local advocacy organizations are asked without warning or financial support to develop new programs for hate crime offenders, they typically cannot be counted on to provide an effective form of community service.

A major limitation of the community service sentencing approach is its lack of formal treatment programs. Having a location for the assignment of offenders is one thing; putting together an effective program to reduce hatred is quite another. Having an offender paint the exterior of a synagogue that he has defaced might return something to the community he harmed, but it is questionable that this activity alone would teach the offender why what he did was wrong. To do that, he would need a program that deals effectively with his misconceptions.

Several such programs have been developed and implemented across the country. The first large-scale program is the STOP program of the Montgomery County, Maryland, Office of Human Relations. Begun in July 1982, STOP was established as a juvenile diversion program, or an alternative to formal court processing for youths arrested for hate crimes.

STOP involves six sessions, including one entrance interview, one exit interview, and four two and one-half hour sessions. In addition, participants are required to do

forty hours of community service. All sessions are conducted by staff from the Human Rights Commission in
conjunction with members of local teen organizations who
act as positive teen role models. The curriculum includes
discussions about the basis of prejudice and racism, the
role of organized hate groups, the impact of bias-
motivated violence on victims, and the legal ramifications
of perpetrating hate crimes. (4)

In Massachusetts, a partnership involving the Anti-
Defamation League, the attorney general's office, Harvard
University, and Northeastern University has come together to design and implement a program for hate crime offenders. Like STOP, the Massachusetts Youth Diversion
and Community Service program was designed to provide
a sentencing alternative for youths convicted of hate
crimes. It is a sixteen-week program that begins with a
needs assessment to identify the major psychological, educational, and vocational needs of each offender. Like
STOP, the Youth Diversion Program educates the offenders through sessions that deal with the impact of hate
crimes on the victims, the cultural differences between
groups, and the legal implications of actions motivated by
bigotry. This program also includes a component of required service to a local minority community program.
Unlike other similar efforts tried elsewhere, the community service component of the Youth Diversion program is
planned ahead of time and included as part of the overall
educational experience of the offender.

Under the direction of the state's attorney general's
office, an alternative sentencing program for youthful hate
crime offenders is now being developed for implementation in all counties in the state of New Jersey. Similiar to
the Massachusetts program, the plan for New Jersey com-
bines a psychological assessment with an agenda consist-

ing of community service and sessions to increase awareness of cultural differences. When implemented, the New Jersey program will be the most extensive of the efforts at hate crime offender rehabilitation to date.

After reviewing the curricula from these and other hate crime offender rehabilitation programs, we believe that a model hate crime offenders' treatment program must include the following elements: assessment, discussion of impact on victims, cultural awareness, restitution/community service, delineation of legal consequences, participation in a major cultural event, and aftercare.

Initially, all offenders should go through an assessment designed by trained professionals (psychologists, sociologists, or clinical social workers) of their attitudes toward minorities in general and their previous experiences with violence. This assessment should identify the extent of offenders' commitment to racist, anti-ethnic, or homophobic philosophy and should allow the program's staff to distinguish thrill hate offenders from their more committed reactive and mission counterparts.

A number of officials who deal extensively with these offenders believe that many come from homes where violence is commonplace. As Lt. Bill Johnston, Commander of the Boston Police Department's Community Disorders Unit, suggests: "These kids come from homes filled with violence. The first time they see a person attacked because they are different is when they see their father hit their mother." To the extent that violent behavior is generalized from home experience to the streets, any effective treatment program must also uncover and deal with a history of family violence, when it exists.

A model hate crime offender program should also explain to offenders how their actions have harmed the victim. To many hate crime offenders, the victims of hate crimes are "different" in the most negative sense; that is, they are regarded as not quite human. It is therefore important in treatment programs to seek to reverse dehumanization of the victims by having the offenders meet their victims and see, in unequivocal terms, just how much pain and suffering they have caused *another human being*. For this purpose, it may be helpful to have victims tell their own story.

Most hate crime offenders uncritically accept a number of false stereotypes concerning the behavior of minorities. Offender programs should attempt to identify and confront these misconceptions. In addition, such programs should seek to promote cultural diversity by identifying and emphasizing the positive contributions made by the members of different minority groups.

Another dimension of a model program involves the offender giving something back to the minority community. This restitution/community service component should be tied to the harm caused to the victim and not simply be dirty work that no one else wanted to do. Ideally, offenders should feel good about the service they provide and should be thanked for their efforts. In this way, offenders will not wind up resenting their experience and may instead use it to feel closer to the minority group whose members they have harmed. One strategy that can be useful in making the victim seem more of a real person is to have offenders participate in a major cultural event in the victim's community.

Additionally, a model program should have a session describing the legal consequences of bias-motivated crime. Many youths who engage in this type of behavior believe they are immune from serious penalties because public authorities share their biased feelings. This perception should be challenged by indicating what legal conse-

quences could result from continued bias-motivated behavior. The presentation of actual case studies where offenders were sentenced to time in prison for bias-
motivated property crimes, for example, has proven to be
a useful technique for beginning a discussion.

The final component of a model hate crime offender
treatment program is an aftercare plan. Developed jointly
by the offender and the program staff, aftercare would
provide continuing support to each offender on an "as
needed" basis. The plan would allow the offender to come
back to the program for support and to continue to deal
with issues not resolved by the basic program.

In addition, any offender treatment program should
have an ongoing evaluation component. Too many programs begin with a series of concepts that have worked in
other contexts but have not been tested in the area of hate
crimes. An evaluation component can determine to what
extent this assumption is warranted and whether portions
of the program should be adjusted.

Conducted by either outsiders or project staff, the
goal of any evaluation procedure is to improve the program. Toward this goal, at a minimum of every six
months, the full staff should spend a day discussing the
successes and failures of their program. From their meeting together, they should then adopt changes in the program to deal more effectively with the failures they might
have experienced. At the same time, they should set goals
for the next six months. Through a process of periodic
evaluation and change, the program is less likely to become "stale" as its clients change.

It should be recognized that model programs are best
viewed as dynamic—in constant flux, as new and more
accurate information is reviewed and incorporated into
programmatic thinking. A fundamental premise of a mod-

el program should be that next year's program will be different—better—in some respects than this year's effort. Having an ongoing evaluation process and an openness to change is the only means for assuring that progress will be made.

We emphasize that sending hate crime offenders through the criminal justice system has at least two possible consequences, potentially at odds with one another. On the one hand, a strong prison sentence sends a signal to would-be hatemongers everywhere that should they illegally express their bigotry, they can expect to receive more than a mere slap on the wrist. In other words, a severe sentence may deter future hate offenses. On the other hand, a lengthy prison sentence—especially in response to a thrill hate offense—may actually harden and reinforce the bigoted attitudes of the youngster who serves time. If prison is a "school for crime," it is surely a crash course in expressing hatred through violence.

Experts on the issue of hate violence have suggested that some hatemongers may watch what happens in an initial hate crime before deciding to take part in the violence. But when judges are facing certain hate crime offenders, they find themselves in a difficult situation. They may want to communicate a strong message, but the offenders—especially in the case of thrill hate crimes—may be first-time offenders who have no strong commitment to violence motivated by bigotry. This type of offender is not typically incarcerated in our present system.

Judges too often have only two real options—either to incarcerate the offender once he has been convicted or to put the offender on probation. Probation is often perceived by the general public as little more than a minor nuisance, and a judge may fear the reaction of members of the victim's community to this perceived light treatment.

What appears to be lacking in certain hate crime cases, if not in the correctional system generally, is some sanction between prison and probation. To be effective, such a program would allow the offender to remain living at home while he participates in an ongoing educational program and, at the same time, works to compensate (in money, service, or both) either the victim or the victim's community.

In our view, tough sentencing is absolutely essential for protecting members of society against hate crime perpetrators who have demonstrated repeatedly that they are beyond rehabilitation and a danger to society. At the other end of the spectrum, however, creative alternative sentencing is crucial for responding to young first-time offenders who may have been influenced not only by their youth, but also by their friends' bigotry, and are capable of making profound reforms. Intermediate sentences—less than prison but more than probation—are necessary for assuring that hate crimes are treated more seriously than ordinary offenses. However, many hatemongers can be rehabilitated—if they are fortunate enough to benefit from a serious, but humane and imaginative, approach to criminality.

CHAPTER 15

Grass Roots

Russell and Laura Jones awoke with a start. It was 2:30 in the morning, and the sound of loud voices outside was unmistakable. By the time the couple checked their children and got to the living-room window, the voices had gone, but not the two-foot cross burning on their front lawn. (1)

In March 1990, less than three months earlier, the Joneses had moved from the inner city into their "dream house," a 100-year-old four-bedroom home in a predominantly white middle-income section of East St. Paul. Their five children would benefit most from the move, they had reasoned—the youngsters would see no more crack houses and violence on the block, only safety, security, and tranquility.

Shortly after moving in, however, disturbing things began to happen. First, the tires on their family car were slashed. A few days later, the windshield of their car was found shattered. Most troubling, a local teenager called their nine-year-old son a "nigger," and, for the first time,

Laura Jones was forced to explain to her child the meaning of racism and bigotry. (2)

One of the most difficult issues for the victims of hate crimes is wondering just how widespread is the bigotry. How many of the other people on the block want them to leave the neighborhood? How many other students on campus resent their presence? How many other teenagers in town will impress their friends with their bigoted behavior? Victims often want to believe that the hate crime against them was the deviant behavior of a few "screwed-up kids," a small number of bigots, but they also fear that these actions reflect the sentiments of the masses.

After the cross-burning incident in St. Paul, the local community came together to send a message of support to the Jones family. Some neighbors brought over pies and cakes. A number of them called to express their outrage and to confirm to Russell and Laura Jones that they did not share, but instead abhorred, the racist attitudes of the defendants. According to Laura Jones, this outpouring of support and encouragement from members of the white community "made the family feel more comfortable." It also sent a broader message to potential hate crime offenders everywhere—a message of racial tolerance and acceptance that directly contradicted the intolerant message that the offenders had sought to communicate.

Unfortunately, communicating a message after a hate crime is committed doesn't always have an ameliorative effect. On the contrary, the community reaction is often defensive and retaliatory. In response to major racial incidents in the New York City area, angry protesters, mostly black, paraded through the streets of the predominantly white neighborhoods—Bensonhurst, Canarsie, Crown Heights—in which the hate crime had occurred. Led by black activists like the Reverend Al Sharpton, large numbers from outside the community marched to dramatize the wrongdoing perpetrated against members of their group.

The accusatory tone of such parades, marches, and demonstrations can have the effect of dividing groups even more against one another. When people of color march through a white neighborhood, they are usually perceived, correctly or not, as indicting the entire community of racism. Moreover, the presence of marchers is taken as additional evidence that "outsiders" are intruding on the neighborhood. In many cases, the demonstration brings out even more intense and dangerous expressions of racism on the part of community members who "stand accused" of crimes they did not personally commit, or perhaps even condone. After Yusuf Hawkins's murder in Bensonhurst, for example, marchers were met by hordes of angry spectators shouting racial slurs and throwing watermelons. After a racial incident in Canarsie, spectators from the community yelled racial epithets at marchers, while a group of white teenagers held up a watermelon from the back of a pickup truck which had been painted with racist sayings.

If it is ineffective for blacks to demonstrate in protest after a black is victimized in a brutal crime of hate, what should be done? Clearly, hate crimes cannot go unchallenged. The community reaction to the cross burning in St. Paul gives us a significant clue.

As divisive as his reaction may be, Sharpton fills a vacuum in community response that ought to be filled by the grass-roots opposition of whites. During the 1960s, whites and blacks joined together in marches, demonstrations, and protests, creating the civil rights movement. In the same way, after the murder of Yusuf Hawkins, the indignant residents of Bensonhurst themselves should

have marched through *their* streets, in unified opposition
to racial bigotry, preferably alongside blacks. After Michael
Griffith was slain, the outraged people of Howard Beach
should have protested the killing en masse. Ideally, more
whites should have sent cards to the family of the victim;
more of them should have baked pies and cakes; larger
numbers should have taken the initiative to assure the
victim's family that they oppose violence, that they celebrate diversity, and that they will not tolerate further acts
of racism in their neighborhood.

We must understand that in every community, there
will be local residents holding a wide range of views on
this issue. Some will regret that the hate incident ever
happened and may be willing to go out of their way to
support the victim, even at some risk to their image
among neighbors or their personal safety. Others will instead sympathize with the offenders and wholeheartedly
support their intentions. But the largest group of residents
will be indifferent; they simply want to go on with their
lives as if nothing has happened. The relative size of each
group will differ depending on the particular community;
and, in those neighborhoods where the group supporting
the offender is especially large, change will be most difficult to achieve.

We believe that the goal of any effective community
response must be to identify those local residents who
support the victim and to work with them toward the goal
of promoting more widespread acceptance of this view
among their fellow community members. Those who are
perceived to be outsiders can hardly expect to be effective
as agents of change. But insiders—friends and neighbors—
can really make a difference at the informal level, especially if they are observed putting themselves on the line
on behalf of the hate crime victim.

One important factor in the community response to a hate crime is the role played by local advocacy groups, those organizations that represent the interests of a specific minority group and attempt to influence public policy regarding issues of interest to its members. Advocacy groups include such national organizations as the Anti-Defamation League of B'nai B'rith (ADL), the National Association for the Advancement of Colored People (NAACP), the National Gay and Lesbian Task Force, and the Asian Society. At the local level, advocacy groups may include local chapters of these and other national organizations as well as other groups including local human relations and equal opportunity councils.

One limitation on groups at the local level is that while some do exist in most communities, not all the minority groups in a particular community are represented by an advocacy group. For example, while a neighborhood may have a very active office of the NAACP, there may be no local group dealing specifically with the problems faced by gay and lesbian residents.

Such local advocacy groups can, however, play a significant role in responding to hate crimes. Initially, the group can provide support for the hate crime victim. As we have emphasized, victims of bias-motivated violence generally feel extremely vulnerable. The local advocacy group can support victims by letting them know that they are not alone and by assisting the victims in their contacts with the police, the courts, and the media. In some communities, local advocacy groups will act as a liaison between the victim and the police and court officials. These advocates will explain each step of the process to the victim and, if necessary, accompany the victim to the police station and to court.

Local advocacy groups can also serve to follow up on

incidents by visiting the police, who may be ambivalent about how to respond to bias-motivated violence. In such circumstances, a call or visit from a local advocacy group might convince the police that a crime is heinous and that it should be investigated seriously. One follow-up strategy employed by the New England regional office of the ADL to sensitize local police to the hate crime problem is to send to them a hate crime report for each anti-Semitic incident reported to the ADL office from their jurisdiction. In addition to working closely with police, advocacy groups can follow up with the local prosecutor's office and the local courts to assure that, once an arrest has been made, the case proceeds swiftly to trial.

Another role advocacy groups can play is to support the police by participating in hate crime training programs. In this way, such groups can directly educate those police officers who will be dealing with issues of bigotry. An important consequence of this collaboration in training, as we have noted, is that members of the local police department and members of local advocacy groups will get to know each other and develop informal communication links that can be mutually beneficial should a major incident occur.

Advocacy groups can also be helpful in collecting and reporting hate crime statistics. Many local organizations offer assistance to victims in completing police department paperwork—a service that can lead to improved data on bias-motivated violence provided to the police. In two states, Maryland and Massachusetts, advocacy groups have their own separate hate crime reporting system. There, local advocacy groups collect information on bias incidents, those occurrences of bias-motivated actions that do not rise to the level of a crime. For example, a racial slur shouted from a moving car could be reported as a hate incident, though it may not qualify as a criminal act.

Another important function of advocacy groups involves support for those government agencies that are doing effective work in their response to hate crimes. It is often the case, particularly in the area of data collection, that the very agencies that are doing a good job will be most severely criticized for their efforts. For example, Boston has been called the hate crime capital of America, because it has a large number of hate crimes reported each year. This label is misleading. The large number of hate offenses reported in the city of Boston is in part the result of advocacy groups and the police working together to encourage victims to come forward and report crimes motivated by bias. One pivotal function that local advocacy groups in Boston play is to stand with the police when it releases the hate crime statistics each year and explain to the local media how an increase in numbers of hate crimes may be a positive result of programs to encourage victim reporting.

Local advocacy organizations can also serve a longer-term function in response to bias-motivated crime. In 1990, for example, the Anti-Defamation League of B'nai B'rith initiated two programs of education, A Campus of Difference and A Workplace of Difference, designed to reduce prejudice. Both programs—one for colleges and the other for corporations and government agencies— were modeled after ADL's earlier educational and media initiative, A World of Difference, under whose auspices teachers in cities across the country were trained to increase their students' awareness of cultural diversity. Workshops in both of these programs are designed to encourage participants to discuss openly issues related to prejudice, discrimination, and diversity. (3)

But even the local advocacy groups are not enough. The response to hate crimes can only be effective if it also receives the inspiration and blessing of community leaders who represent a broad range of constituents, not just those in the victims' group. In their public proclamations as well as their behavior, therefore, presidents, governors, mayors, and other government officials must make it known, in the most unequivocal terms possible, that hate crimes are evil, immoral, and unacceptable—that they simply will not be tolerated in any form. It is not enough for members of the affected group to respond to hate crimes. When an attack is directed against blacks, white leaders must respond. When the crime is against gays, mainstream leaders must react, and so on.

A swift and solid response to an offense will most effectively minimize the potential for future hate attacks. In Hull, Massachusetts, a small coastal community located some eight miles from downtown Boston, city officials recently voted to replace the floor tiles in its town hall that had offended Jewish residents. The floor in question consisted of inlaid tiles containing the image of swastikas, but it had been laid many years before the Nazis came to power, and the swastikas actually were an American Indian symbol of peace and good fortune. The leadership of the town of Hull could easily have become defensive and recalcitrant in reacting to offended Jews in the area. Instead, the floor was covered. In so doing, the community defused a potential crisis. They sent a message of acceptance and respect to its few Jewish residents as well as to any residents who might have considered committing anti-Semitic acts. (4)

Another case of appropriate response on the part of community leadership occurred recently in Wellesley, Massachusetts. In 1990, this affluent community was faced with the charge of racism and bigotry after an incident in which a black Celtics basketball rookie, new to the town as well as the team, was humiliated by local police in what turned out to be a case of mistaken identity. And this was not the first time that Wellesley residents had been accused of bigotry. As mentioned earlier, two young men were convicted in October 1989 of perpetrating hate crimes against blacks and Jews in the town by spray painting racist and anti-Semitic graffiti on driveways and sidewalks. The residents of Wellesley could have easily turned their backs on both occurrences, taking a position of resentment and denial. Instead, 800 Wellesley residents, most of whom were white, gathered for a candlelight march and rally against racism and anti-Semitism. More important, political leaders, including Senator John Kerry and Representative Barney Frank, provided muscle by showing up to voice their support.

Reactions in the aftermath of campus hate incidents can also be tempered by enlightened community leadership. In the fall of 1989, the members of a fraternity at the University of Vermont, upon discovering that one of their pledges was a homosexual, informed the student that he was no longer welcome to become a brother. After finding that the fraternity had discriminated based on sexual orientation, a student judicial board on campus ordered the fraternity to apologize to the gay student, to refund his pledge fee, and to hold in-house educational programs about homosexuality. A rally and march on campus against hate attracted some 400 students and local residents, including the mayor of Burlington, Vermont. He later asked the Board of Aldermen in his town to amend its housing discrimination codes so that college fraternities would be legally prohibited from discriminating on the basis of sexual orientation. (5)

In a major racial incident on campus, hundreds of students at Brandeis University conducted a weeklong boycott of their college bookstore, after thirty black students had accused its managers of having singled them out for scrutiny, based entirely on their race, and treating them all like potential shoplifters. More than 700 students, most of whom were white, signed a pledge, saying that they would not buy from the bookstore until its managers had been fired. In response, the bookstore agreed to replace the managers, institute a new system for handling complaints, make a conscientious effort to hire more black students, and implement a training program for the purpose of increasing racial sensitivity among its employees. (6)

What happens when leadership is slow in responding to incidents of hate? Orléans, France, is a town of some 88,000 people located 110 kilometers south of Paris. In May 1969, students at an Orléans high school began spreading stories that two women in town had disappeared while shopping at a local boutique owned and operated by a Jewish couple. According to the story being circulated among students at the school, the victims had been trying on clothes in a dressing room when they were given injections of some unknown drug that rendered them unconscious. They were then taken downstairs to the basement and imprisoned while waiting to be sold into slavery.

After a few weeks, versions of the same story began to circulate outside of the high school in families, offices, and factories as well. The newer versions were more elaborate than the old. The number of abductions increased from two to sixty. The number of shops responsible for the crimes increased from one to an entire network of half-a-dozen stores in town, most of which were owned by Jews.

At this point, parents and teachers warned teenage girls in Orléans to avoid the boutiques named in the rumor until the matter had been cleared up. There were also anti-Semitic allegations specifically targeting Jewish shopkeepers as the culprits. No kidnappings had actually been reported to the police and none were reported in the local newspaper. Yet the victim count continued to increase, and the story became even more complex and dangerous. Ultimately, the residents of Orléans were convinced that the police and press had been bribed into inaction and that a conspiracy of silence was in effect. An angry crowd formed in front of the shops named in the story to prevent customers from entering them.

Why had these totally unfounded stories about Jewish shopkeepers become a focal point of panic among the people of Orléans? They had been allowed to grow and flourish because of the failure of local leadership in politics, the police, and the press to take a definite stand in condemning the falsehoods. Only when the entire affair had mushroomed into a near disaster did town authorities finally step in. And, when they did—by reassuring the townspeople, discrediting the rumormongers, and writing articles about the false reports in local newspapers—all traces of the false accusations quickly evaporated. (7)

In communities across the country, government leaders must have the courage to take strong positions against acts of bigotry. In the climate of hate so prevalent in the 1990s, however, they cannot count on receiving the support and encouragement of their constituents. Today we hear a great deal about the insidious prevalence of political correctness. But where can you actually find a preference for tolerance and liberalism aside from college faculty meetings or among attorneys of the ACLU. Certainly, tolerance for diversity does not exist to any great extent among those college students who feel squeezed by the growing presence of cultural diversity on campus. Nor does it exist among employees who fear they might lose their promotions, their raises, or possibly their jobs to "outsiders."

In the 1990s, national and state leaders who hope to maintain the loyalty and respect of their mainstream constituents feel pressured to pander to the insecurities of the masses. The more they gripe about "welfare parasites," "reverse discrimination," and "femi-Nazis," the louder the applause they receive from their constituents. At the same time, some leaders are able to rise to the challenge and to take a strong stand against bigotry. In the long run, they may save us from even more bloodshed and violence.

CHAPTER 16

The Coming Crisis

As bad as race relations in the United States may be, we have since the 1950s at least moved in the direction of making some effort, through public policy, to reduce inequality and increase opportunities for people of color, women, the disabled, and gays. Various federal initiatives, including the 1964 Civil Rights Act and, more recently, the Americans with Disabilities Act have carried our society further toward the goal of protecting the rights of minority citizens.

Data on the public's acceptance of such policies and programs have been mixed, however. In fact, public opinion survey reports and hate crime data are apparently at odds. When Americans are asked about their acceptance of racial integration in schools, neighborhoods, and friendship circles, large numbers of them express tolerance for diversity, at least at an abstract level. Yet, almost every advocacy organization reports that hate crimes are on the rise.

In fact, it may well be our relative tolerance for diversity as an abstract principle that, to some degree, has set the stage, during the last few years, for the rise of hate crimes in the United States. To the extent that our policies have indeed worked, we have moved away from questions of what ought to be done in principle and instead have created concrete challenges and threats to the traditionally advantaged position of white males. We have therefore unwittingly provided the breeding ground for growing resentment. In an era of economic stagnation, if not decline, hate crimes may be the price we pay for inclusion.

During the last twenty years, more and more gays have come out of the closet, have demonstrated loudly for equality of opportunity, and have openly expressed their affection for members of the same sex. During the same period, people of color and women have made their growing presence felt in companies and colleges that formerly were reserved almost exclusively for white males. At the same time, emigrants into the United States from Latin America, Eastern Europe, and Asia have arrived in record numbers. A climate of tolerance and inclusion, beginning in the late 1960s, has created more and more *challenges* to the status quo and thus more opportunities for outsiders to be victimized. On college campuses, blacks and whites interact where they previously had not; on the job, women and men work more closely together, increasingly in positions of equality or near equality.

As a consequence, hate crimes are occurring in every region of the nation, including the deep South. For example, the grand dragon of the Tennessee White Knights of the Ku Klux Klan recently pleaded guilty to shooting into a Nashville synagogue to intimidate the Jewish congregation. (1) In Louisiana, a federal grand jury recently indicted five Ku Klux Klan members for civil rights violations arising from cross burnings at schools, a courthouse, the home of a black family, a church, and an apartment building. (2)

At the same time, it should be noted that fewer of the hate offenses described in this book have taken place in Southern states than in any other region of the nation, at least during the last few years. Statistical evidence supports this contention. In both Florida and Oklahoma, states in which hate crimes are reported by police jurisdictions, relatively few such offenses have come to the attention of the police.

The reasons for the relative paucity of hate crimes in Southern states remain a matter of conjecture. Perhaps victims fail to report such offenses out of fear that they will not receive support from, or even that they will be further intimidated by, official sources. Maybe Southerners, recognizing the legacy of slavery as an institution, are more sensitive than other Americans to the plight of minorities living in their region. Or, perhaps people of color in the South simply no longer challenge the status quo, at least not to the extent that they are doing in other parts of the country. Indeed, millions of Southern black Americans, over the last few decades, have relocated to northeastern and western states for the sake of opportunity. While some have found what they set out to secure for themselves, many others have uncovered only more stubborn obstacles in their paths.

During the 1950s and 1960s, at a time of rapid change in the South, violence in the region often occurred in response to blacks demanding their civil rights. For the 1990s, however, the major battleground for equality may have moved out of the South, into New York City, Dubuque, Los Angeles, and Minneapolis—localities in which hate crimes continue to plague many victims.

Public policy aimed at reducing racial inequities has

too often been driven by fear and anxiety rather than by any genuine desire to do the right thing for those members of our society who are caught in the hideous grip of bigotry and inequality. The result has been a "patchwork policy" without long-term advantage. After the urban riots of the 1960s, for example, welfare expenditures were for a time increased in order to stem the tide of urban unrest and disorder. Similarly, in the aftermath of the Los Angeles riots in 1992, proposals for enhancing the quality of inner-city life were introduced with fanfare and publicly debated anew, but few effective measures ever saw the light of day. Our response to a soaring crime rate is typically to advocate law-and-order policies such as the death penalty or longer prison sentences. Consequently, we have doubled the rate of imprisonment over a ten-year period, yet criminal violence continues to skyrocket out of sight.

In a sense, the hatemonger often uses the same logic as our political leaders. The perpetrator *fears* the encroachment of blacks, gays, or Asians; and he acts, often in an impulsive and ineffectual manner, to remedy what he sees as an intolerable situation. The hate crime offender actually commits an act of terrorism, by sending a message to *all* members of his victim's group. If successful, he therefore reduces the immediate threat that he feels coming from those who are different. His hate crime represents a short-term response to more profound feelings of powerlessness and despair that can hardly be eliminated by engaging in an act of violence.

Actually, hate offenses work against the long-term interests of the perpetrators by protecting the true sources of their everyday problems and placing the blame on innocent targets who are located at the margins of society. Hate crimes function to maintain the status quo; they protect our leaders, the people in charge, the men and women who are responsible for making important decisions at the highest levels of society. Blame tends to move away from the top, minimizing the possibility that profound changes could ever occur. For example, a disgruntled teenager who, out of a sense of personal frustration, spray paints homophobic slurs on a government building may temporarily experience some psychological satisfaction, but he comes no closer to succeeding in school or on the job.

In 1830, the largest number of our newcomers were Irish; in 1890, they were German; in 1900, they were Italian; then, they were Canadian. During the 1980s, four out of five immigrants came from Asia, Latin America, and the Caribbean. By 1990, the newcomers were arriving in great numbers from Mexico, the Philippines, Vietnam, China and Taiwan, South Korea, and India. Smaller quantities also entered from the Dominican Republic, El Salvador, Jamaica, Haiti, and Iran.

The foreign-born population of the United States is currently more than fourteen million, by far the largest in the world. Moreover, we are presently in the midst of possibly the largest wave of immigration in U.S. history. Between 1981 and 1990, more than seven million newcomers, for political as well as economic reasons, pulled up their roots and left their homelands to begin new lives in the United States. There will be more newcomers in America in the 1990s than in any previous decade; and the overwhelming majority are Asians, Latinos, and blacks—very few are white.

The continuing influx of newcomers into the United States will have profound implications for the future of intergroup relations. Within a decade or so, multiculturalism will have become a focal point of social change. Indeed, within the lifetime of most Americans living today, the white Anglo-Saxon majority will have become a statistical minority. People of color—Asians, Latinos, and blacks—will increasingly challenge the traditional power structure for jobs, status, and power; they will more and more be demanding to share the wealth of the nation. At the same time, gays, women, and people with disabilities will continue to seek equality of opportunity. In our postindustrial society, there is likely to be growing conflict between groups for scarce economic resources. Prejudice and violence may escalate on a scale never seen before.

By randomly examining hate confrontations of the present, we may be able to catch a glimpse of what crises lie ahead should we fail to improve the climate of intolerance in the United States. In April 1992, on the campus of Olivet College in Michigan, black and white students engaged in what one black sophomore called "a civil war on this campus." There were rumors about groups of black men attacking a white female, confrontations in which racial epithets were exchanged, allegations of Ku Klux Klan intervention, death threats recorded on a telephone answering machine, and a fire set in a dormitory where many of the black students lived. Fearing for their personal safety, many of the black students packed their bags and abandoned the campus. (3)

In February 1990, some 600 blacks marched through the streets of Selma, Alabama, in protest of the decision of the school committee's white majority to fire the town's first black school superintendent. One side claimed his incompetence; the other charged that racism was at work. Black members of the school board walked out; black students boycotted classes while their parents picketed the schools. Angry white parents urged officials to end "mob rule" by ejecting the demonstrators from the school. (4)

At New York's City College (CUNY) recently, a

black historian blamed "rich Jews" for the African slave trade and for a "conspiracy" to defame black Americans through their stereotyped portrayal in Hollywood motion pictures. Down the hall, another CUNY professor, this one white, suggested that blacks were intellectually inferior to whites. (5)

The violent reaction of inner-city blacks in Los Angeles to the not-guilty verdict in the April 1992 trial of police officers responsible for Rodney King's beating provides frightening testimony as to the possibility of extreme forms of racial turmoil. In all likelihood, King had been the victim of a hate crime—police brutality. Unfortunately, the rioters in Los Angeles perpetrated their own hate crimes. A truckdriver was pulled from his truck and nearly killed, simply because he was white. Stores were looted and burned because their proprietors were Koreans or whites. Hoping to protect their property, black shopkeepers in inner-city Los Angeles displayed signs reading "Black Owner." After all the fires were finally smothered and most of the smoke had cleared, more than fifty people had lost their lives and thousands more had been injured.

At a time when affirmative action programs are finally making some difference in the lives of women and minorities, we simply cannot afford to abandon our national commitment to eliminating racial and gender inequities. Nor can we afford to back away from our promise to provide equal access to Americans with disabilities. But we must also be prepared to redesign our policies and programs for implementing change, so that they are more in keeping with the political and economic climate of our times. Otherwise, no one will secure the privilege of a safe and prosperous environment.

During the 1960s, Americans enjoyed a period of unparalleled prosperity and economic growth. Hence, many supported affirmative action programs. After all, if you believe that the "pie" is getting larger, you are more willing to reserve a slice for someone without a piece. In the postindustrial era of the 1990s, however, the pie no longer appears to be growing—if anything, it seems to be shrinking. And millions of Americans who might have supported affirmative action policies twenty years earlier now think about holding on to a slice of the pie for themselves and their own families.

To be responsive to the increased presence of hate-mongers in our society, effective hate crime legislation is important, at least in the short term. Statutes which increase the penalties for committing a hate crime, for example, provide the weapons necessary to keep hardened recidivists behind bars and away from their potential victims. Creative alternative sentences must also be available to reach youthful hate crime offenders *long before* they have become hardened recidivists. At the same time, we emphasize that the criminal justice system—even when it operates at maximum effectiveness—is limited in its ability to stem the rising tide of bigotry and bloodshed. Solutions that work will require that our leaders lay the groundwork by long-term planning to reduce both intolerance and resentment.

Wherever possible, we need more programs and policies that help vulnerable groups without being specifically for them. Rather than base all affirmative action policies solely on race or gender, we might also develop programs and policies of affirmative action to reduce poverty—based, for example, on the neighborhood in which a person lives or the economic conditions of a family. Such programs would still disproportionately benefit people of color and women, who have been historically disadvantaged, without also singling them out; they might well generate less resentment from Americans who have become self-defensive in attitude. Focusing more directly on poverty, we would hope to counteract the perceived inequity in policies that aid racial minorities regardless of income or assets. Struggling to send their own children to college, for example, many middle-class Americans conjure up an image of affirmative action that seems as extreme as it is unfair. They ask, "Why should the son of a successful black doctor receive preferential treatment from college admissions over the son of an unemployed white laborer?" or "Why should a Latino candidate for admission qualify before a comparable white student with a higher SAT score?"

Colleges and universities located in the urban core provide a case in point. Institutions of higher learning are increasingly being regarded by residents of surrounding neighborhoods as symbols of disenfranchisement rather than hope. To reverse this trend, these institutions must change their image from that of exclusivity to access.

Many private universities have long maintained scholarship programs for students who are financially in need. In many cases, aid has been targeted specifically at students representing racial and ethnic minorities. Though effective, such programs are increasingly under attack. Moreover, they often fail to address the particular needs of lower-income families in the neighborhoods in which particular colleges are located.

James Fox and one of the authors, Jack Levin, have recently urged that schools take steps to recruit larger numbers of disadvantaged students specifically from surrounding inner-city neighborhoods. And, in fact, some colleges—Brown University, Northeastern University, University of Pennsylvania—have already begun to direct their scholarship aid in this direction. (6)

The approach that we advocate is based on the philanthropic work of Eugene Lang, who in 1981 "adopted" a graduating class of sixth graders in East Harlem and assisted them financially through college. In the Say Yes to Education program in Philadelphia, for example, more than 100 sixth graders have been promised full college support by the University of Pennsylvania, but only if they finish high school. Similarly, Northeastern University in Boston recently announced a scholarship program targeted at 100 Boston public school children who will be granted full scholarships upon receiving a high school diploma. Each Boston student, now in the sixth grade, will also receive additional academic support through undergraduate student mentors as well as extra help through after-school and summer tutoring.

Aside from the obvious advantage of providing assistance for students almost literally in a college's backyard, targeting aid by residence rather than race has considerable potential as a more acceptable general model. First of all, it illustrates a program that affects a particular group—in this case, people of color—without being specifically for them. Blacks, Latinos, and Asians tend to be clustered in lower-income urban centers and would therefore disproportionately benefit from residence-based scholarship aid. In the Northeastern University program, for example, the population of the targeted school is 58 percent Latino and 35 percent black, with the remaining 6 percent divided evenly between Asians and whites.

Minority recipients of such residence-based financial assistance would, at the same time, be less likely to be stigmatized by such programs. Because scholarship aid is potentially available without regard to race, religion, or national origin, no one group would be likely to be singled out as recipients of special treatment. Aside from shared residence, the common denominator is shared poverty. As a result, resentment toward minority populations would, we hope, be minimized.

One final suggestion for reducing hate crimes in our society is in order. We are convinced of the effectiveness of *coalitions* against bigotry. At the turn of the century, labor unions developed out of a temporary alliance of newcomers who put aside their vast differences to join together for the sake of a common objective—higher pay and better working conditions. In the 1940s and 1950s, the civil rights movement began as a coalition of blacks and whites, many of whom were Jewish, who regarded bigotry as a common enemy deserving of a united response. In the 1960s, a coalition of women and blacks successfully lobbied for affirmative action legislation at the federal level, a goal that neither group would in all likelihood have achieved by itself. (7)

The college campus is, in many respects, a microcosm of the larger society in which we live. Much of what works on campus can also be generalized to everyday life on the job and in the neighborhood.

In addition to organizations that exclusively service the needs of a particular group of minority college students, we need a balance of more cooperative organizations and activities in which diverse members of the student body come together to achieve a common goal. The campus is a highly competitive social environment, much like its counterpart in the business world. Students often see one another as rivals for scarce resources. Only if they are interdependent—forced to rely upon one another for the fulfillment of their important goals—will they begin to recognize their commonalities as targets of bigotry. They are, of course, in competition for better grades, good letters of reference, social relationships, and ultimately career opportunities. At the same time, there are many curricular and extracurricular areas in which cooperation is desirable, if not necessary.

An interesting example of coalition politics on a col-

lege campus is provided by student reactions to a controversial speaker from the Nation of Islam—a Black Muslim
sect—at Trinity College in Hartford. Sponsored by an organization of black students on campus, the speaker was
accused by some Trinity students of making statements
that violated the college's recently established racial harassment policy. Outside the lecture hall, representatives
from a number of different student groups handed out
flyers in which the allegedly racist and anti-Semitic remarks of the speaker were printed. Among those protesting the Black Muslim speaker were students from Hillel, a
Jewish organization, La Voz Latina, a Hispanic organization, College Democrats, and College Republicans.

Their actions paid off, at least in the short term. Trinity's president sent a letter inviting students to attend a
campuswide discussion of bigotry. More than 400 students
of diverse ethnic backgrounds attended, providing an opportunity for them to share their viewpoints and to pressure college administrators into considering alternative
speakers on future occasions. (8)

Coalitions can also have a basis in initiating positive
actions, rather than merely responding to negative actions, on their own behalf. Across the country, groups and
organizations of students at major universities are coming
together—women and men, whites, blacks, and Asians,
Christians, Muslims, and Jews, straights and gays, Latinos and Anglos, able-bodied and students with disabilities—to celebrate the diversity of humankind by holding
lectures, food fairs, and music festivals that highlight the
strengths of *all* of the cultures they represent. As separate
factions on campus, such groups are often viewed as little
more than a thorn in the side of bigotry. Together, however, they represent a powerful force to be reckoned with
by anyone who is intolerant of differences.

Boston Police Hate Crime Tabulations

Table 1. Race, Religion, and Ethnicity of Victims of Racial Violence in Boston—1983–1987

Race	Frequency	Percentage
Black	143	31.6
White	157	34.7
Hispanic	30	6.6
Cambodian	8	1.8
Chinese	7	1.5
Laotian	2	.4
Filipino	2	.4
Vietnamese	53	11.7
Asian (other)	31	6.8
Indian	1	.2
Jewish	3	.7
Other	15	3.4
	452	100.0

Table 2. Race and Ethnicity of Victim/Offender Combinations in Incidents of Racial Violence in Boston—1983–1987

Race of victim	Race of offender[a]				
	Black	White	Hispanic	Asian	Total
Black	6 (5.1)	108 (91.5)	2 (1.7)	2 (1.7)	11.8
White	95 (77.9)	19 (15.6)	2 (1.6)	6 (4.9)	122
Hispanic	4 (18.2)	19 (81.8)	0	0	23
Cambodian	0	5 (83.3)	1 (16.7)	0	6
Chinese	0	2 (100.0)	0	0	2
Laotian	0	2 (100.0)	0	0	2
Filipino	0	1 (100.0)	0	0	1
Vietnamese	4 (11.4)	31 (88.6)	0	0	35
Asian (other)	2 (10.5)	15 (78.9)	2 (10.5)	0	19
Jewish	0	2 (100.0)	0	0	2
Total	111 (33.6)	204 (61.8)	7 (2.1)	8 (2.4)	330

[a] Numbers in parentheses are percentages.

Table 3. Description of Civil Rights Incidents as Recorded by Responding Officers

Offense	Frequency	Percentage
Assault and battery	77	17.7
Assault and battery with dangerous weapon	136	31.3
Vandalism to property	98	22.6
Stoning	13	3.0
Threats	32	7.4
Harassment	14	3.2
Breaking and entering	2	.5
Civil rights violations	10	2.3
Arson	9	2.1
Community disorder	4	.9
Robbery	2	.5
Larceny under $100	1	.2
Racial incident	9	2.1
Armed robbery	12	2.8
Investigating premises	3	.7
Shooting	1	.2
Carrying dangerous weapon	1	.2
Affray or fight	1	.2
Larceny over $100	4	.9
Missing information	5	1.2
	434	100.0

Table 4. Sex of Victims of Racial Violence in Boston—1983–1987

Sex	Frequency	Percentage
Male	321	71.0
Female	131	29.0
	452	100.0

Table 5. Ages of Victims of Racial Violence in Boston—1983–1987

Age	Frequency	Percentage
Under 18	79	19.9
18–29	176	44.3
30 and over	142	35.8
	397	100.0

Table 6. Reason for Incident as Recorded in Investigation by Community Disorders Unit

Reason for incident	Frequency	Percentage
Passing through the neighborhood	100	27.4
Prejudice	57	15.6
Moving into a neighborhood	45	12.3
Driving through a neighborhood	24	6.6
History of discord	23	6.3
Automobile incidents	12	3.3
Want victim to move	11	3.0
Fight or altercation	11	3.0
Working in a neighborhood	10	2.7
Trespassing	6	1.6
Noncompliance with perpetrator	6	1.6
Suspect drunk	5	1.4
Offender not competent	2	.6
Dating a minority	4	1.1
Money	4	1.1
Politically motivated	2	.6
Other	15	4.1
Unknown	28	7.7
	365	100.0
Missing cases 77		

Hate Crime Statistics Act

PUBLIC LAW 101-275—APR. 23, 1990

Public Law 101-275
101st Congress

An Act

To provide for the acquisition and publication of data about crimes that manifest prejudice based on certain group characteristics.

Be it enacted by the Senate and House of Representatives of the United States of America in Congress assembled, That (a) this Act may be cited as the "Hate Crime Statistics Act."

(b) (1) Under the authority of section 534 of title 28, United States Code, the Attorney General shall acquire data, for the calendar year 1990 and each of the succeeding

4 calendar years, about crimes that manifest evidence of prejudice based on race, religion, sexual orientation, or ethnicity, including where appropriate the crimes of murder, non-negligent manslaughter; forcible rape; aggravated assault, simple assault, intimidation; arson; and destruction, damage, or vandalism of property.

(2) The Attorney General shall establish guidelines for the collection of such data including the necessary evidence and criteria that must be present for a finding of manifest prejudice and procedures for carrying out the purpose of this section.

(3) Nothing in this section creates a cause of action or a right to bring an action, including an action based on discrimination due to sexual orientation. As used in this section, the term "sexual orientation" means consensual homosexuality or heterosexuality. This subsection does not limit any existing cause of action or right to bring an action, including any action under Administrative Procedure Act or the All Writs Act.

(4) Data acquired under this section shall be used only for research or statistical purposes and may not contain any information that may reveal the identity of an individual victim of a crime.

(5) The Attorney General shall publish an annual summary of the data acquired under this section.

(c) There are authorized to be appropriated such sums as may be necessary to carry out the provisions of this section through fiscal year 1994.

Sec. 2. (a) Congress finds that—

(1) the American family life is the foundation of American Society,

(2) Federal policy should encourage the well-being, financial security, and health of the American family,

(3) schools should not de-emphasize the critical value of American family life.

(b) Nothing in this Act shall be construed, nor shall any funds appropriated to carry out the purpose of the Act be used, to promote or encourage homosexuality.

Approved April 23, 1990

Notes

1. Reign of Terror

1. Stephen Singular, *Talked to Death: The Life and Murder of Alan Berg* (New York: William Morrow, 1987); also, Philip Lamy, "The Meek Shall Not Inherit the Earth: Survivalism and the American Millennial Myth" (Doctoral dissertation submitted to the Department of Sociology and Anthropology, Northeastern University, July 1991).
2. James Coates, "Trial Opens for 11 in Neo-Nazi Group," *Chicago Tribune*, September 13, 1985, p. 12.
3. James Coates, *Armed and Dangerous: The Rise of the Survivalist Right* (New York: The Noonday Press, 1987).
4. James Coates, "Rightist Hate Groups Put on the Defensive," *Chicago Tribune*, November 9, 1987, p. 10.
5. According to the FBI definition, hate need not be the total motivation but only a partial motivation: "A criminal offense committed against a person or property which is motivated, in whole or in part, by the offender's bias against a race, religion, ethnic/national origin group, or sexual orientation group" (U.S. Department of Justice, *Hate Crime Data Collection Guidelines*, Washington, DC: Federal Bureau of Investigation, 1990).
6. Charles Hynes, speech to Annual Meeting of the Anti-Defamation League, Boston, October 11, 1989.
7. American-Arab Anti-Discrimination Committee, *1991 Report on Anti-Arab Hate Crimes* (Washington, DC, February 1992).

8. Center for Democratic Renewal, *They Don't All Wear White Sheets: A Chronology of Racist and Far Right Violence—1980–1986* (Atlanta: Center for Democratic Renewal, 1987).
9. Ibid.
10. Ibid.
11. Jack McDevitt, "The Study of the Character of Civil Rights Crimes in Massachusetts 1983–1989" (Paper presented at annual meeting of the American Society of Criminology, Reno, Nevada, November 1990).
12. Ibid.
13. George Hacket, "Women under Assault," *Newsweek,* July 16, 1990, pp. 23–24.
14. Bureau of Justice Statistics, *Criminal Victimization in the United States* (Washington, DC: Bureau of Justice Statistics, 1985).
15. Interview with Lt. William Johnston, Boston Police Department, Boston, September 1991.

2. Nasty Pictures in Our Heads

1. Gary A. Tobin and Sharon L. Sassler, *Jewish Perceptions of Anti-Semitism* (New York: Plenum, 1988).
2. Jack Levin and William C. Levin, *The Functions of Discrimination and Prejudice* (New York: Harper & Row, 1982).
3. Alison Lurie, *The Language of Clothing* (New York: Random House, 1981), p. 81.
4. Levin and Levin, *The Functions of Discrimination and Prejudice;* Jack Levin, William C. Levin, and Arnold Arluke, "Powerful Elders" (Paper presented at the annual meeting of the American Sociological Association, Pittsburgh, August 1992); Nel Noddings, *Women and Evil* (Berkeley: University of California Press, 1989); Sam Keen, *Faces of the Enemy* (San Francisco: Harper & Row, 1986).
5. Elinor Langer, "The American Neo-Nazi Movement Today," *The Nation,* July 16/23, 1990, pp. 82–107.
6. Noddings, *Women and Evil;* Keen, *Faces of the Enemy.*
7. Howard Schuman, Charlotte Steeh, and Lawrence Bobo, *Racial Attitudes in America* (Cambridge, MA: Harvard University Press, 1988); Lee Siegelman and Susan Welch, *Black Americans' Views of Racial Inequality* (Cambridge: Cambridge University Press, 1991).

8. Lynne Duke, "Race Relations Are Worsening," in *Racism in America: Opposing Viewpoints*, ed. William Dudley (San Diego, CA: Greenhaven Press, 1991), pp. 17–20.

9. Thea Lee, "Racism Is a Serious Problem for Asian Americans," in *Racism in America: Opposing Viewpoints*, ed. William Dudley (San Diego, CA: Greenhaven Press, 1991), pp. 38–45.

10. Ibid.

11. Richard D. Mohr, "Anti-Gay Stereotypes," in *Gays/Justice: A Study of Ethics, Society and Law* (New York: Columbia University Press, 1988), pp. 21–27.

12. Levin and Levin, *The Functions of Discrimination and Prejudice*.

3. Hatred Is Hip

1. Jeffrey H. Goldstein and Paul E. McGhee, *The Psychology of Humor* (New York: Academic Press, 1972).

2. Marvin R. Koller, *Humor and Society: Explorations in the Sociology of Humor* (Houston: Cap and Gown Press, 1988).

3. John Leo, "Even Lenny Bruce Would Know Better," *U.S. News and World Report*, May 28, 1990, p. 21.

4. William Keough, *Punchlines* (New York: Paragon House, 1990), pp. 194–197.

5. Ibid.

6. Jerry Adler, "The Rap Attitude," *Newsweek*, March 19, 1990, p. 56–59.

7. Fred Bruning, "The Devilish Soul of Rock and Roll," *Maclean's*, October 21, 1985, p. 13.

8. Adler, "The Rap Attitude," p. 59.

9. Brian D. Johnson, "Spanking New Madonna," *Maclean's*, June 18, 1990, pp. 48–50.

10. Anti-Defamation League of B'nai B'rith, Civil Rights Division, "Special Edition," New York, October, 1987; 1.

11. Anti-Defamation League of B'nai B'rith, Civil Rights Division, "David Duke: A Bigot Goes to Baton Rouge," Special Edition, New York, March 1989, p. 2.

12. William F. Buckley, Jr. "In Search of Anti-Semitism," *National Review*, December 30, 1991, p. 32.

13. Eric Alterman, "The Pat and Abe Show," *The Nation*, November 5, 1990, pp. 517–520.

14. David Wild, "Who Is Howard Stern?" *Rolling Stone,* June 11, 1990, p. 87.
15. Ni Yang and Daniel Linz, "Movie Ratings and the Content of Adult Videos: The Sex-Violence Ratio," *Journal of Communication* 40 (Spring, 1990); Edward Donnerstein, Daniel Linz, and Steven Penrod, *The Question of Pornography* (New York: Free Press, 1987).

4. Resentment

1. Coates, *Armed and Dangerous.*
2. Theodore W. Adorno, E. Frankel-Brunswick, D. J. Levinson, and N. H. Sanford, *The Authoritarian Personality* (New York: Harper Row, 1950).
3. Kevin Phillips, *The Politics of the Rich and the Poor* (New York: Random House, 1990); see also Katherine S. Newman, *Falling from Grace: The Experience of Downward Mobility in the American Middle Class* (New York: Free Press, 1988).
4. Lawrence Mishel and David Frankel, *The State of Working America* (Washington, DC: Economic Policy Institute, 1990–1991).
5. S. Levitan, G. Mangum, and M. Pines, *A Proper Inheritance: Investing in the Self-Sufficiency of Poor Families* (Washington, DC: George Washington University, Center for Social Policy Studies, 1989).
6. See, for example, Mark A. Fossett and K. Jill Kiecolt, "The Relative Size of Minority Populations and White Racial Attitudes," *Social Science Quarterly* (December, 1989): 120–176; Thomas C. Wilson, "Interregional Migration and Racial Attitudes," *Social Forces* (September, 1986): 177–187.
7. Colleen Brush, "Report Indicates Rise in Antigay Violence," *Boston Globe,* January 29, 1992, p. 43.
8. Jack P. Douglas, *Deviance and Respectability* (New York: Basic Books, 1970).
9. Fox Butterfield, "Arab-Americans Face Wave of Threats in U.S.," *New York Times,* August 29, 1990, p. A19; Nancy Gibbs, "Walking a Tightrope," *Time,* February 4, 1991, pp. 42–43; Charles E. Cohen, "As the Gulf War Stirs Prejudice, Albert Mokhiber Fights for the Rights of Arab-Americans," *People,* February 11, 1991, pp. 87–89.
10. "Should Punishment Fit the Criminal?" *Newsweek,* June 13, 1983, p. 22; "It Isn't Fair," *Time,* November 14, 1983, p. 46.

11. Charles Leershen, "Busing the Prince of Love," *Newsweek*, November 19, 1990, p. 45; Larry Rohter, "Sect Leader Convicted on Conspiracy Charge," *New York Times*, May 28, 1992, p. A16.

12. David Ellis, "L.A. Lawless," *Time*, May 11, 1992.

13. Southern Poverty Law Center, "Hate Violence and White Supremacy—A Decade Review, 1980–1990," *Klanwatch Intelligence Report #47* (Montgomery, December 1989), pp. 2–3.

5. For the Thrill of It

1. As quoted in David Gelman, "Going 'Wilding' in the City," *Newsweek*, May 8, 1989, p. 65.

2. Interview with Lt. William Johnston, Boston Police Department, Boston, September 1991.

3. James N. Baker, "Hatred in a Tolerant Town," *Newsweek*, October 1, 1990, p. 33.

4. Kevin Sullivan, "2 Arrested in 'Heinous' Racial Assault," *Washington Post*, March 4, 1992, p. A1.

5. Bruce Weber, "Black Children Beaten in Bias Attack, Police Say," *New York Times*, January 7, 1992, p. 3.

6. Gregory Herek and Kevin Berrill, *Primary and Secondary Victimization in Anti-Gay Hate Crimes: Official Response and Public Policy in Hate Crimes Confronting Violence against Lesbians and Gay Men* (Newbury Park, CA: Sage, 1992).

7. Gary David Comstock, *Violence against Lesbians and Gay Men* (New York: Columbia University Press, 1991).

8. Eric Pooley, "With Extreme Prejudice," *New York*, April 8, 1991, pp. 36–43.

9. "Gay-Bash Killing Testimony," *New York Newsday*, November 8, 1991, p. 6; Joseph P. Fried, "Queens Man Describes Hunt for a Victim, Then a Murder," *New York Times*, November 8, 1991, p. B1.

6. Reacting to a Personal Threat

1. Luz Delgado, "Black Family in North End Is Met with Racist Graffiti," *Boston Globe*, July 31, 1992, p. 17.

2. Ronald Smothers, "Hate Crime Found Aimed at Blacks in White Areas," *New York Times*, April 28, 1990, p. 26.

3. Joan Weiss, Howard Ehrlich, and Barbara Larcom, "Ethnoviolence at Work," *The Journal of Intergroup Relations* (Winter, 1991–92): 21–33.
4. Bill Stanton, *Klanwatch* (New York: Grove Weidenfeld, 1991).
5. Anti-Defamation League of B'nai B'rith, *Extremism on the Right: A Handbook* (New York, 1988).
6. Howard W. French, "Hatred and Social Isolation May Spur Acts of Racial Violence, Experts Say," *New York Times*, September 4, 1989, p. 30.
7. Ronald Powers, "Defendant Acquitted of Murder in '89 Racial Killing in Brooklyn," *Boston Globe*, December 7, 1990, p. 13.
8. Jonathan Rieder, *Canarsie* (Cambridge, MA: Harvard University Press, 1985).
9. Ibid.
10. "Long-Held Racial Anxieties Surface Again in Canarsie," *New York Times*, August 4, 1991, pp. 1, 38.
11. "Wilder Says Racism Is on Rise in America," *Boston Globe*, November 25, 1991, p. 9.
12. Greg Smith, "In Iowa, a Burning Hate," *Boston Globe*, November 23, 1991, p. 3.
13. *20/20*, December, 1991.
14. "Klan Leader Visits City Hit by Cross Burnings," *Boston Globe*, December 1, 1991, p. 27.
15. "Cross Burnings Reported in Iowa," *Boston Globe*, November 17, 1991, p. 18.
16. Paul Murphy, "13 Charged with Indian Attacks," *India Abroad*, July 5, 1991, p. 29.
17. Connie Leslie, "We Shall Not Be Moved," *Newsweek*, December 12, 1988, p. 67.

7. Ridding the World of Evil

1. Rod MacDonell, E. Thompson, A. McIntosh, and W. Marsden, "Killer's Father Beats Him as a Child," *Gazette*, December 10, 1989, p. A7.
2. Jeff Heinrich, "A Day of Tears and Hugs and Heartache," *Gazette*, December 10, 1989, p. A4.
3. Stephen G. Michaud, "Something Snapped," *Crime Beat*, October 1992, pp. 27–34, 58–59.
4. Osha G. Davidson, *Under Fire* (New York: Holt, 1993).

5. Stuart Wasserman, "After Carnage at California School, Curiosity, Questions, and Fears," *Boston Globe*, January 19, 1989, p. 1; "Five Children Killed as Gunman Attacks a California School," *New York Times*, January 18, 1989, p. 1; Robert Reinhold, "After Shooting, Horror but Few Answers," *New York Times*, January 19, 1989, p. B6.

8. Organized Hate

1. Langer, "The American Neo-Nazi Movement Today."
2. Southern Poverty Law Center, "Metzger Warns of More Violence," *Klanwatch Intelligence Report #56* (Montgomery, June 1991), p. 1.
3. Southern Poverty Law Center, "$12.5 Million Verdict Holds WAR, Metzgers Liable in '88 Murder." *Klanwatch Intelligence Report #53*, December, 1990, p. 2.
4. Richard A. Serrano, "Metzger Must Pay $5 Million in Rights Death," *Los Angeles Times*, October 23, 1990, p. 1.
5. Southern Poverty Law Center, "Metzger Warns of More Violence."
6. Anti-Defamation League of B'nai B'rith (ADL), *Neo-Nazi Skinheads: A 1990 Status Report* (New York, 1990).
7. Southern Poverty Law Center, "A Year of WAR in the Courtroom and Young Brutality in the Streets." *Klanwatch Intelligence Report #54*, February 1991.
8. Ronald Smothers, "Hate Groups Seen Growing as Neo-Nazis Draw Young," *New York Times*, February 19, 1992, p. A2.
9. Reprinted in Langer, "The American Neo-Nazi Movement Today."
10. As quoted in Southern Poverty Law Center, "Hate Groups Exploit Violence Sparked by Rodney King Verdict," *Klanwatch Intelligence Report #62* (Montgomery, June 1992), p. 11.
11. "ADL Says 'Hate' Shows on Rise on Cable," *Boston Globe*, June 13, 1991, p. 88.
12. Langer, "The American Neo-Nazi Movement Today."
13. Southern Poverty Law Center, "Hate Violence and White Supremacy."
14. ADL, *Extremism on the Right: A Handbook* (New York, 1988), p. 106.
15. Ibid.
16. Southern Poverty Law Center, "Hate Violence and White Supremacy."
17. Anti-Defamation League of B'nai B'rith, *Extremism on the Right: A Handbook* (New York: Anti-Defamation League of B'nai B'rith, 1988).

9. Hate Goes to School

1. Frederick A. Hurst, *Report on University of Massachusetts Investigation* (Boston: Massachusetts Commission Against Discrimination, February 1987).
2. Ibid.
3. Center for the Study of Sport in Society, *Youth Attitudes on Racism* (Boston: Northeastern University, October, 1990).
4. Jean Merl, "Survey of Schools Finds Hate Crime Widespread," *Los Angeles Times*, October 26, 1989, pp. A1, S43.
5. Carl A. Raschke, *Painted Black* (New York: Harper, 1990).
6. Robert L. Gross, "Heavy Metal Music: A New Subculture in American Society," *Journal of Popular Culture*, 1990, pp. 119–130; Raschke, *Painted Black*. To be fair, it should be noted that the majority of heavy metal songs do not focus on violence. Sociologist Heather Walcutt recently content analyzed the lyrics from fifty top-selling heavy metal songs released between August 1991 and March 1992. She found that 20 percent of these songs contained violent or sexist lyrics (Heather Walcutt, "A Content Analysis of Heavy Metal Lyrics," Unpublished manuscript, Northeastern University, Department of Sociology and Anthropology, 1992). Deena Weinstein, author of *Heavy Metal: A Cultural Sociology* (New York: Macmillan/Lexington, 1991), believes that many critics of heavy metal give it a "maximally incompetent" reading. That is, "they have no sense of irony, take things literally, and therefore totally misinterpret the songs." As an example, she cites Ozzy Osbourne's "Suicide Solution," which some critics claim tells kids to commit suicide. But according to Weinstein, "if you read the lyrics, listen to the song, or know who Ozzy Osbourne is, it's a song denouncing alcoholism, a song of lament for a guy who drank himself to death." The problem, of course, is that many twelve- and thirteen-year-old kids are indeed "maximally incompetent" readers who take the lyrics of their favorite songs at face value.
7. ADL, *Neo-Nazi Skinheads: A 1990 Status Report*.
8. Ibid.
9. ADL Special Report, "Skinheads Target the Schools" (New York, 1989).
10. Ibid.
11. Art Levine, "America's Youthful Bigots," *U.S. News and World Re-*

port, May 7, 1990, pp. 59–60; Shelby Steele, "The Recoloring of Campus Life," *Harper's*, February 1989, pp. 47–55.

12. Anti-Defamation League of B'nai B'rith, " 'JAP Baiting': When Sexism and Anti-Semitism Meet," *Special Edition of ADL Periodic Update* (New York, October 1988).

13. Pete Hamill, "Black and White at Brown," *Esquire*, April 1990, pp. 67–68; Levine, "America's Youthful Bigots"; Steele, "The Recoloring of Campus Life"; Ken Emerson, "Only Correct," *New Republic*, February 18, 1991, pp. 18–19; Howard J. Ehrlich, *Campus Ethnoviolence and the Policy Options* (Baltimore: National Institute Against Prejudice and Violence, 1990); "Five Charged in Fatal Beating of Student," *The Enterprise*, August 19, 1992, p. 8.

14. "Bias Beating and a Death Shock a City," *New York Times*, August 23, 1992, p. 36.

15. Cited in Berrill, "Anti-Gay Violence and Victimization in the United States," *Journal of Interpersonal Violence* 5 (September 1990).

16. Hamill, "Black and White at Brown."

17. ADL, *Extremism on the Right: A Handbook*, p. 129.

18. Donald E. Muir, " 'White' Fraternity and Sorority Attitudes toward 'Blacks' on a Deep-South Campus," *Sociological Spectrum* 11 (January–March 1991): 93–103.

19. Andrew Merton, "Return to Brotherhood," *Ms.*, September 1985, pp. 60–65, 121–122.

20. "Anti-Homosexual T-Shirt Prompts Suspension of Syracuse Fraternity," *New York Times*, June 26, 1991, p. B4.

21. "5 Are Disciplined in Racial Prank at Fraternity," *New York Times*, October 22, 1989, p. 44.

22. Merton, "Return to Brotherhood."

23. Hamill, "Black and White at Brown," p. 67.

10. Minority against Minority

1. "Brooklyn Killing Reignites Strife," *Boston Globe*, February 8, 1992, p. 23; "Man Charged in Brooklyn Stabbing Death," *Boston Globe*, February 11, 1992, p. 60.

2. Debra Nussbaum Cohen and Jackie Rothenberg, "Blacks and Hasidic Jews Fighting in Brooklyn," *The Jewish Advocate*, August 23–29, 1991, pp. 1, 25.

3. Adrian Walker, "Black Leader Defends Book Called Anti-Semitic," *Boston Globe*, July 27, 1992, pp. 1, 7.

4. Quoted in Walker, "Black Leader Defends."

5. Jonathan Rieder, "Trouble in Store," *New Republic*, July 2, 1990, pp. 16–22; Ari Goldman, "Other Korean Grocers Give to Those in Brooklyn Boycott," *New York Times*, May 14, 1990, p. B5; Robert McFadden, "Blacks Attack 3 Vietnamese; One Hurt Badly," *New York Times*, May 14, 1990, p. 1.

6. Robert D. McFadden, "Police Now Say Flatbush Attack Wasn't Planned," *New York Times*, May 15, 1990, p. 1.

7. Alex Prud'Homme, Essay, *Time*, July 29, 1991, p. 15.

8. "More Than 200 Arrested in Miami in 2nd Night of Racial Disturbances," *New York Times*, January 19, 1989, p. A1.

9. "Appeals Court Overturns Conviction of Miami Cop," *Jet*, July 22, 1991, p. 18.

10. Prud'Homme, Essay.

11. James N. Baker, "Minority against Minority," *Newsweek*, May 20, 1991, p. 28; "Congressional Probe Urged to Find Root of D.C. Rioting," *Jet*, May 27, 1991, p. 7.

12. Muzafer Sherif et al., *Intergroup Conflict and Cooperation* (Norman: University of Oklahoma, 1961).

13. Quoted in Walker, "Black Leader Defends."

11. Hate around the World

1. Judith Miller, "Strangers at the Gate," *New York Times Magazine*, September 15, 1991, pp. 33–37, 49, 80, 81, 86.

2. Judith Miller, "Out of Hiding," *New York Times Magazine*, December 9, 1990, pp. 70–76.

3. "German Neo-Nazis Firebomb Foreigners' Housing," *New York Times*, August 26, 1992, p. A3; Jonathan Kaufman, "Attacks on Foreigners Daze Germany," *Boston Globe*, September 7, 1992, p. 2.

4. "German Leftists Rally to Protest Hess Mourners," *Boston Globe*, August 16, 1992, p. 21.

5. Chris Wallace, *Primetime Live*, ABC-TV, January 2, 1992.

6. Don Wycliff, "Their Race Problem, and Ours," *New York Times*, January 8, 1989, p. 28.

7. Nicholas Kristof, "China's Burst of Rage: A Show of Racism, and of Something More," *New York Times*, January 8, 1989, p. 3.

8. Wycliff, "Their Race Problem, and Ours."
9. Michael Lerner, "The Motley Pals of Jean-Marie Le Pen," *Newsweek*, March 31, 1986, p. 29.
10. Youssef Ibrahim, "France Pushes Integration of Arab Immigrants," *New York Times*, December 7, 1989, p. A9.
11. Alan Riding, "Attacks on Jewish Graves Jolt France," *New York Times*, May 12, 1990, p. A3.
12. Alexander Stille, "Italy," *Atlantic*, February 1992, pp. 28–38.
13. Charles A. Radin, "Immigrants and Italians Face Strains," *Boston Globe*, February 26, 1992, pp. 1, 18.
14. "African Pupils, Russian Police Clash," *Boston Globe*, August 13, 1992, p. 2.
15. Alan Lupo, "A Hatred That Endures," *Boston Globe*, February 22, 1992; Natan Sharansky, "The Greatest Exodus," *New York Times Magazine*, February 2, 1992, pp. 20–21, 46.
16. Stephen Engelberg, "Poland's Jewish Uproar, and with So Few Jews," *New York Times*, September 17, 1990, p. A6.
17. Miller, "Out of Hiding."
18. Quoted in Miller, "Out of Hiding."
19. Interview with Paul Bookbinder, August 26, 1992.

12. Police Response

1. National Advisory Commission on Civil Disorders, *Report of the National Advisory Commission on Civil Disorders* (New York: Bantam Books, 1968).
2. William Tafoya, "Rioting in the Streets: Deja Vu," in *Bias Crime: The Law Enforcement Response*, ed. Nancy Taylor (Chicago: Office of International Criminal Justice, 1991).
3. National Advisory Commission on Civil Disorders, *Report of the National Advisory Commission on Civil Disorders*.
4. James N. Baker, "Los Angeles Aftershocks," *Newsweek*, April 1, 1991, pp. 18–19; "Panel Probing L.A. Police Wants Chief to Resign: Cites Racism, Violence," *Jet*, July 29, 1991, p. 6; Seth Mydans, "Tape of Beating by Police Revives Charges of Racism," *New York Times*, March 7, 1991, p. A18.
5. "King Protest Turns Violent in Toronto," *Boston Globe*, May 5, 1992, p. 15.

6. Robert Hanley, "26 Arrested in Rampage in Jersey Town," *New York Times*, August 30, 1989, p. B1.

7. "Police Shooting Sparks Violence in New Jersey," *Jet*, September 18, 1989, p. 6.

8. John Kifner, "Teaneck Youths Say BB Gun Was Waved Just Before Killing," *New York Times*, April 14, 1990, p. 1.

9. David Pitt, "Brutality Inquiry Looks at a Police Distress Call," *New York Times*, March 22, 1989, p. A10.

10. "Rights Advocate Maintains Police Beat Him in a 'Sting' He Arranged," *New York Times*, January 16, 1989, p. A11.

11. Arthur L. Kobler, "Police Homicide in a Democracy," *Journal of Social Issues* 31 (Winter 1975): 163–184.

12. *Miami Herald,* March 27, 1983, p. 18A.

13. "Ohio Court Voids Hate Crime Law," *Boston Globe*, August 27, 1992, p. 11.

14. U.S. Department of Justice, *Training Guide for Hate Crime Data Collection* (Federal Bureau of Investigation, 1990). Developing and using a specialized unit or officer who deals primarily or exclusively with hate crimes offers a number of advantages for local police agencies. First, the unit or officer (in smaller departments, one officer may be all that is necessary for the hate crime investigation unit) develops expertise in the phenomenon of hate crimes, which can be applied to future investigations. For example, hate crime officers may become sensitive to the anxieties that hate crime victims face—in particular, to the fear of retaliation from the offender or from the offender's friends. Once alerted to these fears, the officer can provide the victim with additional protection.

   Affording the police more time to determine if an incident is actually hate motivated is a second advantage of a separate hate crime investigating unit. By turning the investigation over to a specialized unit with expertise in conducting hate crime investigations, more time can be allocated to the investigation than would be available to the patrol officer who originally receives the call. Because these offenses are their primary responsibility, the hate crime officers can do a more complete inquiry, including canvassing a neighborhood for witnesses and interviewing the friends and family of any potential suspects.

   A third advantage of a specialized unit is that it offers a check against hate crimes being misclassified by the police during the initial investigation. Many specialized units have a policy whereby they review all incidents that might be bias motivated. In Boston's Community Disorders Unit, for example, the commanding officer reviews all interracial incident reports each day, whether bias is suspected or not. This procedure provides a check on cases that might be missed by the original responding officer, and affords a measure of accountability against bigoted officers who may feel that hate victims are not entitled to protection.

In Boston, for example, the policy works this way. For each case where hate may be a motivation, the responding officer forwards a Boston Police Incident Report Form to the hate crime unit or officer. In addition, all incidents that involve interracial or inter-ethnic crimes are forwarded to the unit as well. The descriptions of these latter incidents are reviewed by experienced hate crime investigators who, if they believe that bias or bigotry might be a motivation, can call the victim or the responding officer to begin an investigation.

A specialized unit also improves the likelihood that an arrest will result in a conviction by encouraging a relationship between the hate crime investigating officers and the local prosecutor's office. Hate crime cases are difficult to prosecute because the state has to prove the offender's intent in addition to elements of the crime that was charged. Specialized hate crime units learn from local prosecutors what types of evidence (e.g., witness testimony, use of defamatory language) are necessary to get a conviction. Once this is understood, the police can gear their investigation to collect the evidence that will be crucial to the case.

The existence of a specialized unit also promotes accountability in the police agency. Presently, in most police agencies throughout the United States, if a victim of hate violence who comes to the police is ignored, there is little that the victim or members of the local community can do. Even if they lodge a complaint with the police chief, the best victims can expect to get is an apology and a statement that the police will try to do a better job next time. Because the object of complaint was the action of a single officer, the police department in question may punish that officer, but no department-wide changes will generally occur. By contrast, if there is a specialized unit or officer on staff, the victim and the community can point to a place where the department is not doing its job and can more forcefully demand system-wide changes.

Finally, the formation of a specialized unit continues to send the message that hate crimes are a priority with that particular police agency. As a result, victims may feel more secure, police may be more careful, and potential offenders may think twice before they break the law.

15. Jack McDevitt, "The Study of the Characteristics of Civil Rights Crimes in Massachusetts 1983–1987" (Paper presented at the American Society of Criminology meeting, Reno, November 1989).

16. U.S. Department of Justice, "Training Guide for Hate Crime Data Collection" (Washington, DC: Federal Bureau of Investigation, 1990).

17. McDevitt, "The Study of the Characteristics of Civil Rights Crimes in Massachusetts 1983–1987."

18. Ibid.

19. Leslie Hatamiya, "Walk with Pride: Taking Steps to Address Anti-Asian Violence" (San Francisco: Japanese American Citizens League, August 1991).

20. Timothy Egan, "New Faces and New Roles for the Police," *New York Times*, April 25, 1991, p. A1.

21. Ibid.

22. Bruce Berg, Edmond True, and Marc Gertz, "Police Riots and Alienation," *Journal of Police Science and Administration* 12 (1984): 186–190.

13. The Law

1. National Institute Against Prejudice and Violence, *Striking Back at Bigotry: Remedies under Federal Law for Violence Motivated by Racial, Religious and Ethnic Prejudice* (Washington DC, 1986).

2. U.S. v. Lee, 935 F.2d 952 (8th Cir. 1991).

3. National Institute Against Prejudice and Violence, *Striking Back at Bigotry.*

4. Southern Poverty Law Center, *Klanwatch Special Reports Outlawing Hate Crime* (Montgomery, AL, November 1989), p. 4.

5. R.A.V. v. St. Paul, 1992 WL 135564 (U.S.).

6. ADL, *1991 Audit of Anti-Semitic Incidents* (New York, 1992).

7. R.A.V. v. St. Paul, 1992 WL 135564 (U.S.).

8. Bureau of Justice Statistics, "Correctional Population of the United States 1985," Bureau of Justice Statistics Report (Washington, DC, December 1987).

9. ADL, *Hate Crime Statutes: A 1991 Status Report* (New York, 1991).

10. National Institute Against Prejudice and Violence, *Striking Back at Bigotry.*
11. American-Arab Anti-Discrimination Committee, *1991 Report on Anti-Arab Hate Crimes* (Washington, DC, February 1992).
12. Ibid.
13. Ibid.
14. Center for Democratic Renewal, *They Don't All Wear Sheets: A Chronology of Racist and Far Right Violence—1980–1986* (Atlanta, 1987).
15. Ibid.
16. Ibid.
17. Ibid.
18. Ibid.
19. ADL, *Hate Crime Statutes: A 1991 Status Report.*
20. Ibid.
21. Ibid.
22. American-Arab Anti-Discrimination Committee, *1991 Report on Anti-Arab Hate Crimes.*
23. Center for Democratic Renewal, *They Don't All Wear Sheets.*
24. Ibid.
25. Ibid.
26. Ibid.
27. Ibid.
28. Ibid.
29. Ibid.
30. Ibid.
31. Ibid.
32. Ibid.
33. Ibid.
34. McDevitt, "Characteristics of Civil Rights Crimes in Massachusetts 1983–1987."
35. William Wallace, "Bias Incident Investigation Unit," New York City Police Department, September 1991.
36. FBI, "Crime in the United States, 1990," August 1991.
37. Francis M. Roche, "Boston Police Department Community Disorders Unit Annual Report," March 1992.
38. FBI, "Crime in the United States, 1990."
39. Office of Florida Attorney General, *Hate Crimes in Florida January 1, 1990–December 31, 1990* (Tallahassee: Florida Department of Law Enforcement, 1991).

40. McDevitt, "Characteristics of Civil Rights Violations in Boston 1983–1978."
41. Wallace, "Bias Incident Investigation Unit."
42. Roche, "Boston Police Department Community Disorders Unit Annual Report."

14. Rehab

1. ADL, *1991 Audit of Anti-Semitic Incidents.*
2. Bureau of Justice Statistics, *Report to the Nation on Crime and Justice* 2d ed. (Washington, DC, March 1988).
3. Interview with Daniel Weiss, Northeastern University, Boston, August 5, 1992.
4. Montgomery County Office of Human Relations, *Handling Hate Violence* (Baltimore, 1989).

15. Grass Roots

1. Peter Myer, "The Case for Hate," *Life,* Fall 1991 (Special Issue), pp. 88–91.
2. 464 N.W. 2d 507 (Minn. 1991).
3. "ADL Finds Increase in Anti-Semitic Incidents during 1990," *The Jewish Life,* Spring, 1991, p. 46.
4. "Massachusetts Town Votes to Remove Indian Swastikas," *New York Times,* January 14, 1990, p. 19.
5. "Fraternity Rebuff Stirs Whirlwind in Vermont," *New York Times,* April 11, 1990, p. A17.
6. "Student Boycott Gains Staff Change at Bookstore," *New York Times,* February 25, 1990, pp. 44–45.
7. Edgar Morin, *Rumor in Orleans* (New York: Random House, 1971).

16. The Coming Crisis

1. "Klan Chief Pleads in Shooting Case," *Boston Globe,* April 12, 1992, p. 31.
2. "Five Louisiana Klansmen Are Indicted in Cross Burnings," *Boston Globe,* August 14, 1991, p. 8.
3. Lynne Duke, "How a Michigan Campus Erupted in Racial Strife," *Boston Globe,* April 14, 1992, p. 3.

4. Ronald Smothers, "25 Years Later, Racial Tensions Revive in Selma," *New York Times*, February 11, 1990, p. 30.
5. Lance Morrow, "The Provocative Professor," *Time*, August 26, 1991, pp. 19–20.
6. Jack Levin and James A. Fox, "Shooting at the Ivory Tower," *Boston Globe*, September 9, 1990, p. C20.
7. Levin and Levin, *The Functions of Discrimination and Prejudice*.
8. "Black Talks Prompt Protest and Complaint," *New York Times*, December 10, 1989, p. 67.

References

Adorno, Theodore W., E. Frankel-Brunswick, D. J. Levinson, and N. H. Sanford. *The Authoritarian Personality.* New York: Harper & Row, 1950.

Allport, Gordon W. *The Nature of Prejudice.* Reading, MA: Addison-Wesley, 1954.

American-Arab Anti-Discrimination Committee. *1991 Report on Anti-Arab Hate Crime.* Washington, DC, February 1992.

Anti-Defamation League of B'nai B'rith. *Combatting Bigotry on Campus.* New York, 1989.

———. *Hate Crimes: Policies and Procedures for Law Enforcement Agencies.* New York, 1989.

———. *An ADL Special Report: The KKK Today: A 1991 Status Report.* New York, 1991.

———. *Liberty Lobby: Network of Hate.* New York, 1990.

———. *Louis Farrakhan: The Campaign to Manipulate Public Opinion: A Study in the Packaging of Bigotry.* New York, 1990.

———. *Neo-Nazi Skinheads: A 1990 Status Report.* New York, 1990.

———. *1989 Audit of Anti-Semitic Incidents.* New York, 1990.

———. *1990 Audit of Anti-Semitic Incidents.* New York, 1991.

Berrill, Kevin. *Anti-Gay Violence: Causes, Consequences, Responses.* Washington, DC: National Gay and Lesbian Task Force, 1986, pp. 1–26.

Blackwell, James E. *The Black Community.* New York: Harper & Row, 1991.

Blauner, Bob. *Black Lives, White Lives: Three Decades of Race Relations in America*. Los Angeles: University of California Press, 1989.

Bureau of Justice Statistics. *Report to the Nation on Crime and Justice* 2d ed. Washington, DC, March 1988.

Center for Democratic Renewal. *They Don't All Wear White Sheets: A Chronology of Racist and Far-Right Violence—1980–1986*. Atlanta, 1987.

Center for the Study of Sport in Society. *Youth Attitudes on Racism*. Boston: Northeastern University, October, 1990.

Clark, Floyd I. "Hate Violence in the United States," *F.B.I. Law Enforcement Bulletin* 60 (1991): 1.

Coates, James. *Armed and Dangerous: The Rise of the Survivalist Right*. New York: The Noonday Press, 1987.

Comstock, Gary David. *Violence against Lesbians and Gay Men*. New York: Columbia University Press, 1991.

Davidson, Osha Gray. *Under Fire*. New York: Holt, 1993.

Donnerstein, Edward, Daniel Linz, and Steven Penrod. *The Question of Pornography*. New York: Free Press, 1987.

Douglas, Jack P. *Deviance and Respectability*. New York: Basic Books, 1970.

Dugo, D., and L. Aragon, "Alert Eyes Spot Hate Crime Evidence." *Law Enforcement Quarterly* (May–June–July 1991).

Eagles, Charles W., ed. *The Civil Rights Movement in America*. Jackson: University Press of Mississippi, 1986.

Ehrlich, Howard J. *Campus Ethnoviolence and Policy Options*. Baltimore: National Institute Against Prejudice and Violence, 1990.

Ehrlich, Howard J. *Studying Workplace Ethnoviolence*. Baltimore: National Institute Against Prejudice and Violence, 1990.

Finn, Peter. "Bias Crime: Difficult to Define, Difficult to Prosecute," *Journal of Criminal Justice* (Summer 1988).

Finn, Peter, and Taylor McNeil. *Bias Crime and the Criminal Justice Response: A Summary Report Prepared for the National Criminal Justice Association*. Cambridge, MA: Abt Associates Inc., 1988.

Garofalo, James. "Bias and Non-Bias Crimes in New York City: Preliminary Findings." Paper presented at annual meeting of the American Society of Criminology, Baltimore, November 1990.

Goldstein, Jeffrey H., and Paul E. McGhee. *The Psychology of Humor*. New York: Academic Press, 1972.

Governors Task Force on Civil Rights. *Report on Racial, Ethnic, and Religious Violence in California*. Sacramento: California Department of General Services, Office of State Printing, 1982.

Hatamiya, Leslie. *Walk with Pride: Taking Steps to Address Anti-Asian Violence.* Handbook prepared for Coro Foundation. San Francisco: Coro Foundation, 1991.

Herek, Gregory, and Kevin Berrill. *Hate Crime: Confronting Violence Against Lesbians and Gay Men.* Newbury Park, CA: Sage, 1992.

Hodge, John L., Donald K. Struckmann, and Lynn Dorland Trost. *Cultural Bases of Racism and Group Oppression.* Berkeley, CA: Two Riders Press, 1975.

Hurst, Frederick A. *Report on University of Massachusetts Investigation.* Boston: Massachusetts Commission Against Discrimination, February 1987.

Jenkins, William D. *Steel Valley Klan.* Kent, OH: Kent State University Press, 1990.

Keen, Sam. *Faces of the Enemy.* San Francisco: Harper & Row, 1986.

Keough, William. *Punchlines.* New York: Paragon House, 1990.

Koller, Marvin R. *Humor and Society: Explorations in the Sociology of Humor.* Houston: Cap and Gown Press, 1988.

Lamy, Philip. "The Meek Shall Not Inherit the Earth: Survivalism and the American Millennial Myth." Doctoral dissertation, Northeastern University, July 1991.

Langer, Elinor. "The American Neo-Nazi Movement Today," *The Nation*, July 16/23, 1990, pp. 82–107.

Lee, V. "Legislative Responses to Hate-Motivated Violence: The Massachusetts Experience and Beyond." *Harvard Civil Rights-Civil Liberties Law Review* 25 (Summer 1990): 287–340.

Leiberman, Michael. "The Hate Crime Statistics Act." *Anti-Defamation League of B'nai B'rith Bulletin*, May–June 1990, p. 1.

Levin, Jack, and James A. Fox. *Mass Murder: America's Growing Menace.* New York: Plenum Press, 1985.

Levin, Jack, and William Levin. *The Functions of Discrimination and Prejudice.* New York: Harper & Row, 1982.

Levin, Jack, and Jack McDevitt. "A Typology of Hate Crimes." Paper presented at annual meeting of American Society of Criminology, New Orleans, November 1992.

Levitan S., G. Mangum, and M. Pines. *A Proper Inheritance: Investing in the Self-Sufficiency of Poor Families.* Washington, DC: George Washington University, Center for Social Policy Studies, 1989.

Los Angeles County Commission on Human Relations, *Intergroup Conflict in Los Angeles Schools: Report on a Survey of Hate Crime.* Los Angeles, 1989.

Lurie, Alison. *The Language of Clothing*. New York: Random House, 1981.

McDevitt, Jack. "The Study of the Character of Civil Rights Crimes in Massachusetts (1983–1989)." Paper presented at annual meeting of the American Society of Criminology, Reno, November 1990.

McDevitt, Jack. *The Study of the Implementation of the Massachusetts Civil Rights Act*. Boston: Northeastern University, Center for Applied Social Research, 1989.

Massachusetts Executive Office of Public Safety. *Hate Crime in Massachusetts Preliminary Annual Report: January–December 1990*. Executive Office of Public Safety and Criminal History System Board, Crime Reporting Unit, 1990.

Mishel, Lawrence, and David Frankel. "The State of Working America," Economic Policy Institute, 1990–1991.

Mohr, Richard D. "Anti-Gay Stereotypes." *Gays/Justice: A Study of Ethics, Society and Law*. New York: Columbia University Press, 1988.

National Gay and Lesbian Task Force. *Dealing with Violence: A Guide for Gay and Lesbian People*. Washington, DC, 1986.

National Institute Against Prejudice and Violence. *Prejudice and Violence: An Annotated Bibliography of Selected Materials on Racial, Religious, and Ethnic Violence and Intimidation*. Baltimore, 1985.

National Organization of Black Law Enforcement Executives. *Final Report: Racial and Religious Violence: A Model Law Enforcement Response*. Washington, DC, 1985.

Newman, Katherine S. *Falling from Grace: The Experience of Downward Mobility in the American Middle Class*. New York: Free Press, 1988.

Noddings, Nel. *Women and Evil*. Berkeley: University of California Press, 1989.

Olzak, S. "Political Context of Competition: Lynching and Urban Violence." *Social Forces* 69 (December 1990): 395–421.

Padgett, George. "Radically Motivated State Enforcement and Federal Civil Rights Remedies." *The Journal of Law and Criminology* 75 (1986): 103–138.

Phillips, Kevin. *The Politics of the Rich and the Poor*. New York: Random House, 1990.

Raschke, Carl A. *Painted Black*. New York: Harper, 1990.

Rieder, Jonathan. *Canarsie*. Cambridge, MA: Harvard University Press, 1985.

Schuman, Howard, Charlotte Steeh, and Lawrence Bobo. *Racial Attitudes in America*. Cambridge, MA: Harvard University Press, 1988.

Siegelman, Lee, and Susan Welch. *Black Americans' Views of Racial Inequality.* Cambridge: Cambridge University Press, 1991.

Singular, Stephen. *Talked to Death: The Life and Murder of Alan Berg.* New York: Morrow, 1987.

Southern Poverty Law Center. "Hate Violence and White Supremacy—A Decade Review, 1980–1990." *Klanwatch Intelligence Report #47.* Montgomery, AL, 1989.

Southern Poverty Law Center. *Klanwatch Special Report; Outlawing Hate Crime.* Montgomery, AL, 1989.

Sniderman, Paul M., and Michael Gary Hegen. *Race and Inequality: A Study in American Values.* Trenton, NJ: Chatman House, 1985.

Sparks, Richard F. *Research on Victims of Crime: Accomplishment, Issues, and New Directions.* Crime and Delinquency Issues: A Monograph Series. Rockville, MD: National Institute of Mental Health Center for Studies of Crime and Delinquency, 1982.

Stanton, Bill. *Klanwatch.* New York: Grove Weidenfeld, 1991.

Taylor, Nancy, ed. *Bias Crime: The Law Enforcement Response.* Chicago: Office of International Criminal Justice, 1991.

Tobin, Gary A., and Sharon L. Sassler. *Jewish Perceptions of Anti-Semitism.* New York: Plenum Press, 1988.

U.S. Department of Justice. *Hate Crime Data Collection Guidelines.* Washington, DC: Federal Bureau of Investigation, 1990.

———. *Measuring Crime.* Washington, DC: Bureau of Justice Statistics, 1981.

———. *Training Guide for Hate Crime Data Collection.* Washington, DC: Federal Bureau of Investigation, 1991.

———. *Uniform Crime Reporting National Incident-Based Reporting System: Volume 1—Data Collection Guidelines.* Washington, DC: Federal Bureau of Investigation, 1988.

Ward, Benjamin. "Hate Crimes: The Police Response in New York City." *The Police Chief* 53 (1986): 46–47.

Weiss, Joan C., and Paul H. Ephross. "Group Work Approaches to 'Hate Violence' Incidents." *Social Work* 31 (1989): 35–39.

Wexler, Chuck, and Gary Marx. "When Law and Order Works: Boston's Innovative Approach to the Problem of Racial Violence." *Crime and Delinquency* 32 (1986): 205–223.

Wilson, William Julius, ed. "The Ghetto Underclass: Social Science Perspectives," *The Annual of The American Academy of Political and Social Science* 501 (1989): 1–233.

Index